CHANGING FAMILY LIFE IN EAST AFRICA
Women and Children at Risk

CHANGING FAMILY LIFE IN EAST AFRICA

IN EAST AFRICA

Women and Children at Risk

Philip Leroy Kilbride
and
Janet Capriott

THE PENNSYLVANIA STATE UNIVERSITY PRESS
University Park and London

HQ
792
.A422
K55
1990

Library of Congress Cataloging-in-Publication Data

Kilbride, Philip Leroy.
   Changing family life in East Africa: women and children at risk /
Philip Leroy Kilbride and Janet Capriotti Kilbride.
      p.   cm.
   Bibliography: p.
   Includes index.
   ISBN 0-271-00676-5 :
   1. Children—Africa, Eastern—Social conditions.   2. Family—
Africa, Eastern.   3. Quality of life—Africa, Eastern.   4. Mothers—
Africa, Eastern—Economic conditions.   I. Kilbride, Janet
Capriotti.   II. Title.
HQ792.A422K55   1990
304.2′3′09676—dc19   90–2961
                                                                   CIP

This book is dedicated to Candice,
who is a drop of rain in the dry season

CONTENTS

PREFACE

This is a book about children, more precisely "children of value." Our concern here is to show through ethnographic description how children in East Africa overall are now experiencing a more threatening existence than was once the case in the very recent past. This is so even though there have been significant advances in medical care, a reduction in infant mortality rates, and educational opportunities not dreamed of before. The modern threat to East African children comes from the human social environment, primarily from their parents and other relatives who are reacting to threats to their own economic and social well-being. For this reason, although this book concerns children as its subject matter, significant attention must focus on environmental factors, particularly changing kinship roles as understood in the context of economic transformation of society. Among the key environmental parameters concerning children to be discussed in this book, none is more important than the woman's role as wife and mother, especially as this role is juxtaposed in relation to the status of men. The book's organization illustrates this structural thesis. While one may not contend that "women and children" necessarily "belong together" as a given "natural unit," it cannot be denied that the mother-infant dyad is now the empirical social dyad everywhere basic to human societies as known to anthropologists (Goodenough 1970), more basic even than the nuclear family of husband-wife-children. When the mother-infant dyad is superseded, it is usually other female relatives of the child who assume caretaking responsibilities.

Many children in East Africa now experience an unfavorable environment not unlike that described for many children in the industrial West. On the other hand, like children in Colonial United States, for example, traditional East African children rarely experience what we have come to identify as "child abuse" (Demos 1982). The modern industrial world in both the U.S. and East Africa has not proven to be favorable to the child's quality of life. This book is, therefore, "comparative" with the simultaneous interest of understanding childhood in both regions of the world. Due to similarities of economy, such a comparison is particularly useful. East Africa, however, provides a striking *cultural* contrast, one where "genuine" family experience there is worthy of retention in modernity, and possibly emulation here in the West. Viewing the family from this cultural perspective might create a renewed commitment to diverse family arrangements here in the Western world as a means of enhancing the status of children. "Absolute" assumptions about the "naturalism" of the nuclear family, about monogamy, or about child-absent life-styles in the West all serve to work against the interest of children. Thus our attention to "children of value" in East Africa should be of interest to both Americans and East Africans. In any case, there are numerous economic and other structural links between these two areas (tourism, coffee export, international corporations). For example, providing formula samples for infants who are traditionally breast fed resulted in increasing intestinal distresses due to the difficulty of maintaining sterile bottles in rural areas (e.g., the Nestle controversy).

A second broad theoretical concern in this book, necessary to interpreting the tragic plight of the world's children today, is to confront the social reality of what Wallerstein (1974) refers to as the "modern world-system." This international global structure originated in the European, capitalist economy of the sixteenth century with subsequent capitalistic penetration of the pre-industrial, pre-modern area of the world (Wolf 1982). The approach here will not be concerned directly with the "penetration" of capitalism in East Africa but, rather, we as ethnographers will examine the *consequences* of such penetration as perceived, as it were, locally from the ground up. From this vantage point, penetration is best described as "delocalization" (Pelto 1973), a key term to be developed later. Our assumption of a "world system" based on capitalist economy also accounts for a world process known as "feminization of poverty" that is occurring not only in the USA (Sidel 1986) but also in regions of the older "colonial" empires (Etienne and Leacock 1980). Children too have suffered greatly as women's status has suffered from global poverty (Werner 1979). In sum, our specific theoretical interest in children, particularly their quality of life, would be incomplete without consideration of the child's "system network," minimally to include the "mother," the community, and the nation, and maximally to include the "modern world-system" (Gordon 1980).

Anthropologists are often interested in "quality of life" issues, particularly as they affect the "peoples" studied, many of whom now live in such settings as reservations, slums, and refugee camps. The solutions to such widespread oppression have been various. Some scholars work to develop socioeconomic theories to account for such "oppression" (neo-Marxist analysis); others develop action-oriented projects built around host populations' expressed concerns; still others prefer to work on land litigation cases. Most hope to contribute to a theoretical development of "applied" or "issue-oriented" theory (Goodenough 1966, Foster 1969, Pelto and Pelto 1978).

This book also examines the question of "quality of life" very directly. The authors believe that cultures differ in "relative happiness" for their members, although this is hard to measure. The anthropologist Sapir wrote about a "genuine" culture as contrasted with a "spurious" one as follows:

> The genuine culture is not of necessity either high or low; it is merely inherently harmonious, balanced, self satisfactory. . . . It is, ideally speaking, a culture in which nothing is spiritually meaningless, in which no important part of the general functioning brings with it a sense of frustration, of misdirected or unsympathetic effort. (1962:90)

It may be argued that the capitalist penetration in East Africa has produced a movement away from a more "genuine" culture toward that of a more "spurious" one. This book will attempt to show that this is especially true for women and children. In agreement with J. Henry and others, we believe that contemporary U.S. society can also be broadly characterized as a "spurious" culture for many if not most Americans, irrespective of region or class (Henry 1963). This is so because the modern world system and an associated life-style known as "modernity" (Berger 1977) have not generated significant "caring" institutions comparable to those of the premodern family and community. One of the primary institutions under threat in East Africa, for example, is the "extended family." This social unit has been identified globally as the "most basic" human "moralnet" known to mankind (Naroll 1983). It will be shown that this is true of East Africa, too, where moral erosion is threatening children with child abuse and neglect in a hostile modern environment.

Finally, the authors hope that their material will suggest certain policy steps to politicians, academicians, religious leaders, and others who believe that action is in order. Some policy recommendations concerning women, children, and family interrelations will be suggested in the last chapter. It shall be argued from our data, however, that a holistic concept of broad, environmental interaction is required so that policy does not isolate women, children, and family into a kind of "natural unit." A cultural approach is necessary to avoid this trap. Daniel P. Moynihan, who has noted that for the first time in America's history, children are the poorest age group in the population, states:

> Do we care? A certain plausibility attends the proposition that the failure is likely to be considerably affected by how we answer. I believe we ought to care. But given the equivocal nature of much research, the absence of any direct political stirring, and the absence of any easily available resources, the question Do we care? will be answered in the first instance by our ability to state with some concision just what it is we would do if we did. (1987:101)

What we have done in our studies is to employ a *cross-cultural approach* to children, one that is based on what we have identified as an *"interactive ethnography."* Whatever policy steps are taken in Kenya, the United States, or elsewhere should be grounded in cross-cultural, empirical, experiential life situations, for which such methodology is indispensable. This is so because every person or society is like *every* other one, like *some* other ones, and like *no* other one (after Kluckhohn 1949).

The first section of this book sets out its theoretical approach and interactive methodology. The modernizing of East African society is also described in this section. Our materials are drawn primarily from the interior areas of the East African region, although we argue for their regional typicalness. Section 2 describes the cultural context for "children of value" by focusing on the life cycle, with particular reference to infancy and childhood. In this section, a "genuine" cultural context for men, women, and children is presented. The third section sets out our argument that modern culture is less economically favorable for women compared to men. One consequence of such modern problems as teenage pregnancy, absent-father homes, and overburdened extended family obligations is a pattern of child abuse and neglect.

Throughout this book, the term *Ba*ganda refers to the group of people who live in Uganda in the region formerly called *Bu*ganda. An individual member of this society is a *Mu*ganda. *Ki*ganda refers to things pertaining to the Baganda; their language is *Lu*ganda. *Ki*Swahili (Swahili in English) is a language spoken widely in East Africa. On occasion, the term *Abaluyia* is used to refer to the *Samia*, who, along with several other groups, are Abaluyia. Pseudonyms have been used in all cases where informants are named.

ACKNOWLEDGMENTS

Our professional and personal debt to others is immense. The field materials in this volume were gathered over an eighteen-year period from 1967 to 1985, involving ten research visits to Uganda and Kenya. These repeated visits ranged from several months to three extended periods of more than a year each. It is therefore difficult to acknowledge all those upon whom this book, considered by us to be an overview of our work, depended upon in one way or another for its completion. Nevertheless, we attempt here to provide some sense of our gratitude, although we hope that those not mentioned explicitly will understand that our task cannot be complete given the duration of our study and limitations of space.

We are grateful to the National Science Foundation, National Education Association, National Institute of Mental Health, and the Wenner-Gren Foundation for research funding. Bryn Mawr College has regularly provided endowed funds for Philip Kilbride and students to visit Kenya for research projects. We thank Lady de Freitas for her generous gift to the college in support of African studies. Janet Kilbride thanks her former colleagues in the Department of Human Development at the University of Delaware for their encouragement and support of her research endeavors.

Our various projects in East Africa were undertaken while we were Associates of the Makerere Institute of Social Research, Makerere University, Kampala, Uganda, and the Institute of African Studies, University of Nairobi, Nairobi, Kenya. We thank these fine universities and also the governments of Uganda and Kenya for research clearances. Many public and private persons in East Africa have provided advice and help in our research, as well as living arrangements. In particular we thank officials of the Kako Secondary School in Uganda and the Medical Mission Sisters and many others associated with the Nangina Hospital in Kenya.

Our research assistants have been indispensable, as will be obvious later. For assistance in our earlier research in Uganda, we thank Joseph Busuulwa, Charles Lule, and Leone Lule. John Bukenya is thanked for his help in getting us started in Uganda. Those who provided us with extensive long-term assistance in Kenya are Gertrude Lwanga, Solome Ouma, and Ridah M'Mbone.

Many scholars have shaped our intellectual style although this is difficult to precisely disentangle. Dr. Michael Robbins and Dr. Irene Harms, during our graduate school days at The Pennsylvania State University, provided us with a strong sense of the importance of research method in all social inquiry. The Anthropology Department at Penn State nurtured in us a respect for and love of fieldwork, while the Department of Human Development there provided us with respect for and love of families and children. Professor Robbins, additionally, offered us his personal friendship. Whatever merit this book has would not have been possible without his support and intellectual influence, first at Penn State and later at the University of Missouri where he was Philip Kilbride's doctoral advisor.

Dr. Janet Hoopes of the Department of Human Development, Bryn Mawr College, is thanked for her guidance of Janet Kilbride's doctoral research. Dr. Matthew Yarczower, Department of Psychology, Bryn Mawr College, is given special gratitude for his intellectual contributions as a research colleague. In recent years, Robert Washington and Michael Krausz have regularly "team taught" courses with Philip Kilbride on Afro-American Heritage and Philosophical Anthropology, respectively. Some of the ideas for this book emerged while teaching with these two esteemed colleagues.

Bryn Mawr undergraduate and graduate students have offered us insights and/or data. Among graduate students, we thank Diana Putman, Maria Cattell, Stevie Nangendo, Kusimba Makokha, and Carolyn Friedman. Several undergraduates have provided research reports in conjunction with their student projects in Kenya. Among these the outstanding work of Erin Heath, Gertrude Fraser, and Nancy Davis were significant to us. Barbara Herr was helpful in Uganda. Dr. Robert Rubinstein is thanked for his excellent editorial suggestions. Dr. Peter Rigby's comments were especially helpful in our efforts to improve our last chapter where the work of Rodney (1974) was recommended.

Needless to say there are countless Ugandans and Kenyans who responded in one way or another to our attempts to better understand them and their culture. In chapter 2 their various roles are assessed. We simply state here our gratitude to each and every one who cooperated with us. We hope that in some small measure our efforts to provide here our view of them (and ourselves) will be of some practical merit to East Africans (and also to Americans). There can never be any book without editorial assistance. For this we thank Holly Taylor, Sarah Woodbury, Jennifer Spruill, Deanne Bell, and Stevie Nangendo.

Finally, our parents, who are now grandparents, provided us with financial and emotional support throughout our student days (and beyond). The distinctly "pro" extended families tone of this book is therefore to some extent inevitable. We accordingly extend our love to Mr. Philip and Mrs. Natalie Kilbride and to Mr. Armand and Mrs. Mary Capriotti. Moreover, we have experienced the joy of late initial parenthood (in our forties) such that this book should also be construed to some extent as a celebration of that event. We accordingly dedicate this book to Candice Maria Kilbride, specifically, and to the other children of East Africa and America.

To all those mentioned above (and many others), we thank you, although the responsibility for what follows is entirely our own.

SECTION 1

1
INTERPRETIVE FRAMEWORK
Comparative Functionalism

S ome twenty years ago, the authors first traveled to Uganda, East Africa, to engage in cross-cultural study. East African cities, like those in other parts of the developing world, give a physical appearance of similarity to the Western world. There are luxury hotels, elegant restaurants, paved highways and modern transportation including taxis. However, a taxi ride in Uganda, as we soon discovered, is very different both physically and ideologically from a taxi ride at home in the United States. Soon after our arrival, we departed from Uganda's major city of Kampala for a more remote area of the country where our actual fieldwork was to take place. We had anticipated spending about three hours on a 90-mile trip, considering that the taxi was semiprivate and the major roads were good. Although our start was an early one, only half our distance had been traveled by lunchtime—a meal which remained uneaten as we waited amongst chickens, bananas, and other produce which by now shared the taxi with us. Our notes are incomplete concerning the rest of the trip, but we did eventually reach our destination. That particular taxi ride is not necessarily typical of all taxi trips in East Africa, as the high rate of accidental deaths caused by speed would attest. Nevertheless, while this trip was obviously stressful to our Western need for rapid movement from point A to point B in a given amount of time, it afforded us a beginning understanding of a different concept of time. Our traveling companions and driver, not as oriented to clock time as we, perceived the trip as a series of social events such as stopping to see a father's sister here or a mother's brother there as well as an opportunity to obtain chickens or produce from an assortment of friends. We were to discover later that much of life in East Africa revolves around social events such as funerals, weddings, circumcision ceremonies, and clan-naming ceremonies. To these local experiences have been added the Christian rites, including Christmas and Easter, as well as more recently created national holidays. The taxi experience sensitized us to many other cultural differences that became further elaborated and reinforced over our years in Kenya. Initially, in both our personal ethnographic lives and intellectual thought, it became necessary to overcome our culturally derived training to experience life, and therefore, to think about it, in a worldview metaphor replete with quantification, cameras, clocks, and other deper-sonalized activities. We even felt guilty about interactions that could inter-fere with our pursuit of perceived objectivity. Much later, in the familiar cultural terrain of our library at home, we were in a position to concur with Walter Ong's (1969) reiteration of the relativity of human experience. Our experiences in East Africa led us to agree with him that some cultures are oriented around "events" while others perceive reality as "worldview." Ong writes of worldview that it reflects the

> marked tendency of technological man to think of actuality as some-thing eventually picturable and to think of knowledge itself by analogy with visual activity to the exclusion, more or less, of other senses. Oral or nonwriting cultures tend much more to cast up actuality in comprehensive auditory terms, such as voice and har-mony. Their "world" is not so markedly something spread out be-fore the eyes as a "view" but rather something dynamic and rela-tively unpredictable, an event-world rather than an object world . . . (1969:634)

Philip Kilbride's study of pictorial depth perception among the Baganda provides a good illustration of cultural differences. In collaboration, with M. C. Robbins and H. Leibowitz, he showed that seeing depth in pictures, so much a part of our Western visual worldview that it was assumed to be an unlearned human ability, involved learning pictorial visual perceptive cues such as object size, superimposition, and others not used by most Baganda (Kilbride and Robbins, 1969; Kilbride and Leibowitz, 1982). Thus, for example, an object appearing in a photograph that one would identify as a "railway track" (perspective cue) is perceived frequently in Uganda to be a "hill," "roof," "camera tripod," "ladder," or some other object that goes "up" and "down" rather than "back." A picture is, of course, a two-dimensional surface such that our perception of depth is entirely symbolic and not necessarily real or "correct." Kilbride also found that as Baganda became more modernized, assuming a worldview technology learned through formal education, they too acquired pictorial depth-perception skills. Ugandans, of course, perceive three-dimensional visual space the same as all humans do. Nevertheless, their two-dimensional pictorial perception does suggest a different symbolic visual "sensotype" as suggested by Ong, Wober, and others (see Wober 1975).

Two additional examples of the deculturalizing we found necessary in order to more fully appreciate the East African experience will be provided. The first example is drawn from Janet Kilbride's research interest in 1967, when she undertook a verification of some earlier reports (Marcelle Geber 1958, Geber and Dean 1957) on the precocity of African infants. Baganda infants were assessed by means of standardized tests of motor development, involving ages of attainment of skills such as sitting, crawling, and walking. It was found that one area in which the Baganda were particularly advanced was that of sitting skills. During a subsequent field trip several years later, it was discovered that sitting is a meaningful cultural experience for Baganda infants for which they are trained and for which they receive much attention upon accomplishing. Thus sitting is not only a landmark in Baganda infants' motor development, as it is for American infants, but a burgeoning social event marked by a ceremony (Kilbride & Kilbride 1974).

Our second example of unlearning cultural expectations is what Philip Kilbride has come to identify as an interactive ethnographic method; it is derived from some fieldwork he did in 1976 concerning ideas about intelligence among the Samia of Kenya. His understanding of intelligence then was to say the least considerably more developed than the ethnocentric opinion in some scholarly circles that Africans, who often score low on IQ tests, are therefore not very bright, if not childlike, in their reasoning (see Cryns 1962). One may also recall that around the time of this fieldwork, Arthur Jensen (1969) still received serious attention for his argument that a genetic difference in intelligence existed between blacks and whites. What Putman and Kilbride (1980) discovered among the Samia did not of course unseat these perjorative ideas. It does not take a study to do this, only a willingness to live and to learn from Africans or Afro-Americans. Cultural differences in the definition of intelligence were nevertheless discovered. People the Samia identify as being intelligent (*omukesi*) are considered so because of a facility for successfully performing activities important for the functioning of the social group. Emphasized as constituting intelligent behavior are the ability to resolve conflict, inventing a novel agricultural technique, or other activities where mastery is necessary for group survival in everyday life. There are, of course, individual differences, as in any society, but performance is not quantitative, and it is more socially oriented compared to the major equation of intelligence with academic performance in the United States.

In general, this finding is in agreement with the observation by Olsen and others that "intelligence as we know it is a skill in a cultural medium" (Price Williams 1975:62). In particular, the Samia observations agree with those of Mundy-Castle who, while researching in Ghana, developed the notion of "social intelligence," comprising "such skills as involved in tact, sensitivity to social atmosphere, social and intersexual lore, unself-consciousness, guidance of behavior in accordance with accepted social values," in contrast to Western "technical intelligence" (Kingsley 1976:15). Social intelligence is adaptive in societies like Samia where people and not mechanical devices are significant for getting on in life.

Surprising too was the Samia's view that slowness was the most important aspect of intelligent behavior. Speed, especially in taking tests, is so dramatically a part of our own experience of assessment of intelligence that it would be useful to reevaluate our cultural equivalence of intelligence with speed. This is, of course, difficult in a society where fast-food restaurants, computers, stopwatches, drive-in banks, and numerous other "timesaving" devices and practices are in evidence. Among the Samia, the phrase, "Quick to table, got burnt teeth," aptly illustrates their disdain for nondeliberative haste.

In the pages to follow, the authors will set out other materials which comprise their present understanding of East African childhood and family life. While the frame of reference will be children, a consideration of them requires that considerable attention be paid to the family. These two subjects are closely interwoven in some ways no longer true for much of American society. A cross-cultural study inextricably involves values, as the above examples are intended to initially show. These materials serve to illustrate a theme which will be evident throughout this book, that is, how a universal human nature interacts with cultural values to produce cross-cultural similarities and differences in experience (see Bourguignon 1979). Related to this question is the way in which an ethnographer's own values structure interaction with hosts who have their own values to produce what we believe is a descriptively valid account of social life in another culture. In brief, the finding that East African infants proceed through the same developmental phases as their Western counterparts, albeit at a faster rate with differential emphasis on specific skills, and that the Samia possess a domain of human behavior broadly recognized as intelligent and in many ways similar to our own, leads us to concur with Clyde Kluckhohn (1949) who as stated earlier believes that cross-cultural study shows that every person is like no other person, like some other people, and like all other people.

Our descriptions and interpretations of East African family life, particularly its focus on children, cannot be understood apart from our intellectual position on the relativistic-universalistic issue of human cultural analysis and cross-cultural study. One of the key methodological ideas now current in social-science circles is the awareness that social facts do not exist "out there" apart from an interactive context, one that includes both the observer and the observed who, to a great extent, "construct" meanings through a process of social interaction. Thus, to assume that a study is "value free" would not be tenable. This awareness is now commonplace in anthropology and sociology, although logical positivism cannot be said to be entirely unseated (the assumption that "facts" are out there to be discovered by a neutral observer). In family studies research, a recent book by Feldman and Feldman (1985) reviews a number of topics in family study with an explicit recognition that such study is not value-free. Writers from contrasting points of view about the "goodness" or "badness" of such things as divorce, wife swapping, computerized dating, or monogamy openly identify their perspectives as grounded in personal experience, religious beliefs or other influences without recourse to value-free rhetoric. Likewise, the present book is not one which claims a value-free agenda. Its concern is to describe and interpret *the authors'* understanding of family life in another culture, an understanding that is perhaps itself best understood as emerging from interactive ethnographic research. The objective is not to translate life as experienced by East Africans themselves. This is best accomplished by indigenous writers and scholars. Rather we seek to communicate those ideas about family in East Africa which represent our consciousness as influenced by our own value backgrounds in combination with numerous interactions with East African people and their values in many social contexts over nearly two decades. This, we believe, will provide a meaningful perspective for *both* East Africans and Euro-Americans since "outside" accounts can be insightful. Our research role is, of course, best labeled as that of the "insider-outsider" or "marginal native" (Freilich 1970).

Importantly, the assumption of "objective" facts "out there" should not be entirely absent. Interactive ethnography based in a constructionist frame need not reject the idea that a considerable portion of human experience is common or "universal." We hold with universalists such as Hollis (1982), Horton (1982), and Hallowell (1955) that *all* accurate ethnographic descriptions will reveal, if completeness is the goal, some construal of universal transcultural experience. For example, we know of no culture where "intelligent" behavior cannot be *locally* contrasted with its opposite or in which infants and children do not pass through "stages," however they may be defined locally. Thus our own philosophical "commitment" is to an epistemological viewpoint that is closer to universalism than it is to relativism.

Our description of family life in terms of social science would not necessarily negate a description by other scientists whose views of the "facts" are "different," provided they too were explicit in their method and "up front" whenever possible about the place of human values in their description and interpretation (e.g., ours is an interactive ethnography). According to our criteria for social science, there is, therefore, a legitimate, epistemological place for many, but not all, descriptions and explanations of African family life.

Relativistic Universalism

Those specific theoretical ideas which have emerged as useful tools for interpretation in the course of the authors' ethnographic work will now be made explicit. The selection of a theoretical perspective should also be viewed as an interactive process not unlike that between host populations and respective researchers. One's selection is determined by what seems reasonable given interactive social experiences in the field and the available repertoire of alternative theoretical perspectives as mediated by one's own personal background. For example, we are predisposed to favor "functionalism" given our humanistic and religious backgrounds and consequent hope of "improving" dysfunctioning social orders. Our observation of East Africans as behaving "functionally" or "pragmatically" may be influenced by this predilection, but hopefully not unreasonably so. In contrast, we are not likely to advocate "structuralism" in most forms inasmuch as such a perspective often requires little social interaction, is exclusively cerebral, and is not particularly preoccupied with applied issues. Our theoretical perspective of relativistic universalism predisposes us in a theoretical and therefore comparative direction towards the view that process can be expected to regularly recur across all cultures if predisposing social conditions are similar. This is, of course, the primary assumption of social science, as opposed to, for example, extreme humanistic scholarship which is, by comparison, less "theoretical" on the whole.

Our central theoretical principle is drawn from A. I. Hallowell's work (see, for example, 1955). This pioneering anthropologist was a recipient of the Viking medal for his ethnographic and profound original theoretical work among the Ojibwa Indians of North America. Hallowell believes that all human cultural experience is biopsychologically grounded in a "self" awareness that serves to orient persons in a temporal, spaciogeographical and social field (this is universal). The self-orientations are, however, culturalized by experience such that each society provides for its members through cultural learning—what he called a "behavioral environment." (This is relative.) The Ojibwa Self can journey back to the mother's womb or visit other sacred locations during what we would call "dreaming." The Ojibwa human person often became extremely fearful of frogs, for example, compared to bears, since supernatural persons could reside in the former (Hallowell 1955:172–82). In U.S. society, the behavioral environment does not often include spacial and temporal experiences such as these! Hallowell cast his relativistic social constructionist theory squarely in an evolutionary-universalistic frame. He argued that early hominid cerebral development at some point provided a basis for "self" awareness which has remained ever since fundamental to and a precondition for cultural experience. Hallowell writes, "I believe that we must assume that the functioning of any human society is inconceivable without self-awareness, reinforced and constituted by traditional beliefs about the nature of the self" (1955:83).

Nevertheless, it would be incorrect to overstate Hallowell to mean simply the "individual" as isomorphic with self in all cultures. The universality of naming, for example, is a self-anchoring device, but in many societies in Africa and elsewhere, one's name is anchored more in a social group than in an "interior" experience of individuality. Thus Hallowell also informs our respect for social constructionism. His work broadly guides our commitment to a "relativistic-universalistic" perspective as a beginning point in cross-cultural study. Anthropologists working on questions of cross-cultural child development typically have, like Hallowell, begun with an assumption of universalistic process as a functional context for their analysis of child development (Whiting and Whiting, 1975). The pioneer anthropologist Margaret Mead made an important reference to socialization as a set of species-wide requirements made of human beings by human societies and to enculturation as a process of learning a specific culture in its uniqueness (1963:187).

More recently, LeVine describes three goals common to parents everywhere:

1. The physical survival and health of the child, including (implicitly) the normal development of his or her reproductive capacity during puberty.
2. The development of the child's behavioral capacity for economic self-maintenance in maturity.
3. The development of the child's behavioral capacities for maximizing other cultural values—for example, morality, prestige, wealth, religious piety, intellectual achievement, personal satisfaction, self-realization—as formulated and symbolically elaborated in culturally distinctive beliefs, norms, and ideologies (1977:17).

Both Mead and LeVine have provided a key conceptual orientation for the present work.

While having universal properties, child development always occurs in a socio-cultural context which is interactive with the child. Among the Baganda, for example, the social smile is relatively advanced in its expression among three- to six-month-old infants. Sociability is a Kiganda cultural value which begins early and is continuously reinforced in the wider society. In this society, adults rely on numerous social strategies for advancement in a stratified kingdom where "personalism" is the key social context. Thus a major parental goal of Baganda parents is for their children to become expert in interpersonal manipulative strategies. Techniques of training infants and children, to be described in another chapter, will reveal this parental attitude. Our previous studies of the sensorimotor development of Baganda infants have led us to the conviction that rate of development in this area is, to a great extent, influenced by socio-environmental factors. This is not to deny that the basis of sensorimotor development in the individual is under the constraints of human biology. There is, however, no reliable evidence in the literature to suggest that the advanced rate of sensorimotor development displayed in Baganda infants can be accounted for by biological or genetic factors. While research on Baganda newborns has revealed that Ugandan infants (compared to British) show a significant advance in skull hardness, lanugo hair, and nail texture (Parkin 1971), no generalized maturity was detected. These differences, moreover, have no direct or obvious relationship to infant behavior (Super 1981). Geber and Dean (1957) have reported a pattern of precocious head control for Ugandan newborns, but other researchers have failed to replicate this finding (Warren and Parkin 1974). Presently, all available evidence argues for biological factors operating in Baganda infant development primarily as species-wide or universal adaptations which facilitate human infant development everywhere.

Species-wide variations in the rate of infant sensorimotor development are generally not extreme under "normal" environmental conditions. In addition, the course of this development is not easily deflected from its genetically prescribed path (see Scarr Salapatek, 1976, for a discussion of canalization of infant sensorimotor development). Our own studies of Baganda infants have emphasized the importance of experiential conditions and their impact on infant development as adaptations to a total socio-cultural milieu. Nevertheless, no simple, single-effect causal argument from culture to behavior seems justified. That is, one should not assume, as did many earlier studies of culture and personality, that the child is born a *tabula rasa* who is subsequently molded or shaped along whatever behavioral lines a given society may emphasize (see Spiro, 1978, for a criticism of such studies). Extreme cultural relativity ignores biological universals (and even cultural universals).

Contrary to the above view, our studies provide evidence that the Muganda infant develops within broad biological constraints which are probably universal (see Freedman, 1974, for a discussion of universals). Our material on the social smile, for example, shows that Baganda and Samia infants, although precocious in later smiling skills, display the initial social smile at about the same age as do infants from other cultures. By four months of age, when the frequency of infant smiling reaches a peak, cross-cultural differences have been reported (Super 1980). It seems likely that the smile, once activated, facilitates attachment between baby and caretaker; why this behavior is not evident at birth is poorly understood. Freedman, however, believes that the pre-smiling phase tends to foster the "potential advantage of a relatively loose mother-infant attachment in the first months, when a large percentage of infants die, particularly in subsistence cultures; presumably, the depression and pain caused by infant death after attachment could impair future childbearing" (1974:39). Izard (1978) suggests that, from the infant's vantage point, the initial phase of non-discriminatory smiling may be adaptive from an evolutionary-biological perspective "in that it invites care and attention from anyone who can attend" (397). We will later discuss the positive affective behaviors (including face-to-face looking, smiling, and vocalizing) exchanged between Baganda mothers and their infants. Although societies vary in the intensity of affect between mother and infant, it is likely that a minimum degree of positive maternal affect is necessary for infant care to occur at all. Infant smiling appears to be an important reinforcer for positive maternal feelings and behavior.

Delocalization

Our second theoretical framework is drawn from the literature on "modernization." Considerable cross-cultural study has investigated social and economic transformation which has occurred around the world as a consequence of the appearance of such things as the nation-state, literacy and formal education, urbanization, and industrialization. One of the tensions in modern Kenya concerns a gradual "delocalization" of economy as the old agrarian-based economies gave way to a modern economy with national and international connections (see E. Wolf 1982). Poggie and Lynch (1974) believe that economic delocalization is a chain of complex events which results when food, energy sources, and services which had formerly been provided within the local setting are transferred into market-exchange commodities, most of which originate from sources outside the local area. Pelto (1973), who extensively uses the term delocalization, showed how Skolt Lapp social organization was transformed as the local reindeer energy source was largely replaced by petrol-dependent snowmobiles. The new technology created, for example, the "haves" (snowmobile owners) and the "have nots." He most recently reports that the automobile is rapidly replacing the snowmobile as coveted local technology (1987). In the same book,

Bernard and Pelto (1987) provide further ethnographic examples of "delocalization." These cases can be viewed as forming a continuum of "localization" and "delocalization" as comparatively small-scale regional tribal and village economies variously respond to more inclusive economic forces in the modern internationally based world economic system. Forced "relocation" as among Bikini Islanders (Kiste 1987) or the Plateau Tonga (Scudder and Colson 1987) necessitates abrupt and extreme delocalization. In comparison, Bernard observed among Greek fishermen that "for awhile it appeared that sophisticated new diving equipment such as scuba gear and portable decompression chambers would provide the answer to the industry's difficulties. Surprisingly, just the opposite is the case—the sponge industry is vigorous again because its technology was primitivized" (Bernard 1987:170).

Less dramatic than relocation and primitivization are the probably far more frequent "intermediary" cases such as those among the Baganda of Uganda who experienced many new international and national events directly through the radio and mass media, powerful communicative means of delocalization (Robbins and Kilbride 1987). In Western Kenya, Wagner (1949) observed the earliest stages of "westernization" (cultural delocalization) in the 1930's. He observed that eleusine was the most precious crop, which "tastes to the Africans like sugar to the Europeans." Young people and Christians, however, he noted, preferred maize. Thus changes in food preference may be seen as an early indication of cultural delocalization. Today in Western Kenya (and elsewhere in East Africa), a more serious form of delocalization, based on a cash economy, land shortage, and the migration of men, has had a profound impact on family structure, female power, and the previous rationale for reproduction. Modern delocalization of the economy involves change from a scene where local crops are grown exclusively by subsistence technology and controlled by men and women to a predominantly male-dominated, monetary, national economy based on wage labor and cash crops grown for sale "outside." This economic delocalization has made many women, particularly those without education, economically worse off than their counterparts in the past.

A process of "moral delocalization" closely paralleling this economic delocalization can also be observed in Kenya. Powerful religious, educational, and legal quarters in modern Kenya declare, for example, that polygny is "wrong," that infanticide (and abortion) is "illegal," that "unnatural" birth control is "sinful," and that women are primarily "responsible" for child care. Such a moral climate would, no doubt, seem quite foreign to Wagner's informants even if they could not articulate how each of these "crimes" or "sins" works against the interest of a majority, if not all, women who have little "rational" choice in such matters affecting female belief and practice.

Today the traditional ethical role of "elders" as moral entrepreneurs has declined through what is here called moral delocalization. Modern figures, such as church ministers, priests, teachers, or secular authorities, sometimes promote values inappropriate for the local context, if not for locations outside it. For example, the Western Province has the highest birth rate in the world, and 62% of the population of Kenya is under eighteen years of age (Onyango and Kayongo-Male 1982). Nevertheless, some institutions possessing moral authority in this region are opposed to the use of "unnatural" techniques of birth control. Likewise, polygyny (traditionally permitting a form of child spacing by a post partum sexual taboo) has been disapproved (Hillman 1975). Interestingly, the "elders" often decry the new economic and moral order, often without a sympathetic ear from delocalized moral entrepreneurs. Recent research in the Western Province, for example, has shown that traditional *Baswala Kumuse*, "teachers of wisdom," who are active as funeral orators, or singers, "criticize young working people for not clothing or otherwise caring for their parents (the child-parent relationship is a pervasive theme) . . . and comment on the pervasive individualism of present-day Kenyan societies" (Wanjala 1985:89). Nevertheless, delocalization has rendered powerless traditionalists such as the *Oswala Kumuse*.

In a recent theoretical statement, it was suggested that "the unidirectional nature of basic technological evolution is matched by the unidirectional nature of socio-cultural delocalization" (Bernard and Pelto 1987:266). Accordingly, in East Africa it is unlikely that future cultural evolution will, either by conscious planning or accidental "adaptation," revert to a tribal, agrarian, localized past—even if it could be shown that women and children are worse off at present than formerly. What in fact is occurring there is an ideological encounter between various local and external ideologies and associated moral codes. The concept of moral delocalization as developed here would include the rapid growth of Christianity and Islam with associated sacred relics and pilgrimages to distant places such as Rome or Mecca. This religious developmental process would appear to be unidirectional in the main but certainly not linear. Moral delocalization is best thought of as dialectical, as in related ideas such as cultural or cultural-religious revitalization (Wallace 1970) or cultural neo-traditionalism (Rogers 1969). These and similar processes are well-known cultural dynamics involving synthetic interaction between local ideologies and external ones. Additionally, however, the concept of delocalization recognizes the importance of a world-wide perspective, one that transcends an exclusive focus on local "tribal" or "village" dynamics. Moreover, a power dimension is the primary explanatory focus in delocalization analysis.

In East Africa, as elsewhere in Africa, religious delocalization has witnessed the growth of numerous "independent" churches. These often split from "parent" (European) churches precisely to maintain local beliefs (Sangree 1966). In Western Province Kenya, for example, the "church of Israel" and the "Legion of Mary," respectively, represent a tolerance for polygyny in the one case and a veneration of the curative process of a sacred woman in the other. Kenyan theologians such as Mbiti (1986) consider indigenous African beliefs about God, for example, to be similar to Christianity, thus serving to provide theological support for a delocalization of traditional religious beliefs. Okot p'Bitek (1972) on the other hand, views East African spirituality as "atheistic" and primarily materialistic, and not a "pre-adaption" for Christianity.

In modern East African society, sexual knowledge, practice, and moral responsibility have also been delocalized. It can be argued that this process works primarily against the interests of women. Localized East African sexual practices had been embedded in a system of moral obligations which maximized male and female sexual pleasure and social responsibility (cf. Kisekka 1976). In a recent paper, Worthman and Whiting (1987) document that the pool of "unwed" mothers appears to be increasing in a Kikuyu community, particularly among those who have significant amounts of formal education (e.g., the more modern). The modern school and associated values have replaced the traditional *ngweko* rituals as a major peer socialization setting. The *ngweko* custom (Kenyatta 1984) was a form of lovemaking involving an apron used by women to protect their private parts. Sometimes sexual relief was experienced but "petting" would appear to have been the ideal. Worthman and Whiting state that boys were ostracized from further participation in *ngweko* by their peers if they broke the rules. The Church of Scotland mission disapproved *ngweko* so that most of the educational functions of the practice have been lost. They conclude:

> By means of a sacred ceremony, the parental generation transferred to youth the responsibility of regulating premarital sex and initiating the process of mate selection . . . When this system had been

secularized by edict and the introduction of western schooling, both the regulations of premarital and mate selection appear to have been destabilized, at least temporarily. We suspect that this effect of modernization is not unique. (1987:163–64)

It will be argued in this book that normative (and positive) inter-related patterns of child care remain to some extent in East Africa today, as do a reliance on the extended family for support, a subsistence economy with women and men as agriculturalists, and a moral system with elders as moral leaders. Nevertheless, a systematic breakdown in this social pattern is becoming apparent with the advent of a monetary economy through "delocalization." One consequence of this is that child abuse and neglect are becoming more prevalent, not only, for example, in Western Provinces, but throughout Kenya—particularly in Nairobi (Onyango and Kayongo-Male 1982), as well as in Uganda. It is important to note that many males have less power than in the past, due, as in the case of women, to changing social, educational, and economic circumstances associated with delocalization. For this reason, some men are necessarily avoiding the burdens of expensive child-care responsibilities. Nevertheless, the focus of this book is the modern condition. Such a condition is, as we shall see, particularly stressful for women, given that the gender imbalance in power is far more threatening than in the past, when social control was more in the hands of the collectivity and less individualistic.

Power

A third theoretical focus to be emphasized is the significance of social power in understanding modern family life and childhood in East Africa. We would agree with those who have assayed to portray economic delocalization in the developing world by showing how women overall have experienced a loss of social power beginning with the colonial policies of imperial power (cf. Etienne and Leacock 1980). As these studies show, moral delocalization concerning judgments about female decorum, responsibility, and rights should not be understood apart from considerations of economy and power. Consequently, the present study builds upon an earlier one in East Africa, where Philip Kilbride considered economic and power contexts of the disvalued occupation of "barmaid" among contemporary Baganda of Uganda. This will be fully discussed in chapter 8.

In brief, it was found that barmaids are negatively labeled by members of "respectable" Ugandan society. Kilbride (1979) established that Baganda barmaids conform to Goffman's (1963) view of the stigmatized individual as one who is not accorded the respect and regard that "uncontaminated" aspects of her social life would lead others to extend and the individual to anticipate receiving. The powerless position of the barmaid derives from her position as an unmarried and marginally educated woman in a modernizing society like Uganda where wealth and authority are primarily in the hands of married men and where formal education is required for access to modern jobs. Married women are especially hostile to barmaids, who are perceived as representing a threat to the wife's economic interests by being a drain on her husband's financial resources. In pre-modern times in Uganda, it would appear that the only female role that was stigmatized was that of barren women (cf. Roscoe 1911). The emergence of a new category of "troublesome" female behavior (among others, such as prostitute) represented an overall loss of female prestige compared to the agrarian past. Previously, most Baganda women enjoyed different but productive symmetrical economic roles relative to men and also reproductive prestige (Kilbride 1979).

Functionalism

Another significant theoretical orientation used here is that of "functionalism." It will be shown that family and child experiences cannot be understood apart from a holistic, systems perspective. The emergence of, for example, child abuse and neglect in modern Kenya or the traditional emphasis on a socially alert infant among the Baganda are by themselves incomprehensible unless interpreted as the dysfunctioning or functioning of behavior or human practice in terms of broader socio-economic and cultural contexts. As has been shown above, we believe that economic delocalization has had significant consequences for family life and childhood. Thus we argue that some elements of socio-cultural structure are more "causative" than other domains of experience. This view departs from earlier functionalist research (e.g., Harris 1968) which treated *all* features of a sociocultural system as more or less equally functional in the overall maintenance of society. The reader familiar with ethnological theory will no doubt recognize that considerable contemporary social theory is derived from a similar attempt to identify that economic aspect of a sociocultural or psychocultural system which seems most central for understanding the overall functioning (or dysfunctioning) of the system. Some examples are Steward's "culture core," Marx's discussion of the relation between "base" and "superstructure," and Whiting's "maintenance system." Here the authors will not attempt a "cause and effect" functional *explanation* by means of a large-scale universalistic comparative study (e.g., Rohner 1975), but will, rather, provide a functional, ethnographic analysis or *interpretation* of their data.

Yarrow, Pedersen, and Rubenstein (1977), who are psychologists, have suggested that anthropological studies that rely mainly on describing global variables of the environment in portraying the "normative child" and the "modal mother" rarely mention the range of variations within a given culture (cf. 558). Nevertheless, they recognize that concentrating only on those specific child-care practices which are apparently related to specific infant behaviors provides the researcher with an incomplete picture of the infant's behavior. It ignores behavioral meanings in terms of the larger cultural context. Yarrow, Pederson, and Rubenstein (1977) state:

> It is clear that such basic variables as amount of kinesthetic stimulation or encouragement of gross motor activity will be influenced by the society's and the caretaker's modal values and idealized images of the young child. Similarly, the patterns of contingent responsiveness are likely to be affected; the culture that values stoicism may not sanction rapid responsiveness to the infant's distress. (560)

Likewise, Carew (1980) while advocating a "functional, microanalytic approach" to the study of child-care environments, fears that the growing use of this method might ignore the connection between these functional systems and broader societal systems. She states:

> Studies of this type seldom go beyond child development considerations to address issues that sociologists, economists, and anthropologists might think vital to the interpretation of results (such as differences in economic, social, and political resources and differences in cultural norms and expectations, and values as factors influencing behaviors). (171)

The general functional assumption the authors assume in their research is that of holism. According to the "holistic" view, a society's total design for living is composed of constituent parts, such as institutions, values, and material artifacts. Cultural analysis has revealed that such constituent elements tend to be interrelated such that, for example, a society functions more or less as a total system. A change in one institution is likely, therefore, to have functional consequences for other institutions in that society. For instance, a change in marital form from polygyny to monogamy may have created the emergence of the occupation of barmaiding in Kiganda society (Kilbride 1979). In this occupation, unmarried women function in many respects as co-wives formerly did by providing sexual and emotional outlets for married men. Thus an understanding of a leisure-time or recreational institution is enhanced by our understanding of changes in the marital institution. Functionalism as a theoretical approach seeks to understand the interconnections that obtain among cultural institutions and to reveal "functions" that are served for the total system by each constituent institution.

While anthropologists no longer accept some of the assumptions made in classical functionalism, much of psychological anthropology remains functionalistic inasmuch as human psychological properties such as values, perceptions, cognitions, and, indeed, behavioral functioning throughout the entire life cycle are assumed to be best understood in a causal sense by reference to antecedent or consequent events in a total psycho-socio-cultural system. Finally, contemporary functionalism as an orienting principle has much to offer for understanding modern East African human practice in terms of group phenomena understood at the macro-socio-cultural level emphasized in much of anthropological theory. The authors wholeheartedly agree with Goodenough, who states, "The fundamentally functional orientation of anthropological science is appropriate to its subject matter. But we must not forget what our orientation is or neglect its implications for theory and method just because it comes naturally to us" (1970:122).

Child Abuse and Neglect

Another body of literature has been influential in the development of our functional interpretation of our findings, especially those concerning the contemporary problem in Kenya of abused and neglected children. To date, research in the West has established that economic unemployment is associated with increased abuse. At the psychological level, the abuser tends to have a history of being abused, inaccurate knowledge of appropriate child capabilities, poor impulse control, and an alcohol or drug problem. Children who are exceptional (e.g., premature, handicapped) are comparatively more vulnerable to abuse. We will argue here that our cross-cultural material provides strong functional theoretical support for those holistic theorists who claim that the etiology of child abuse is best understood from a "systems" or "ecological" perspective (Bronfenbrenner 1974, Garbarino 1976, Kent 1979). This approach emphasizes that lack of social supports and deficient economic employment, for example, are powerfully predictive societal level risk factors for child abuse. Specifically, the "systems" approach in America, and also it would appear in Kenya, "calls for radical change in these social conditions which predispose people to abuse, such as inequalities of wealth, education, opportunities and quality of life" (Kent 1979:638).

Anthropological research on child abuse importantly emphasizes the need to *define* child abuse for cross-cultural comparison (Korbin 1981). Should culturally appropriate but painful initiation ceremonies in New Guinea be called abuse (cf. Langness, 1981)? Although it is often socially approved, is joint parent-child suicide in Japan abusive (Wagatsuma 1981)? A sociobiological perspective highlights the "rational" context in which some instances of infanticide may contribute to the overall adaptive potential for the group (Gelles and Lancaster 1987). Infanticide is thus viewed as "benign neglect" in South America where stronger infants are fed at the expense of weaker ones (Johnson 1981). Infanticide in Western Kenya was traditionally permitted in some societies under certain conditions. Thus it is imperative that "child abuse" be defined in a fashion appropriate to the culture in question. On the whole, anthropological work would seem to support relativistically inclined child-abuse theorists who define child abuse, for example, as "when the child suffers non-accidental physical injury as a result of acts—or omissions—on the part of his parents or guardians that violate the community standards concerning the treatment of children" (Segal 1979:580). In the United States, does the new knowledge that newborn infants experience pain to a much greater extent than realized previously make circumcision without an anesthetic agent now abusive?

The ecological or systems approach mentioned above requires that theoretical consideration of child abuse and neglect be conceptualized in a holistic environmental context. Historical analysis further affords a process approach to the consideration of suspected social etiological forces if such have changed over time and if child abuse and neglect rates have also changed over time. For example, Demos (1987) shows that child abuse was minimal in Colonial America compared to present-day America. Lack of data dictate that the present study cannot discuss child abuse rates in Kenya but will argue more confidently that social power has, in fact, decreased for both women and children in the modern context. There is also no difficulty in documenting, as attempted later (and by others), the empirical fact of child abuse and neglect as a phenomenological, local Kenyan category in the modern experience. Cause and effect cannot be proven, but a hypothesis of cause can be formulated on the basis of previous social-science theory and, in Kenya, on the basis of associated historical occurrences of increased social powerlessness for women and children as well as the present vulnerability experienced by women as abusers and neglecters and by children as victims.

It would appear generally that in societies where collective (e.g., national, family, neighborhood) rather than individual moral responsibilities are emphasized, child abuse can be greatly curtailed or even eliminated. Thus child abuse is rare in "traditional" Africa (LeVine and LeVine 1981) and in rural Kenya, in particular, where the extended family or clan is important (Fraser and Kilbride 1981, Kilbride 1986). Even research in the United States, where kin or neighborhood bonds are comparatively weak, has found that, "Families isolated from relatives and friends show higher rates of violence than do other families, probably because people with relatives and friends can turn to them for help and also because relations and friends can intervene if the situation deteriorates too far" (Strauss and Gelles 1970).

Any comparative, functional interpretation must be concerned with the issue of "functional equivalence" (Price-Williams 1975). Are seemingly different human practices able to perform similar functions? Do similar beliefs, practices, and customs across cultures have contrasting functions? An extreme social constructionist assumption, of course, would obviate the very enterprise of cross-cultural functional comparison. Its emphasis is on the human capacity's seemingly infinite ability for arbitrary symbol construction of meaningful webs of significance (Geertz 1973, Benedict 1959). We are likewise sensitive to the need for "thick description," but we prefer to ground our description in a view of human nature that admits of, following Hallowell, a significant universal dimension in cultural organization or human experience. We have tried to argue this above. Nevertheless, cultural diversity is profound and the task of identifying "functionally equivalent" practices is difficult. This task will be attempted later when we consider the "evil eye" as a traditional form of child abuse in Kenya.

Finally, we believe that our theoretical preference for functionalism is not inappropriate for interpretation of East African cultural materials. Quite to the contrary, this preference has grown out of our interaction with our informants. Most of the daily concerns of our informants have been related to "manifest function" or pragmatic concern for the likelihood of an action serving some perceived personal or group objective. Illustrations will be presented in later chapters. Our experience is in strong agreement with Okot p'Bitek (1971), who writes specifically about African religion contrasted with European Christianity:

> African religions are not so much concerned about the *beginning* and the *end* of the world, they are rather more concerned with the good life here and now, with health and prosperity, with success in life, happy and productive marriage, etc. They deal with the causes of diseases, with failures and other obstacles in the path of self-realization and fulfillment (62) . . . The Nilotes [for example] are concerned not with ontological definitions but with dynamic function. (72)

In chapter 2, we will set forth the operational activities that constitute for us those requirements and field techniques linking our fieldwork with the theoretical framework developed in chapter 1.

2

INTERACTIVE ETHNOGRAPHY

A Cultural Approach to Comparative Child Study

Interactive ethnography is a particular kind of ethnography emanating from our previously discussed focus of theory on the conscious reality. This reality is largely constructed from social interaction although not to such an extreme as to preclude cross-cultural understanding and universalizing theoretical generalization. That is, we attempt with Hallowell to develop a frame of reference for viewing the individual in another society in terms of "the psychological perspective which his culture constitutes for him and which is the integral focus of his activities, rather than to content ourselves with the perspective of an outside observer who may even pride himself on his 'objectivity'" (1955:79). We would extend this "phenomenological" frame to the interactive context between researchers and host community and thereby construe our enterprise as constituting interactive ethnography. The subject of our study is, therefore, the experienced world of East African family life as it is understood through our "gaze," which is shaped by our own cultural backgrounds, our theoretical disciplinary interests, and our host communities' perceptions and actions toward us (Stoller 1982). It is always problematic to judge the extent to which the phenomenological reality of another experience is approximated, but to do so is our primary objective. The interactive style of ethnography is maximized to do this as much as possible.

Our methodology contains the following four requirements to best provide a "meaningful" transformation from "their" experience to "our" theoretical concepts. The term "meaningful" here is taken to suggest in some sense "accurate" rather than the "only," or even "the best," account possible. We take the domain of methodology to be "the logical steps and requirements whereby ethnographers convert the stuff of raw observation into abstract anthropological conceptual structures" (Pelto and Pelto 1978:XIV). First, steps must be taken to use data-gathering techniques that ensure that our materials are *cultural* and not idiosyncratic or unduly individualistic. Second, our techniques must ensure that one can, in principle, through familiarity "get at" *genuine* social interaction. Technique here refers to the realm of concrete, hands-on practices associated with data collection. Genuine is taken to be behavior that is spontaneously expressed or otherwise naturalistic. A third requirement is that every effort must be made to let the community and its members "speak for themselves" through their own words and deeds. Importantly and fourth, the group's words and deeds are always filtered through the gaze of the fieldworker, and therefore the interactive context at the heart of all ethnography must be elevated to a primary methodology concern. We turn now to specifically consider each of these four broad methodological principles or requirements which have informed the present study.

Cultural Analysis

The serious student of cultural study faces an immense array of definitions and approaches to the study of culture even though the concept is "the cornerstone of the discipline of anthropology" (Langness 1975). In fact, little progress has been made in reaching a consensus since the day that Kroeber and Kluckhohn (1952) rehearsed several hundred definitions. Our approach can best be situated in the broad landscape of cultural analysis by briefly indicating what our study is *not* attempting to do, at least explicitly, although we have learned much from these approaches. We do not here view East African social life as a bundle of symbols (a sign that stands for something else) although much of such life is, as in all societies, symbolic. Such an approach tends to understate concrete experiences and associated affective states, removing analysis far from the realm of people's experiences. At worst, the symbolic system so described is often not even grounded in local meanings, but a product of the student's own "brilliance." (For this reason many "symbolists" in our experience, particularly those of the structuralist sort, generally evaluate each other in terms of relative brightness rather than the quality of their data.) In any case, our East African friends are not disposed to symbolic analysis, preferring instead a functionalist/experiential analysis of their own social life. We have learned much, however, from the argued need to pursue what Geertz (1973) has called, "thick description" (extended experiential learning in our terms), although we do not study "symbolic action" in the present study. Human action is not construed by us here as "standing for something else" but as human action in its own concrete terms as conscious experience. At the other extreme are those who are not in "search of meaning" (symbolic study) but who are more aptly said to view their fieldwork activity as serving to explain human behavior as institutional life. From the latter, we borrow the concern for methodology and functionalism but with a preference for functional interpretations rather than explanations (probably not a possible objective in analysis of human practice). Compared to the symbolist, the cross-cultural researcher produces very "thin" descriptions of local experiences, symbols, lives, or other phenomenological accounts. Description is almost wholly in reference to code sheets, checklists, survey questions, or other tests often prepared *before* entrance into the field. Significantly, these two approaches share a hearty respect for "other people's" lives and behavior as rational products of either their own "meaningful" symbols on the one hand or as a "functional" response to environmental, historical, or economic forces on the other hand. For this reason, we have learned from these two perspectives, although our approach is more phenomenologically grounded than is either of these. Like them, however, it also assumes rationality and purposefulness in the social life of "the other." We reject approaches that are "structural," believing with Geertz that they are overly cerebral, and that they do not, in principle, require much interactive fieldwork (since, for example, it is assumed *a priori* by Levi-Strauss [1962] that social life is composed of "oppositions" where locus is in the "unconscious mind"). Similarly, Freudian studies which construe social life as symbolic of underlying "unconscious motivations" or certain Marxian assumptions that phenomenological experience is "false consciousness" are too abstract although we do not, or would not, know how to falsify their assumptions (since they are not descriptions of concrete behavior but are inferred from such behavior).

Nevertheless, Marxists and Freudians have taught us much about contradiction, paradox, and authority such that our awareness of the significance of economy and power at the theoretical level of our interpretation owes much to their insights. We are here attempting, as already indicated, to follow up on the pioneering work laid out some years ago by A. I. Hallowell. Our view of culture is that it is "constructed" from experience producing a behavioral environment as culturalized. The behavioral environment is "symbolic" but is also grounded in universal functions necessary for collective life in a specific environment and appropriate for its biologically conditioned human carriers. This universal-particularistic, symbolic/functional perspective seems most appropriate to us since its point of theoretical departure is the *direct* (not symbolic) conscious experience of life's events as mediated by a society's symbolic, cultural, and collective heritage. For this reason, Hallowell's book was entitled *Culture and Experience*. In the field of sociology, the theoretical work of Peter Berger (1977) has proven insightful, including both his numerous insights on "modernity" and his articulation of "paramount reality" or the experience of "consciousness" as a key area of sociological study. Our understanding of culture is also indebted to Gregory Bateson (1979), one of the most brilliant theorists of our age (also interestingly and surprisingly neglected, as is Hallowell). To Bateson, we owe our concerns for cultural holism or "systems" assumptions without necessarily taking it in the communicative direction that he did. Rather, his consuming concern can be reduced to his plea that one should search for "the pattern that connects" (1979) however unconventional the perceived connection may appear. We attempt here to show connections among such seemingly unrelated practices as barmaiding, the crawling of infants, and the social role of a grandmother! This is not a very "conventional" grouping of social categories in the child development literature, but we shall show that these "connections" are arguably patterned. Finally, our view of culture is "historical," and we also assume that it is primarily inculcated through learning or enculturation. We reject sociobiological reductions of cultural behavior to the level of gene (Sahlins 1976). Rather, culture is the learning property of a social group; nevertheless, as we shall see in the next chapter, much of cultural context "diffuses" from one society to another. Cultural life in East Africa, for example, can now be said to possess a strong regional pattern such that numerous practices in family life and childhood can be found all over the region. We will return to the concept of diffusion and regional culture when we provide in the next chapter a rationale for our regional East African, rather than "tribal," focus. We have introduced here our view of cultural study, one which requires an interactive methodology in ethnography.

It is clear that variation exists within any society so that not all individuals conform to those normative patterns that are operationally defined by the ethnographer to be "cultural." Indeed, much controversy centers on precisely how much "shared" behavior ever exists in a society. In other words, is culture a "replication of uniformity" or an "organization of diversity" (Wallace 1970)? For our purposes, culture technically includes all approved actual behaviors thought possible or reasonable within a society irrespective of how many individuals actually practice such behaviors. In actuality, however, most cultural practices turn out to be what "most" people desire, do, or think is proper behavior. Among the Samia, for example, it is an acceptable possibility to be a polygynist although most men are not. Polygyny is, therefore, a cultural standard even though it is not a common practice or experience. On the other hand, although there are some Baganda who do not, most Baganda do eat steamed plantain (*matooke*). Eating *matooke* is, therefore, both an approved behavior and a probable cultural practice.

Following Hallowell, the cultural realm can be referred to as constituting a "behavioral environment" which serves as an orientating frame for individual experience. The interactive ethnographer enters into an informant's behavioral environment through experienced thoughts, words, actions, and feelings. Interactive ethnography occurs at the individual or small-group level of actual experience. Moreover, the interactive context necessarily includes the ethnographer's experience (perception and cognition) as influenced by his or her own behavioral environment. It should, therefore, come as no surprise that any ethnographic description of "culture" can, in principle, be no more than a "version" of a society's ongoing collective social action. Great debates in the ethnographic literature are largely illusory, concerned as they are to show that, for example, Mexican peasants are really "aggressive" or not (Lewis-Redfield debate), or that Zuni Indians are "peaceful" or not (Benedict-Eggan debate; Pelto and Pelto 1978). The search for the "representative" cultural experience is also illusory since no ethnographer, in practice, ever does transcend personal interactive context. Nor is a behavioral environment the "sum total" of each ethnographer's "distorted" view of the "real culture." Rather, interactive ethnography, as opposed to, for example, "etic" counting of heads, artifacts, or "behavioral" events (e.g., Harris 1964), holds that the "behavioral environment" is a subjectively understood meaningful context. This includes people, symbols, and artifacts as a permissible or reasonable social basis for a particular person's experience. Experience is individualized whereas permissibility or reasonableness is a social standard. The philosopher N. Goodman (1978) has discussed what he calls "world versions" in Western science which are in and of themselves quite different, but equally reasonable, "accounts" of reality (e.g., the behavioral environment). Kuhn's (1962) thesis on scientific revolutions is another example of this line of thought. In interactive ethnography, too, there has emerged more than one "version" of East African social life.

Research Techniques

We turn now from methodology to the level of research technique where we have used a research strategy which is dictated by our view of culture as experiential on the one hand and as approved, but variable, behavior on the other. A major aspect of our work, therefore, can best be stated as a concern for a "quantitative/qualitative" mixture of research procedures (Pelto and Pelto 1978). This is especially important, for example, in a large-scale complex society such as the Kiganda, which numbers over two million people and is therefore potentially replete with intrasocietal variation in cultural practice. Focusing intensively on a small number of "key informants" or specific situations will result in very valuable contextual, qualitative information but will be meaningless in the absence of a concerted effort to ensure their "cultural" representativeness or acceptability within the larger sociocultural universe of which they are a part. On the other hand, simply to rely on social-survey procedures may be unproductive unless meaningful variables are included in the formal questions to be asked of a large number of people. Nothing comes out of a social survey that has not already been put into the instrument. Essentially, what does emerge is a verification (or rejection) of insights that the researcher, through interaction, had more or less intuitive feelings about *before* using the formal procedure. The best survey is prepared only after considerable informal experience with individual members of the host group. For example, we have always prepared and/or revised our survey and interview materials while in the field with helpful suggestions from African research assistants and informal discussions with many other local people.

Sometimes informal interactive procedures enable researchers to "induce" or discover new variables, customs, or experiences not previously known. For instance, one afternoon we were relaxing with some adult Baganda in the courtyard of their rural home. The mother of the house was peeling *matooke* (the staple plantain) while another companion was sitting quietly nearby. The children were speaking to each other in what appeared to us to be another language, perhaps *Lusoga,* spoken by a neighboring ethnic group. After some probing, we discovered that the children were "speaking backwards," a custom known as *ludikya.* For example, "omusa-jja" means man in *Luganda;* whereas in ludikya man is "jjasamuo." What is, in fact, a widely practiced language game among the children became known to us, as it were, only by being "on the scene." Children will not engage in *ludikya* unless they are sufficiently relaxed around "visitors." Indeed, many significant behaviors become observable only when informants are behaving naturally. Since *ludikya* had not been previously described in the literature, our "informal" involvements were necessary to discover it and other significant customs.

Through our various informal procedures of participation, observation, and informal interviewing, we gradually acquired a fund of insider information. This data was generally stored in field notes, tapes, or "inside our own heads." In the last instance, we ourselves became "sensitized" research instruments insofar as we were subsequently capable of asking meaningful questions or even behaving properly (or culturally) according to local standards (cf. Powdermaker 1966). Moreover, we began, to a considerable degree, to experience the more subjective emotional aspects of Kiganda culture. For example, during our first field trip, we took a brief safari to the game reserves in Kenya. Like most Americans, we were deeply interested in observing wildlife and other natural beauties available in East Africa. Baganda, however, rarely visit game reserves, nor are they particularly interested in observing wildlife and other "natural" beauties; they would rather spend their time socializing with other people. EuroAmericans who visit Uganda do so primarily to observe wildlife and rarely to interact with Ugandans. This preference appears quite strange to many Baganda. The Kiganda value of "sociability" surfaced repeatedly in other behavioral contexts as our fieldwork proceeded, thus verifying our initial impression that this was a core value of Kiganda social life.

Formal or more quantitative techniques which were used included such things as a household census, surveys on attitudes or preferences, inventories of household possessions, structured interviews, psychological tests, and thematic essays. One important component shared by these and other formal procedures is their being administered to a relatively large number of people. The obvious strength in quantitative techniques is their more extensive and comprehensive coverage of the topic in question than is possible with mainly qualitative, informal strategies. As we indicated above, a major use of formal research is to establish the range of behavior or "variance" pertaining to any particular insight or discovery accruing from informal inquiry. For instance, as part of a larger study of pregnancy, infancy, and childhood, we discovered that women, but not men, sometimes consume soil (geophagy). A survey dealing specifically with soil-eating later revealed that geophagy is particularly common during pregnancy and that women less frequently ingest soil when not pregnant.

A second methodological requirement in interactive ethnography is the need to use techniques which will maximize familiarity between researcher and host communities. That is, a strong temporal commitment must be invested in research to provide an opportunity for behavior to be genuine, trustful (if not factual), and more fully representative of all or most situational contexts. The researcher changes over time, as does the paradigmatic foci of one's discipline. The research process constitutes a dialogue among these dynamic components: the research population, the researcher, and the disciplinary concerns (particularly when "funding" is required). We will now address two of our techniques from the vantage point of enhanced familiarity as seen from a temporal perspective.

The first broad technique to be discussed is that of participant observation (Malinowski 1953, Spradley 1980). This technique involves actually living in the research area for extended periods of time and, whenever possible, personally participating in cultural events. Such participation is imperative as a strategy to provide a chance for obtaining the empathy and rapport necessary for interactive ethnography. Importantly, in anthropology, "to understand a strange society the anthropologist has traditionally immersed himself in it, learning as far as possible, to think, see, feel, and sometimes act as a member of its culture and at the same time as a trained anthropologist from another culture" (Powdermaker 1966:9). In our fieldwork in East Africa, we have lived in a village, a town, a small city, and both suburban and urban (Nairobi) environments. We have visited and lived in local homes and attended numerous funerals, weddings, parties, and church services (mostly Catholic), as well as recreational establishments such as night clubs and local bars. We have eaten and enjoyed African food and have regularly retained "cooks," nursemaids, and research assistants who have lived with us and, in most cases, become our friends and informants. These experiences overall have served in every opportunity to ensure that familiarity was maximized. We have used these informal opportunities to study Luganda and Swahili, mastering them certainly well enough to "use" for purposes of rapport and, eventually after field stays of a year's duration, to obtain simple interview material. Nevertheless, we are fortunate that English is widely understood in our research areas, being a national language in Uganda and Kenya. Research assistants have served as interpreters for conversation of a specialized or technical sort.

Participation can be thought of in two broad ways. The first is "just plain living there." Listening to the radio, shopping, reading newspapers, visiting and being visited, etc. are all, for the anthropologist, learning experiences. A second use is when participation becomes more focused on a problem, something that generally occurs later when problems are more clear to the researcher. In our case, we eventually engaged in friendships which sometimes resulted in being "taken home." This is often an important symbol of friendship in East Africa, where "strangers" are usually not taken home. On one occasion, for example, Philip Kilbride was taken to rural Western Kenya by an urban Luyia man and his two friends. The trip provided him with a chance to observe the extent to which rural and urban ties are generally quite strong in Kenya (cf. Ross and Weisner 1977). At "home" (the city is not yet home for most East Africans), the friend/informant behaved much like an obedient son, not showing his "elders" much about his "urban" side (e.g., frequent preference for bars and night life). Moreover, he was erroneously assumed to be wealthy, and many wondered why he had not given more to the construction of local schools and roads. On the trip home, one traveling companion assumed a rather "haughty" air as he "ordered" people about, implying that they were too "slow" for such an "important" city man.

Participation also provides the researcher with an opportunity to "reciprocate" in the context of "exchange." Being perceived as "wealthy" Europeans (erroneously, like our unfortunate friend above), we have given money for *harambee* development projects, paid school fees for children, and given jobs to people. Our role as "wealthy, friendly outsiders" has even been used by a friend to enhance his own career in business. As we subsequently discovered, he told some of his competitors that Philip was a "rich American" and was now "behind" him. He was, therefore, motivated to involve Philip in his daily activities, which afforded an opportunity to learn much about how the "modern man" makes use of traditional values to achieve success in business. The following episode involving this man will serve to illustrate how interaction occurred in a specific instance of participant observation. Here we illustrate a motivated social relational style to be later considered as a core value in East African family life and childhood.

In Uganda, the "big man," whether a chief, clan head, or modern businessman, seeks out followers whose numbers become a mark of his importance and prestige. For persons of lesser means, to be seen with the right people is to gain status and prestige among peers. This pattern can be seen in the following account of an overseas business trip undertaken by an upwardly mobile businessman, whom we shall call Paul. Prior to Paul's departure for England, several friends organized a "going away" party at his home. About forty guests (university students, nurses, bureaucrats, accountants, etc.) attended the gathering, which included alcohol, dancing, and so on. The following day Paul's elder brother and his daughter drove some eighty miles to the airport in Entebbe to see him depart. Since his journey was to last about one month, it was considered sufficiently long to warrant such a tedious drive. His mother, who lived in Kampala, made the twenty-mile trip to Entebbe, along with about twenty friends from the previous night's party. Unfortunately the chartered plane did not depart, so the entire entourage returned to the city. After a repeat performance the following day, several members of the entourage privately expressed their consternation and suggested to me that perhaps Paul, their friend, and, in some cases, wealthy patron, should purchase a regularly scheduled ticket. This is precisely what he did, primarily to defray the growing belief that perhaps he could not afford the difference between charter and regularly scheduled fare (about 300 dollars).

Accordingly, Paul's next flight was to depart in about a week's time. During the week before his departure, Paul encountered a number of friends around town and on several occasions in bars. He requested that his friends make the trip to Entebbe to "see him off." One such person had been staked by Paul to a sum of money to get started in his own business, so probably for this reason he readily agreed to go. Several other people were otherwise occupied. As it turned out, Paul's departure was witnessed by about twelve people, including his brother, whom Paul had provided with a car to make the trip from Masaka. His mother also attended. While at the airport, Paul was able to arrange through a friend for permission to board the plane from the V.I.P. sitting section. He was then escorted to the plane and, while waving to his friends, boarded it.

The above account is but a modern example of a traditional pattern.

Traditionally a successful chief, for example, was one who was able to attract clients through his reputation for fairness, generosity, and ability to settle conflicts among his clients. His reputation and his source of revenue varied in proportion to the size of his following. Success in the business world similarly requires public confidence and, to use one informant's term, "dignity."

A second technique we used to maximize familiarity is that of the "repeated visit" (Foster et al. 1979). Not only spending long periods of time in the field but often doing this over a long period of time (20 years in the authors' case) is an indispensable technique. Over this "living" period of time, we have changed in the minds of our hosts from an ambiguously married (childless) couple to a "mature" family of three. The bar and night-club scene have been thoroughly experienced as have the "honored" seats afforded at church and harambee meetings for those with professional status and/or white hair. At home the discipline of anthropology has embraced empiricism, moved "beyond empiricism," adopted sociological models, reembraced cultural analysis, and so on. Our experiences in East Africa have reflected this, but we are often "behind" the theoreticians, many of whom have not invested as heavily as we (and others) have in "repeated visit" fieldwork. The repeated visit, or "just plain living there" for extended occasions, provides a maximum opportunity for "fortuitous" events to occur and provides us occasions to learn from them. One such example will be considered later, when we describe in some detail a case of attempted infanticide which we stumbled upon one day while visiting a nearby location. Here we will discuss a stressful situation that occurred in 1972–73 when Idi Amin was the President of Uganda. This period provided an opportunity to observe Ugandans themselves in a novel situation and also to learn more about how East Africans perceived us. The following newspaper accounts will serve to recapture for the reader some sense of the social environment which prevailed during the early years of Amin's rule. All are from the *Voice of Uganda* (formerly *Uganda Argus*), the English-language newspaper published in Kampala.

"The Misguided Policies of Nyerere"

President Nyerere criticised General Amin for sending away British Asians from Uganda, saying no Asians should leave Uganda and that the three months given to Asians with British passports is not adequate. (August 23)

"Scramble for Business—The Big Rush on Forms Starts"

There was a scramble for application forms for the acquisition of businesses belonging to nonUgandan Asians leaving Uganda. (August 31)

"President Amin Spells Out Tactics for the Economic War"

So that Ugandans can help to achieve economic emancipation, the Government has slashed drinking hours in order to create efficiency on the job with longer relaxation on weekends; divided the country into nine Provinces; introduced a five day working week system, and banned teenage dances. (September 11)

"They Plan to Assassinate Me Before Deadline"

General Amin says, "Britain is accused. The British government in collaboration with British Asians and Israelis and some other western countries are planning to assassinate me before the 90 days deadline for the departing British Asians . . ." He stressed that if British troops or white Europeans land in Uganda soil they will not only be a very good target . . . but they will also endanger the lives of other European nationals living in Uganda. "We are waiting," he declared. The President said he knew that there are over 7,000 British Europeans in Uganda and said that all these people must be marked completely now . . . The President added that "we are ready to welcome any invaders whether or not they are Israelis, who are also white as are the British, and they will be a very good target." (September 6)

One of the consequences of Amin's Uganda was a distancing between ourselves and our Ugandan hosts. From early September, 1972, through the remaining ten months of our fieldwork, we experienced an overt form of social isolation which precluded the kind of social interaction essential for informal observation and participant observation. On a more personal level, being deprived of frequent and intense association with many of our informant/friends denied us the kind of recreational relief to which we had grown accustomed. It was, of course, necessary for Ugandans to be cautious in their public movements with whites. At this time, there were several incidents where African women were arrested and detained for their association with whites. A number of Europeans were deported (a 90-year-old Roman Catholic priest, several doctors, one researcher, and a Jewish-American businessman, for example). It was equally necessary for the anthropologists to avoid getting their informants into a position of being accused of "harboring guerrillas."

Perhaps the psychological state of the population can best be communicated by describing a most startling occurrence. Several days after the invasion from Tanzania, Janet Kilbride was in Kampala shopping with a Ugandan friend. A disturbance was heard up the road and rumors as to its cause began circulating. Suddenly, everyone started running away. Being white, and therefore a "good target," Janet joined the exodus as the Asian shopkeeper chased everyone out of his shop so that he could close it. In a matter of twenty minutes or so, many thousands of Ugandans had fled the city, leaving it almost totally abandoned. Philip Kilbride was at the University, where he watched people streaming out of town. One Ugandan said, "The Israelis have come;" another said, "The city is aflame." We never did discover the immediate reason for this mass hysteria at a time when things were reported to be, and on the surface appeared to be, "back to normal." During this time we were not visited by our friends.

Research in a stressful situation potentially provides an opportunity for the ethnographer to discover new ethnographic insights which might escape attention in more normal circumstances (see, for example, Whitten 1966). Our research experience afforded us an opportunity to observe the reactions of many Baganda to a situation that we considered politically and economically stressful. Our informants and other Baganda friends, however, were not as concerned as we were about what to us were clearly "stressful" circumstances. This striking, incongruous reaction to the same situation enabled us to derive some insight into the values of our host population.

To us the prevailing political situation was not unlike a despotic kingdom. That is, absolute rule by decree, arbitrary expression of power, and reports of the disappearance and torture of many Asians and Africans, all contributed to our anxiety and consternation. With the exception of concern by many Baganda over the alleged disappearance of other Baganda, there was a marked degree of unquestioning (public or private) acceptance of governmental policy. Traditionally, Baganda political institutions conformed to the despotic kingdom model (L. Fallers 1964). Their relative "adaptation" to the policies of Amin's government are probably best understood as a cognitive, premodern-derived disposition to tolerate despotic rule.

A lack of pity regarding the Asians was of significance to us. Although lack of pity or empathy seemed to characterize virtually all Baganda irrespective of residence, age, educational level, income, or gender, there were notable exceptions to this pattern (e.g., some clerics and university-educated Baganda bravely expressed in public their opposition to the Asian policy). Many writers have, in fact, attributed a marked degree of "treachery" to the Baganda. For example, the European explorer Mackay (1892: 183) heard Baganda boys laughing at the sight of a man having his throat cut by the kabaka's (king's) executioner. The anthropologist Richards states: "Ganda kings, unlike most other Bantu rulers, were admired for destroying their own subjects, and not only for ferocity against their enemies" (1964:276). The model provided by Baganda kings seemingly influenced other aspects of the social order. Richards for example, also notes that

> the right to inflict punishment seems to have been considered an essential attribute of fatherhood. "To beat a child is not to hate it" is a common proverb. "Why would a child dislike his father for being severe?" said one informant. "He would just say it is my father." "Of course my father punished me" said a girl essay writer, "how else would he display his authority over me?" (1964:262)

Whereas approval of treachery and a relative absence of sentimentality seems to be importantly related to the social order, such sentiments may transcend a sociopolitical frame of reference. LeVine (1970), in the course of a survey of personality traits pertaining to Africa, suggests that lack of pity and sentimentality in social relations is typical of many African agricultural societies.

LeVine (1970) also feels that in these same African societies there is an emphasis on material transactions in interpersonal relations. Many of our informants would agree with this notion; that is, Baganda themselves often describe their relationships to others in terms of the type of material transactions involved. The importance of materialism to Baganda became quite evident to us during the departure of the Asians. The Baganda perceived the situation in primarily material terms, buying up with gusto furniture, cars, radios, televisions, etc. from the departing Asians. (That this value is clearly not "African" exclusively or "Kiganda" in particular is highlighted by the fact that we also purchased a radio and some other goods from several Asian families.)

We will offer a final observation. The president explained the basis for the expulsion of Asians by reference to a dream he experienced. Elsewhere, Philip discussed the importance of dreams for prognosticating the future among Baganda (Kilbride 1974). It was instructive that none of his informants responded negatively to his systematic probes about the many references to dreaming by their President. What Europeans considered an "irrational" strategy in the determination of affairs of state was perceived as acceptable behavior by our informants. A previous research finding was thereby confirmed through the public prominence given to dream prognostication by the head of state.

Our perceptions of the Ugandan scene during 1972–73 were often, but not always, at variance with our African hosts. For example, on the matter of our interpretations of "value" reported here, several university-educated Baganda have offered their assessments. Consistently, there has been concurrence with one exception. These Baganda feel that there was widespread sympathy among Baganda for the expelled Asians. Fear of reprisals prevented the overt manifestation of sympathy which was privately felt. Our Baganda informants also point out that there are a legion of *Luganda* words and expressions for sympathy, pity, and condolences (e.g., *bambi, kitalo*). These are particularly appropriate at funerals, which is an obligatory social function in the life of a Muganda. Moreover, one informant said "probably as much as 90% of the total commercial advertisements on radio Uganda are daily taken up by *Luganda* announcements of deaths and the sick. Absenteeism from the office is most of the time due to funeral attendance." Moreover, one Muganda commented, "The Baganda are highly sophisticated, if also sometimes furtive, people. They have, among other things, a rare capacity to suppress and sublimate their feelings in times of stress. During oppression they are able to sing their master's voice. Just recall the flattery they heaped on Obote and contrast that with the ecstatic jubilation they exhibited at his downfall. You would not think these were the same people."

The Interactive Context

We turn now to a discussion of our third requirement in interactive ethnography, namely that East Africans be given, as the above example shows, every opportunity to "speak for themselves" or concretize their experience at the phenomenological order of their perceived reality. More explicitly, the third requirement in interactive ethnography is for the interactive context to permit or provide every opportunity for the community members to show or reveal their culturally constituted style of life, point of view, or values. In practice, however, the researcher's "gaze" is always implicated in such a way that the interactive context involves selective perception by the researcher (and also community members). For this reason, the process of interactive encounters must maximize every opportunity to reveal "their" and not the researcher's own perspective. The use of appropriate technique is crucial on this issue.

One useful technique involves the researchers themselves. Patience and "just plain listening," either as a regular practice or through the use of "open-ended" questions while interviewing, are essential practices. Personal style sometimes involves a process of "unlearning." This can be illustrated by an example. The researchers became annoyed when one of their research assistants, a bright sociable young woman, administered 50 structured interviews, following her instructions to "question 50 people" by asking the first of 50 questions on the interview to one person, the second question to another person, the third question to still another person, etc. Original joy at a "job well done" turned into disappointment. Then, fortunately, a colleague well known for his work on relativism, advised us to abandon the assumption of exclusive logical positivistic method and to also assume the girl herself was rational and somehow logical. In so doing, we learned the extent to which linear thought and serial mathematical notation had captivated our imaginations. In fact, the answers were all quite interesting and provocative even if not mathematically or statistically elegant.

In chapter 10, we shall report on another technique in which Kenyans indicated their perceptions of the most and least desired traits of selected family roles (e.g., grandmother, grandfather, co-wife). Another important technique was the life history (Langness and Frank 1981). Through the medium of "lives," some of our best-known informants provided their own accounts of remembered events in their past personal experience. In later chapters, we shall present vignettes on family life drawn from these materials. The technique of participant observation provides a good opportunity to spontaneously gather information on "lives." While traveling home with a close Ugandan friend, Philip learned much about events from his friend's childhood through conversations with this friend and other members of his family, recalled in the location of their occurrence.

At this point we will examine the fourth and final requirement in interactive ethnography. This is a necessary one because the East African perspective is always mediated through our gaze. One needs to be aware of one's own cultural background and how this may, in principle at least, affect the research process. We suggest that a process of introspection is useful at all stages of research (cf. Riesman 1977). What follows is a brief account of what we, at the conscious level, believe are "values" which have influenced our interaction with East African people.

It is now widely acknowledged that personal values, personality factors, and other social factors are inextricably intertwined with all levels of social research. This can be seen from entry into the profession to construction of a research problem to selection of methodology to operational decisions about "facts" to include or exclude in publication. In anthropology, "the reflexive" movement of the '60s and '70s challenged the very practice of anthropology as simply an extension of "imperialism" or "colonialism" and in need of "reinvented" revision or possibly abandonment. In this climate, attempts were made formally to develop a set of criteria that would sensitize a fieldworker to "ethical" dimensions such as the need to protect the privacy and rights of the host population (Hymes 1974). For those who perceived values as indeterminate in all research but still problematic, an attempt was made to "manage" them in the service of a more complete "objectivity" in fieldwork and cross-cultural theoretical conceptualization. The Peltos (1978), for example, are strong advocates of the clear need to "operationalize" terms and also to blend "art" and "science" in fieldwork.

That explicit recognition of the fieldworker's cultural and social background is an important factor in shaping one's fieldword is not a surprising fact for "minority" anthropologists. The Ghanaian Owusu (1978) has provided an excellent critique of the research efforts of Anglo anthropologists working in his country. Many believed that they were studying local values and symbols even though they did not learn indigenous languages. In Owusu's view, anthropology cannot survive in Africa unless it abandons its Euro-centric concerns and works along with most African anthropologists toward a critical synthesis of facts of human suffering and the value of human dignity. He states:

> When Rodney Needham was recently interviewed concerning the future of anthropology in Africa, his answer, in part, in keeping with my own position, was that anthropology's only justification would be its ability to contribute something to the well-being,

happiness, and order of the peoples in those regions. . . . (Owusu 1976:20)

Many other minority anthropologists have written about the cultural determination of ethnographic study. The Afro-American Jones (1970) believes that theories fabricated by middle-class professors, which assume classic "functional" equilibrium of society, appear rather misplaced to those at the bottom of the social scale for whom social change is of primary importance. The Indian anthropologist Pandey (1975) was able to discover previously "hidden" dimensions of the life of Zuni Indians who treated him differently because he was a non-white. Jane Goodale (1971) was one of the pioneering figures in the "woman's movement" to reinterpret previously male perspectives on social life. She provided an account of Tiwi (Australian) marriage patterns as they were understood by women. Marcus and Fisher (1986) have attempted to address some of these interpretive issues in their edited book. In one essay, it is argued that our disciplinary categorization of the !Kung San hunters and gatherers is really a social construction which views them as dehumanized members of an "evolutionary stage." Fortunately, anthropologists are now attempting to work values *directly* into their research, rather than merely excluding them as something to be controlled or "factored" out. R. Naroll even advocated an explicit "moral" commitment in theoretical anthropology to such ideals as "peace," "happiness," and the construction of a world political order to be based on scientific humanism (1983).

The practice of "interactive ethnography" learns from all those above while at the same time further emphasizing that, along with Devereux (1967), social interaction can be productive of cultural insights if one is aware that "others" are structuring their interactions to some extent in terms of their own values and also their perceptions of the ethnographer. In Philip Kilbride's early research in Uganda, in collaboration with M. C. Robbins, he used to feel anxiety whenever they sat around the house talking with their Muganda Cook. He was eager to get "into the field" where the Baganda were to be found in their "natural" environment (villages, chief's houses, plaintain gardens). The same attitude about "proper" habitat can be extended to social interaction itself. Interactive ethnography assumes that the mutual interactive process to a great extent "creates" the reality perceived by anthropologists in their interviews, observations or participations. The anthropologist's personality is only part of the story.

An examination of our own values and personalities and how these factors and the interactive context have shaped our view of East African family life will now be considered. We sketch here only a brief portrait of our values and how we believe our informants perceived us in these terms. In this way, the reader can obtain a better sense as to why our "gaze" was so focused during our years in East Africa (see the relativization of "gaze" in social research as analyzed by Stoller 1982). Our interpretive position concerning the African experience later emphasizes the centrality of having children in family life, religious experience, and much else of existential import. Fertility is, however, much more then simply biological reproduction. The basic orientation is one of social reproduction to actualize one's position in a social context such as extended family, clan, or ethnic group. Thus, in our view, a social-relational style is emphasized through life as people actualize the culturally constituted experiences designed to render adults and their children ever more socially relevant. Having children and then socializing them through such events as sitting ceremonies, circumcision ceremonies, and weddings reveal attributes associated with economic wealth, power, and social prestige. Our interpretation would hold that this system is under peril at present due to the forces of modernization. What needs to be here stated is *why we* might be inclined to "positively" value such things as having children, socio-relational style, disdain for the forces of modernity, exclusive association between sexuality and monogamy, and what strikes us, in general, as an orientation to pragmatics, instead of dogmatism, in matters concerning family morality. To this list, by no means complete, could be added our desire to "defend" women and children from harmful oppressive social practices due to modernization. We thereby perceive that our research constitutes an issue-oriented enterprise of assumed utility (Messerschmidt 1981).

Our position is that these personal values have to some extent been influential in shaping our view of East Africans and their view of us. This does not mean that we have simply "invented" their experience as a reflection of our values. Rather, interactive ethnography seeks to incorporate research techniques from the literature devoted to the building of an "objective" methodology and thereby, whenever possible, to control personal biases. This need not also imply agreement on the assumption of achieved objectivity. In this way, readers can evaluate to what extent one writer's version is to be preferred over another writer's account. The methodology of interactive ethnography, with its four broad requirements, is intended to assist the reader in this evaluation. More specifically, our own values reflect in part our upbringing as Roman Catholics, especially our value of having children and protecting the family, particularly children. Our appreciation for African pragmatism probably reveals our rebellion against the "dogmatic" church in which we were raised before the Vatican II revolution. A freer marital morality in America, including optional polygyny as modeled after East Africa, remains for us an ambivalent domain—one that compels our focused attentions later. This ambivalence is probably due to anxiety over extramarital sexuality. Such is no doubt very Catholic (certainly Irish Catholicism produces great sexual anxiety; see Messinger 1969). Our hope to "improve" social conditions through social action which is "right" (i.e., assist powerless women and abused children) is a very Catholic thing to advance (among numerous other ideologies).

The African sense of community which we believe is still strong but under peril would seem to constitute a polar opposite to the Western experience of individualism (see Hsu 1983). We ourselves have never been comfortable with "competition," "individualism," and "racism." American materialism and African materialism are quite similar (LeVine 1970), however, and we are more understanding of this materialism. Janet (Capriotti) Kilbride's background as an Italian American nurtured in her a love of extended family and children that made good sense to her in the East African context. The *interactive* style of fieldwork would appear to be more easily undertaken by one who is basically an "extrovert." Primary reliance on reflexive "introspection" as a research strategy is not appealing to us, nor is it in our view very useful for phenomenological understanding as opposed to structuralist insight (Riesman 1977). In East Africa, we have been perceived variously and sometimes inadvertently as colonialists, missionaries, Catholics, teachers, and medical doctors. We have also been viewed as rich people and, of course, never fully as insiders. Nevertheless, we have many reasons to believe that our attempt to be "interactive" was generally successful in that we note with some confidence that we have always (some ten times) been welcomed back with enthusiasm and friendship.

Some specific illustrations of how this interactive process worked in our research to create for us our perceptions of East African social life will now be presented. Earlier in this chapter, we discussed a business trip undertaken by a person who was later to become a key informant on many aspects of *Kiganda* life. This informant's initial motivation to interact with Philip Kilbride was Philip's potential to be for him a "wealthy" American businessman. Friendship with such a foreigner would, in principle, motivate his Ugandan business competitors to "count him in" whenever business ventures were contemplated. This, in fact, did occur after Philip "went along" with his "status." In time, some Ugandans came to believe that Philip's *father* was very wealthy; why else would he not spend large sums of money himself? This informant has a rich imagination such that for him Philip was part of his fantasy life (see Herdt, 1982, on cultural systems as fantasy). He spent large sums of money in Philip's presence and usually had an entourage of admiring followers, particularly attractive women. Any inclination to label Africans as "materialistic" on other accounts was certainly not discouraged by interactions with this businessman.

In 1972, Janet Kilbride was looking for a research assistant to help in her study of the sensorimotor development of Baganda infants. As circumstances would have it, the wife of the aforementioned businessman was a trained nurse and midwife who was not at that time working. During the course of their work together, the two women became close friends, sharing with each other their disappointment at not having any children. While both were feeling pressure from family members to begin a family, the nurse's concern was greater in that she had been married for five years (a very long time for not conceiving in Kiganda terms), and her husband was being pressured by family and friends to marry a second wife or to divorce her if she refused to accept this. Janet assured her that working around infants would help her to conceive (something she had heard from her own ethnic mythology). While she did not really believe in this, her nurse friend apparently did. During the course of our field stay, the nurse did in reality become pregnant. She and our businessman friend are now the proud parents of five children. Such firsthand observations of family life helped us to understand more fully how important children were to the Baganda for many reasons.

Janet's personal attraction to infant research, her focused conversations about it with Africans, and her eventual admiration for Kiganda cultural practices concerning infants cannot, therefore, be completely divorced from her *own* interactions with her nurse assistant and other women. What most East Africans *take for granted* we have elevated to the title of section 2 of this book, namely "Children of Value." Our point here is not to disavow our views as solely constructed out of our background and the only motivation for interaction with our informants. It is, rather, in the spirit of ethnographic improvement to alert the reader to the often ignored, controlled, denied, or at best implicit assumption (in "our" culture or "compared to us" statements) that the interactive context is trivial. It is not. For this reason, interactive ethnography has "requirements" other than the simple recognition of interactive context. We conclude our illustration with an example of how interaction was implicated in our efforts to understand child abuse, a subject to be considered in section 3.

One day in May, 1985, while preparing to "bow out" (Freilich 1970), the authors observed a large crowd gathering at the local secondary school. Joining the crowd, they arrived just in time to see a newborn infant being lifted out of one of the school's pit latrines. The infant's mother, Sarah (a pseudonym), who had attempted the infanticide, was being hustled into her dormitory for interrogation by local officials and nurses while we observed the proceedings and a crowd continued to gather outside. Through observation and interviews, we followed this incident and its aftermath for several weeks, sometimes with the assistance of a local nurse. Settings included school, hospital, jail, and home situations. Discussions were conducted with the girl herself, various members of her family, police, school officials, and many other members of the general public. It became clear through personal involvement with Sarah and her family that our "bridgehead" into their social field (Hollis 1982) was one of mutual self-interest. Financial assistance for the infant's needs was offered and eagerly accepted in exchange for the chance to acquire "data" by involving ourselves in their present misfortune.

Throughout our encounter with them, we all cooperated as agreed although we resisted continuous attempts, though understandable, to take on added economic responsibility for the mother. It was indeed apparent that she was suffering from economic deprivation and related powerlessness to control her own fate. She seemed a passive depository for decisions concerning her but made by others such as relatives, the police, school officials, and so on. Her male relatives were also feeling monetary obligations, not in terms of their own personal needs, but in relation to stresses associated with extended-family responsibility for helping Sarah and her infant. Their social power potential and responsibility were greater than Sarah's (and her mother's) and probably for this reason they appeared to be under almost as much personal stress as Sarah herself concerning their family tragedy. The most "powerless" actor in the above episode is, of course, the infant. This is so because he has little apparent value for his mother and his absent father.

In the present case, we discovered the germ of the theoretical argument developed in this book, namely, that women and children are comparatively more socially "powerless" in modern Kenyan society than was apparently true in the recent "traditional" past. It will be shown later that traditional female power, especially in private domestic situations, accrued primarily as a consequence of economic factors such as childbearing and food production and distribution. An economic basis for female power is, of course, not unusual for women living in gathering and hunting or horticultural societies (Friedl 1975). Sarah, and many young girls like her, face a modern world where relatively expensive formal education and subsequent paid employment are necessary for economic success.

We conclude this chapter with a commentary on why we believe that this type of book is useful, namely, because it is an account of East African family life as understood by "outsiders" such as ourselves, with their own "interactive" personal histories. We therefore pose to the reader the question of the need for a book on East African family life written by a non-African. We will first address our Western audience and then consider the same question from the perspective of an East African reader.

In the United States today, there is considerable cultural conflict concerning proper definitions of the family, marriage, and childhood experience. Various "alternative forms" of the family can be found, for example, in some West Coast locations (e.g., Weisner et al. 1983), but in general United States society still holds to its European-derived ideal of the nuclear family for the expression of sexual gratification, economic cooperation, and childrearing. Cultural pluralism in the United States increases differences caused by religion, class, or educational levels. For instance, extended family ties are quite active among Italian-Americans; Afro-Americans are comparatively more accepting of "illegitimate" children and less accepting of the abortion route chosen more regularly by their Euro-American counterparts. Presently, issues of homosexual marriage, surrogate motherhood, and abortion receive heated political and theological attention. Divorces hover around the 50% mark, posing problems for children, and sociologists continue to warn of a feminization of poverty in the context of lessening male contributions for child support.

In this landscape, it is little wonder that some students of family-life issues are calling for explicit recognition of values in the ongoing research process on family. We attempt here to do precisely this—a task made more obvious when one is attempting to understand the family values of another society. We therefore believe that our materials will provide some insights of applicability to the U.S. scene while also serving to illustrate a method, namely interactive ethnography, useful for the incorporation of a value perspective in social research on the family and children. Our cross-cultural analysis has the advantage of approaching another culture, but always through the eyes of a Westerner so that our observations here should, in principle, be maximally applicable to those of *our* culture. Foreign anthropolgists who offer insights about our culture unseen by us "natives" offer an advantage of a different sort. It is this "outsider" advantage that we bring to our African audience. Various terms such as "insider-outsider," "marginal native," and "professional stranger," etc., capture the meaning intended here.

In East Africa, this book will serve several purposes. First, there are already available good "insider" accounts written by East Africans. We will refer to some of that literature later. Our own materials are "interactive," as we have explained, and should be taken as an "outsider" account which we would hope will be meaningful to the insider audience by highlighting things which an outsider perceives in the context of a comparative cultural perspective. Our second purpose is political. We seek to write about the *regional* East African cultural experience rather than the tribal or national, believing that numerous cultural practices, especially in family and childhood experience, "cross-cut" these "modern" creations. It is hoped that a developed sense of "cultural unity" may serve to alleviate tensions created by nationalism and tribalism. Finally, one of the great strengths of African society is in the field of social relations (Kaunda 1966). Traditional family and childhood is part of such institutional strength. We elucidate this strength in the second section of this book so that Westerners and East Africans can ponder the nature of our "positive" approval of this particular human experience. Finally, the last section of this book is intended to identify some social problems associated with modernization. We know from personal experience in Uganda and Kenya that East Africans care about such problems. Some of these local views will be examined in the next chapter.

As stated earlier, social life everywhere is replete with contradiction, dilemma, and unresolved wish fulfillment. In East Africa, these frequently painful experiences are often played out against the backdrop of "modernization of tradition," a subject to be discussed in the next chapter. How can one be "African" in a society which widely condemns, for example, polygyny and extramarital sexuality and encourages an "otherworldly" metaphysical reality (Okot p' Bitek 1972)? How can one be a good "clansman" but also save money for one's own children? How can one be a good "grandmother" but also cope with the burden of caring for too many grandchildren? We have found that a systematic monitoring of the East African news media, press, and literature (particularly novels) has been our best technique for establishing the range of experiences which are felt as contradictions of the sort mentioned above. Novels have been particularly useful for disclosing the affective dimension, something true of literature everywhere. Such titles as *Petals of Blood, My Wife Made Me a Polygamist, The Minister's Daughter, The Prostitute, What Does a Man Want?* and *What a Husband,* provide only a brief sense of the sort of titles that attracted us.

3

MODERNIZATION OF TRADITION
Cultural Persistence and Change in East Africa

W e consider here the socio-cultural context in East Africa, specifically Uganda and Kenya, from the perspective of major historical events which have occurred and whose effects can be seen currently in the region quite apart from our personal presence there. Our interactive ethnography is to be situated in this historical context, the same social history that each East African person finds at birth and out of which he too must fashion his own behavioral environment.

The East African cultural region was formerly known as British East Africa, which included Kenya, Uganda, and Tanzania. This total area is fairly large, or about five-and-a-half times as large as the British Isles. There is considerable climate variation in the region, which includes coastal forest, grassland, and desert ecology. In general, the most significant feature is rainfall variation and a more or less constant temperature. Thus there is usually some sequencing of a rainy season with that of a dry season (or seasons). Shortage of water is, therefore, more significant for understanding the region's ecology than are extremes of temperature.

The area of Buganda in Southern Uganda is not unusual for locations west of the Rift Valley where we have conducted much of our work. Located on the northwestern side of Lake Victoria, Buganda is a fertile area on the equator with an elevation of about 4000 feet and a climate of the tropical savanna or modified equatorial variety. Rainfall is sufficient to allow the growing of crops throughout the year, and thus there is little need for food storage. Most Baganda are peasant cultivators whose main subsistence crops are plantains, sweet potatoes, yams, and cassava. Their main cash crops include coffee, tea, and cotton. Both males and females clear the land, but the primary responsibility for cultivating subsistence crops lies with Baganda women and sometimes hired male porters (*abapakasi*). Men usually take control of commercial farming, trading, fishing, and other wage-earning occupations.

Human settlement in East Africa is of long standing. Some believe that East Africa was the original home of mankind (see Leakey 1981). Ancient civilizations of Egypt, Southern India, and Arabia maintained trade connections with East Africa as early as 3,000 years ago. These contacts were greatest along the East African Coast, giving rise to the *Waswahili* people and the *KiSwahili* language (Pritchard 1977). Indigenous peoples of East Africa included the Bantu, who expanded into the area at least five centuries ago, and Nilotic and Hamitic people from the West and North. Contemporary populations show various racial admixtures of all these historic population movements. There is considerable admixture of cultural practice through trade, warfare, and intermarriage. The nineteenth and twentieth centuries are characterized by intensive European penetration into East Africa, which began much earlier in 1498 by Vasco de Gama of Portugal. It is the European penetration that initiated the "modernization" process which is the subject of our concern in this book. Previous contacts involved African and external peoples, all of whom were of the "ancient" world and quite similar in many cultural respects. As we saw in chapter 1, this European penetration set in motion that worldwide process known as modernization which everywhere resulted in an encounter between "ancient" preindustrial family-based civilizations and modernity which includes, for example, individualization, literacy, formal education, and the nation state.

The present work focuses on the nations of Kenya and Uganda. Each of these nations presently contrasts with Tanzania, where socio-economic development has been modeled on a socialist ideology. Nevertheless, the "traditional" cultural context to be described below was commonly found over the entire East African region. To be sure, there are and were numerous intra-regional cultural differences, but our focus here is on family and childhood experiences which were generally shared across community, national, and ethnic boundaries. Specifically, however, our actual fieldwork is confined to the Western Province of Kenya and the adjacent area of southern Uganda. For evidence concerning broader regional cultural affinities, we have relied exclusively on secondary sources.

Many Ugandans and Kenyans today live in small towns and trading centers and in cities such as Kampala-Mengo and Nairobi. Kampala-Mengo, a modern city of several hundred thousand, grew up on hills where Baganda kings resided in the late 1800s. Beginning with the completion of a rail link to the port city of Mombasa, Kenya, in 1901, and continuing up to the present, East Africans have experienced the effects of increasing urbanization and industrialization. Therefore, despite a relatively brief period of contact with the outside world, many profound changes have occurred in social and economic areas of life. For example, in Uganda, Baganda living in Kampala-Mengo are distributed with other Ugandans among housing estates, low-income temporary settlements, and middle- to upper-class residential areas in the city's periphery. Rural Ugandan economic life remains largely agrarian although a desire for cash and increased participation in modern life is a salient dynamic in rural Buganda (Robbins and Kilbride 1974). One can observe some individuals who live in modern homes, wear western-style clothing, and speak a foreign language residing within walking distance of others who retain a traditional circular home, wear barkcloth clothing, and speak only *Luganda*.

The modernization process has overall resulted in both cultural persistence and change. In this chapter, we will try to consider some of the baseline cultural experiences which in East Africa are historically thought to constitute "Tradition" and which we are here calling "Africanity" (Maquet 1972). Using older ethnographic and ethno-historical material concerning life as it was lived several generations ago in addition to our own observations, it will be possible to show both cultural persistence and change in Uganda. A historical profile of social life in a western Kenyan village area, along with our own, will also serve to illustrate a similar synthesis. This chapter will conclude with a focus on the delocalization process with examples gleaned from East African mass media and literature.

Before proceeding, however, we need to clarify our rationale for considering here an East African tradition as a meaningful unit of description. We have set before us the task of describing certain family life experiences—a cultural perspective that emphasizes, for the most part, *similarities* of custom rather than ethnic differences typically found in social organization, economy, or political arrangement. To be sure, "tribal" units did exist in some form prior to the modern era. Nevertheless, there is no doubt that tribalism and tribal boundaries were exacerbated or even created during the colonial period. The Baganda, for example, numbered several million prior to colonial times and were a strongly organized socio-political unit centered in the Kingly institution. This "tribe," or ethnic group was assisted by the British by means of a policy whereby the Baganda were supported in their territorial claims over neighboring societies such as the Bunyoro. The Abaluyia "tribe" in the pre-colonial era was a loosely interacting network of villages and clans, all of whom used the term *"mulembe"* (peace) as a greeting along with sharing numerous other similarities of language and culture. There was considerable diffusion or spread of ideas and lifeways through trade, intermarriage, and warfare among these peoples and also the neighboring Luo (Were 1985). The British created the Abaluyia ethnic group for administrative purposes, and a sense of "tribal" affinity has been stimulated ever since in response to the label Abaluyia as applied to them for administrative purposes. In a recent book, Ambler (1988) shows that a regional rather than tribal model best characterizes the Central region in the nineteenth century. He states:

> Across the region a series of similar exchange relationships joined settlements in the dry areas . . . with communities in higher areas . . . Such trade connections spread out in every direction, creating an evolving complex of interlocking and overlapping networks of economic interdependence that by the second half of the nineteenth century constituted a coherent regional exchange system. (1988:57)

The modern nation state, a recent creation of only 25 years, bears no strong relationship to tribal boundaries. The Abaluyia, for example, are found in Kenya and Uganda, the Maasai in Tanzania and Kenya, and the Somalis in Kenya and Somalia. Added to this is the considerable evidence to suggest that even "tribes" in Africa of long standing, such as the Baganda, eventually owe their political and economic cohesion to external trade and conquest forces, such as the Arab incursion into the East African interior and the Atlantic slave trade (Wolf 1982). Thus it should come as a surprise that ethnic groups or tribes in East Africa are often considered as significant "real" social groups that in turn give rise to social cleavage and conflict (see *The Standard,* August 2, 1985). What is often overlooked in historical study and political ideology is the extent to which different tribes possess, in fact, many similarities in custom, created from a common historical heritage. Through numerous contacts over hundreds of years resulting from the "Bantu expansion," there has emerged in Africa a cultural complex of traits which writer J. Maquet (1972) refers to as "Africanity." For this reason, he suggests that social research in Africa needs to move beyond "global" units such as tribes to develop descriptive categories for cultural practice which crosscut tribes.

Colonialism too has constituted a common regional experience which has served to produce cultural uniformity among ethnic groups. In the preface to a book entitled, *A Century of Change in Eastern Africa*, the editor writes:

> The attempt to deal with a single social system in its entirety, which was characteristic of midcentury social anthropology, now seems to be out of favor as the other studies in this volume indicate. Instead there is a tendency, on one hand, to attack broad social phenomena common to a great variety of the African population as the result of a common experience such as the colonial presence or, on the other hand, to investigate situations on the local level among a limited number of people. (Arens 1976:04)

Based on our research in two nations and among several ethnic groups, along with our reading of the literature, we believe that the domain of family life and childhood displays many similarities throughout the East African region (and certainly for some practices throughout other places in Africa). We believe that some family practices can be thought of as part of a "ModCult" (our term meaning psycho-sociocultural unit or region) that would include the present-day region of former British East Africa encompassing Uganda, Kenya, and Tanzania. Other such geographic cultural units would be, for example, North America and Japan. This study is hopefully a beginning in future cultural classification, involving, as it does, only our own fieldwork and selected reference to societies in Uganda and Kenya. Should the idea of "ModCult" be accurate, it could potentially serve as an intellectual basis to create unity where the older idea of "tribe" now creates dissension. Although we focus on similarity, there are, of course, significant cultural differences among "tribes." For example, even among the Abaluyia some groups practice circumcision and others do not. Nevertheless, considerable regional cultural similarities are due to historical contacts producing a common area heritage, including the recent experience (circa 1900–60) of political control by the British and associated penetration of British institutions, language, and other customs (e.g., teatime is even popular in rural areas).

Regional cultural similarity is also in evidence because culture, in general, is "adaptive." Pre-modern "traditional" East African cultural practice was very "people-oriented" (Maquet 1972, Kaunda 1966) because the economic order was of a subsistence type with no dependency on machines, literacy, or draft animals. Instead people's labor provided economic cooperation and production. Historically, such a human-labor-intensive system of production often, in Africa, evolved into complex kingdoms or stratified societies that centralized control of people's labor and the distribution of goods and services. Thus East African "Africanity" is a cultural form with a regional, geographic base understood by the historical dynamics of both adaptation and diffusion through trade and conquest (Ambler 1988). It should be noted that kinship relations constitute a significant unit of economic adaptation in East Africa. The extended family, for example, still persists as an element in regional East Africa, but as this volume will show, it is presently under peril.

The dynamic aspect of East African regional uniformity is best understood in the context of the modernization process which will be considered in this work from the perspective of delocalization, particularly moral delocalization. We will argue here that through a process of "delocalization" traditional ideas about "proper" behavior are frequently replaced by moral imperatives from "outside." At the same time, economic delocalization has also weakened the moral power of the clan, extended family and other social groups with moral authority over parents and children. In the terms of R. Naroll (1983), the "moralnet" (family, neighborhood, village) is being eroded. By means of a cross-cultural survey, he found that this erosion was related to a dramatic increase in social problems such as alcoholism, suicide, child abuse, and divorce. We turn now to a brief discussion of tradition concentrating on local East African views of their own heritage.

Tradition as Local Knowledge

In the previous chapter we have considered modernization in East Africa from the technical, anthropological, theoretical perspective of delocalization, often referring to cultural description and theorizing by non-East Africans. We now consider the notion of cultural heritage (or Africanity) from an exclusively indigenous intellectual perspective. Some ideas about cultural heritage and persistence held by local scholars will be noted. There are numerous scholars working on "tradition." One thinks, for example, of the work on the East African English language by A. Mazrui (1975) which shows that East African English is in need of a different label if what is meant by English is the King's English. One also thinks of the efforts of the great novelist, Ngugi Wa Thiong'o, to write modern novels in his own Kikuyu dialect. In the domain of music, Wanjala (1985) studies traditional music forms in village life today. The educational psychologist Otaala (1973) contrasts African traditional education as functional in comparison to modern values of critical questioning of tradition as they persist today. There are, of course, many pioneering cultural historical studies and tribal ethnographies which are still relevant today (Kenyatta 1984, Osogo 1966). The indigenous literature on the Baganda is, for example, immense. From the cultural studies of Kiganda culture (*mpisa*) by the Prime Minister Sir A. Kagwa (1952) up to the autobiography of King Freddy Mutesa (1968), there are numerous accounts in English and *Luganda*. Throughout these studies there is evidence of a strong sense of African tradition described in terms of tribal culture or a broader East African heritage. While many other local scholars could be mentioned, we will focus now on the views of four who are most directly pertinent for our work.

The historian G. S. Were has worked to advance the notion that the concept of "tribe" and tribal cultural identity has been overstated in the fields of historical, sociological, and anthropological inquiry. By culture, he means the totality of a group's values, norms, traditions, customs, and language (1985). He states that "the contention is that since in the not-too-distant past our ancestors moved freely and widely, interacting with one another and with various environments, a lot of lending, borrowing and fusion have constantly been taking place. As a result there are many common characteristics, particularly among neighboring ethnic groups" (1985:7). Gideon Were (1985:6) quotes with approval the research findings of Japanese researchers working among six ethnic groups: "as the result of . . . frequent population movements across ethnic boundaries, diffusion and incorporation of many cultural traits among linguistically and socially different peoples seemed to have occurred in various degrees." To be quite specific, Were in various writings considers his central question to be, Are ethnic and cultural identities in African history mythical or real? He believes cultural identity (the more generic) to be more significant than ethnic identity (the more specific and fluctuating) (cf. Were 1982). Thus, our attempt here to combine *cultural* materials gathered from several ethnic groups so as to provide a description of regional cultural uniformity in family life, for example, is locally substantiated.

Perhaps no better cultural expression than oral literature can be found to illustrate both persistence and change in modern East African regional culture. In Kenya, T. Liyong faced the problem of how to retain a sense of "growing up in traditional East Africa" when presented with an inherited colonial English syllabus not suited to the African situation (1972). With some colleagues, he decided to emphasize African oral literature as the core of the literature department at the University of Nairobi. He states,

> The students' initial reaction was: oral literature, What is that? We told them that it was the cultural information and values transmitted mainly by the spoken word . . . in societies where writing was not yet the order of the day: folktales, legends, myths, beliefs, songs, poems, proverbs, tongue twisters, puns. . . . and all the other ways of imparting group knowledge to the young and new members. (1972:VI.)

Liyong's various projects to gather oral literature from various ethnic communities has put him in a good position to detect communality at the level of regional popular culture. He concludes that "there are more similarities in East African (indeed African) mini-cultures than dissimilarities" (1972:VII).

Cultural themes found in oral literature indicate a strong sense of persistence. Liyong writes:

> I don't think our sense of manhood has changed much. You were a man when you were an adult, head of your own family which you managed well so that there was no famine, little quarrel; you were a good host . . . What has changed are the fields in which we distinguish our manhood. For example doing well in school has replaced the seasonal generational intensive passing out parade . . . what it all proves is that the essence of the African is still there. (1972:xi)

Another student of African literary and cultural expression is Okot p'Bitek. His famous song poems (e.g., *Song of Lawino,* 1966) use a traditional idiom to decry the destructive forces of modernism contrasted to the more genuine traditionalism. His work on religion quoted earlier is part of an epistemological position which rejects most of western scholarship, particularly anthropology, as being ethnocentric and self-serving. The concept of "primitive" culture, for example, did often appear in the papers and books concerning cultural practices of African people. Further, his extreme relativistic position rejects even the possibility of universalism which might link African and European cultural expressions together in some form of synthesis. He therefore rejects attempts to argue that traditional African religion is broadly similar to, say, Christianity and can be replaced (with some retention) by the latter.

We agree with p'Bitek that traditional cultural values are, on the whole, more "genuine" than their modern delocalized counterparts. We applaud his poetically stated opposition to, for example, the brutal role of the army in *Song of Soldier* (He lived in exile from Uganda) or to modern man's frequent aping of Western aesthetic values (*Song of Lawino*). While we will argue in this book that traditional African values concerning children are genuine in comparison to those of the modern West, we are not as "relativistic" as p'Bitek, who suggests that everything culturally African should be defended from *any* modern (usually Western) inroads. Nevertheless, we would agree, along with many African scholarly and popular views, with the following sentiments expressed by p'Bitek:

> Thus, most contrary to the African idea that everybody must marry . . . have a family (and for a man, the more wives and children he has the better), . . . schools were built, and upbringing—which should mean instilling into the young the values of their people . . . was christened "education" which now passed on only foreign ideologies . . . The medical student was made to swear the oath of some ancient Greek medicine man as if all medical knowledge came from Europe. Those who studied "food sciences" never thought of farming the African mushrooms and white ants. . . . (1986:15)

Overall we find in the writings of p'Bitek keen observations, beliefs, and cultural practices that unify East Africans into a common regional culture. His nationalistic concerns are suggestive of many political applications of cultural study that are part of a reflexive tradition now quite common in African universities.

Our discussion of traditional heritage concludes by focusing specifically on social organization pertaining to women's work and children's place in society. As we will argue in the third section of this book, it is precisely this area of experience that is becoming delocalized. We consider here a recent piece by the Kenyan historian R. Nasimiyu (1985). Above we argued that East African economy was previously organized in a production process which, when compared to the present, was characterized by a more symmetrical division of labor by gender. This economy contained economic roles for children as well as for men and women. R. Nasimiyu (1985) has written about the Bukusu (Abaluyia) production process at the time just prior to the colonial era (late ninetenth century). She states that land was a major resource and was communal property. Individual rights were restricted to privilege of access and use. Families and clans controlled access to land. Members of a family or clan used common grazing fields, salt-licks, and streams. Women were not allocated land as individuals but were given land to use by their husbands. Nevertheless, Nasimiyu states, "It was also the responsibility of a husband to allocate sufficient land to each wife, which she occupied and used as a right and was not subjected to her husband's whims . . . women had virtual control and monopoly of crop production and distribution of surplus if there was any" (1985:54). Men controlled the land and also cattle, which was the responsibility of men and boys. Once again, with cows as with land and crops, women controlled the products of cattle and goats such as milk, butter, and ghee, while men controlled the producers. In this essentially non-competitive economy, agriculture was a small-scale subsistence system. Technology was horticultural, with iron tools such as digging implements.

Marriage and childhood must be understood in the above economic context. Kinship relations of blood and marriage determined access to land and human labor. Polygyny and fertility increased the pool of laboring kinsmen. Nasimiyu writes, "It is important to point out the fact that the hoe being the major farm implement . . . the supply of labour was readily available from the children and other members of the family, mainly the women" (1985:61). Men cleared the fields whereas planting was done by women and children. Nasimiyu further states "a man knew at all times which fields were held by which of his wives, and he was expected to assist each wife in the heavy agricultural labour required in the fields" (1985:61). Men made iron implements and women produced pottery. These and other products were exchanged through barter, there being, of course, no all-purpose monetary medium of exchange. In conclusion, Nasimiyu writes,

"We can say that women assumed important roles in the pre-colonial Bukusu economy. They featured prominently in the fields of agricultural production and exchange. In terms of land, Bukusu women were granted considerable authority . . . " (1985:64).

Because land was plentiful in nineteenth-century East Africa, human labor was the essential technological imperative throughout the region. Women, therefore, were valued as sources of labor and producers of future laborers. In Central Kenya, for example, women were sometimes pawned in exchange for foodstuffs or livestock (Ambler 1988:62). The extent, however, to which women actually worked in comparison to men is debated. Kitching (1980), for example, argues that both male and female labor was underutilized in nineteenth-century Kenya.

To construe Nasimiyu's observation in our terms, we note that agrarian pre-capitalist economy in Kenya was *localized*. Main crops were African ones such as eleusine, sorghum, simsim, and others. The social relations of production were kin-based, as were the consequent *moralnets* that governed morals associated with marriage, childbearing, and exchange. It is this economic and moral order that now is in a process of delocalization. A people-oriented, social-relational society is in transformation in response to mechanization, urbanization, and other modern social forces. Power relations were clearly tilted in favor of the men in their roles as husbands and elders. In particular, property was inherited through men, and land was in the hands of clans with their male leadership. Comparatively, it is known that gender-power relations in society are related to such factors as inheritance (J. Goody 1983); the distribution, not necessarily just simple production, of resources (Friedl 1975); and differences in public and private political or authority roles (Rosaldo and Lamphere 1974). We can infer that pre-modern Abaluyia gender relations were favorable to men on these and other counts. Nevertheless, the modern monetary economy and the Westernized educational system, to both of which men have greater access, are thus presently even more unfavorable to women, who as Nasimiyu has observed, had considerable economic power in the past (even if not comparable to that of men). This gender imbalance of power is felt most by the illiterate or little-educated rural woman and her unemployed or underpaid urban counterpart. To mention only one area, a woman in her contemporary role as "co-wife" has no legal right to inherit from her husband, nor do her children. When both husband and wife are employed in Nairobi, for example, it is only the husband who is given a "house allowance." The area of gender-power relations will be our subject of study in chapter 8.

Cultural Persistence: Ethnographic Observations

Delocalization is a process that involves *persistence* of tradition and even creation of new cultural forms. Such creativity, known as neo-traditionalism, could be seen in Uganda where, for example, women adapted the traditional dress, the *Basuti,* to the miniskirt, giving rise to the *minibasuti.* The use of scientific terms and concepts in Swahili is another example. We turn now to consider the delocalization process from the perspective of cultural persistence and neo-traditionalism, taking one example from Kenya and another from Uganda. The persistence of traditional family values in modern Kenya will be discussed first, followed by the retention of social values in modern Uganda as derived from a pre-modern kingdom there. These two cases show the regional cultural synthesis of old and new that the previously discussed term *ModCult* is intended to capture.

Our first example of persistence of social practice and cultural value is taken from an agrarian region of Western Kenya not far from where Nasimiyu conducted her own fieldwork. The modern economy is greatly delocalized, with a modern dependence on cash crops (e.g., maize), fertilizer, and transport to distant markets in exchange for money. Nowadays a small proportion of men are resident locally in comparison to the past. We will consider later the negative consequences of this delocalization for children and women. Nevertheless, things would be worse if it were not for considerable cultural persistence of values favorable to women and to children.

Family

Our research in Western Kenya shows that kin or extended family rights and duties are very salient. This cultural ideology of kin-based support groups is no doubt retained from pre-modern times. Table 1 describes a portion of the census data which we collected from sixty-five homes (all Abaluyia) from two villages in the Matunda area. At the time of our census, these villages contained one hundred occupied homes of which sixty-seven were Abaluyia. Inspection of Table 1 reveals that only 20% of these homes

Table 1   Abaluyia Family Structure in Sisal Estates

Family Type	Number of Homes	Percent
Non-Extended		
Nuclear monogamous	13	20.0
Composite polygamous (husband present)	3	4.6
Composite polygamous (husband absent)	1	1.5
Stem (woman and children)	7	10.8
Total	24	36.9
Extended		
Stem (woman, affines and consanguines)*	17	26.2
Nuclear plus at least one consanguine*	15	23.1
Composite (at least two nuclear families extended by generation)	5	7.7
Composite (polygamous and extended by generation)	3	4.6
Stem (man, children, and grandchildren)	1	1.5
Stem (solitary person)	0	0.0
Total	41	63.1

*especially grandchildren

contained the monogamous, nuclear family, with only one husband, one wife, and their children present. Another 4.6% are composite polygynous families, containing a husband, his wives, and their children. One family was a composite polygynous family with the husband absent. In addition, 10.8% are stem families consisting of a mother and her children. Thus 36.9% of our sample could be classified as non-extended families. Nevertheless, the continued importance in Abaluyia society of the extended family, in its various manifestations, is supported by the fact that the remaining households, that is, 63.1%, consist of extended families.

Table 1 lists the various forms of the extended family and their frequency of occurrence. The most frequent type of extended family is the stem family, consisting of a female-headed household (husband absent) with her affines (relatives by marriage) and her consanguines (blood relatives), especially grandchildren (26.2%). This is also the most frequent type of household structure in our sample. The second most frequent type of extended household and the second most frequent in our sample is the nuclear plus at least one consanguine (23.1%). It should be noted that in both of these extended family types, the consanguine is most often a grandchild. Overall, more than half of the homes in our census, or thirty-three homes (50.8%), contain at least one resident grandchild. Twenty-two of these houses do not have the grandchild's father living there although in twelve of the twenty-two homes, the child's grandfather is present. In fact, in the majority of our homes (40), the husband is in residence (61.5%). In some of the homes without a husband, there is a grown, unmarried son present. Significantly, however, ten of the twenty-five stem families (40%) contain three generations and do not have any husband present. We will return later in this book to problems associated with female-headed households and the presence of grandchildren without their parents in many local homes.

We also will show later how extended family ties include obligations to assist related children who are in need of assistance. This tendency must be understood within the broader context of family (both affines and consanguines) seen as a support network in times of crisis such as sickness, death, food shortage, and so on. In our social survey referred to above, we asked respondents to report how frequently, for what reasons, and by whom they are visited and whom they visit in the rural areas from which they have migrated. Family was mentioned by nearly all respondents and exclusively so. Only three mentioned friends and family, while sixty mentioned family only. The frequency of visits ranged from once every several years to several times a month, with most reporting several visits per year. The most common reason (mentioned by nineteen respondents) for being visited was to obtain food from them in exchange for money, farm labor, or food from Western areas. One respondent, for example, states that "I am brought bananas, cassava, and millet in exchange for maize." Other reasons given for being visited include, 'to see the family,' 'to attend a funeral,' and 'to visit a sick relative.' Residents also make visits to their former homes almost as often as they are visited. Relatives constitute, by far, the main category of persons visited. Reasons for visiting are to attend funerals; to attend circumcision ceremonies; to visit sick relatives; or to just plain visit. Only one respondent, however, reported traveling to obtain food from her relatives. Overall, these materials clearly show the significance of family relationships, including extended family ties, in the economic, social, and ceremonial lives of Western Kenya.

Our Ugandan example refers to what many writers and scholars have frequently commented on as a remarkable persistence of Kiganda cultural institutions, particularly those relating to the kingdom (cf. L. Fallers 1964). This is not surprising because until 1967 the Baganda were organized into a centralized kingdom. The dynamics of this system constitute a necessary beginning context for a description of modern social relations and adult cultural values. In Buganda, the kingship was richly embodied in cultural tradition and individual sentiments and behavior. Tribal history, songs, venerations to the king, and numerous other concrete and symbolic expressions make of the Baganda what one anthropologist referred to as "The king's men" (Fallers 1964). Governmental authority was organized from the top; that is, the king (Kabaka) made direct appointments to subordinate political offices (cf. Roscoe 1911; L. Fallers 1964). Stratification and status inequality were, therefore, important elements in the Kiganda status mobility system. This system, in addition, was also characterized by social mobility. Goldschmidt (1965), for example, has stated:

> Each officer in the government served explicitly at the pleasure of the Kabaka (king) as his appointee—promoted, moved, disposed or decapitated by him. This created a high degree of social mobility; it was literally true that a peasant's son could rise to the highest level of status and power, short of the Kabakaship itself . . . Mobility was one major dynamic of Buganda. (1965:785)

This combination of stratification and status inequality, on the one hand, and social mobility, on the other, produced in Buganda a specific configuration of adult cultural values concerning social relations.

In a study of adult Baganda values, Doob (1964) found that a majority of traditional Baganda (e.g., "minor leaders" and "followers") expressed agreement with the statements "a chief should always be obeyed" and "leaders rather than people are more important for progress." Only a minority of his "modern" Makerere University educated leaders, however, expressed agreement (cf. 346–347). Obedience to and respect for authority are not unexpected personal qualities in a society marked by social stratification and status inequality. The dynamic of social mobility, however, poses much more than passive obedience, deference, and respect for authority figures "above" ego. Rather, upward mobility in Buganda requires an active social manipulation of others, both those above and those below ego in the social hierarchy. Traditionally, a peasant could improve his position by convincing the king that he was worthy of "promotion." For example, ideally, Baganda boys were sent by peasant families to the king's palace where they could serve as "pages." Proximity to the center of power provided an opportunity not only to learn the arts of political intrigue, but also to catch the eye of a potential benefactor. A clever page could theoretically rise to the position of *katikkiro* or prime minister. Girls, too, were sometimes given by peasant families to the king in the hopes of winning his favor. A favorite royal concubine or wife could become the mother of a future *kabaka* or otherwise win favors for her family.

Social mobility depended upon a Muganda's ability to become socially involved and facile in the skills of interpersonal manipulation. Concerning this point, Richards (1964) observes:

> A client was, of course, admired for his deference, loyalty, and efficiency. An inferior was praised for his skill in cajoling and manipulating those above him, by the expert use of the arts of submission or, as Baganda would say, by their knowledge of "the art of being ruled" -*kufugibwa*, . . . [o]ld men telling their life histories, will describe with approval behavior involving ostentatious humility, cleverly turned compliments and the nice practice of courtesies to a lord. (273)

In contrast, "a lord who was persuasive, quick in retort and not easily silenced was, and still is, admired, and such attributes were obviously useful in a competitive society like that of Buganda" (Richards 1964:271).

While the values described above are derived from the pre-modern era in Buganda, there is clear evidence that these values persist today. The post-independence period (1962-present) in Uganda has seen increased urbanization and industrialization. Even remote areas of the country have become increasingly more interdependent, with international capital networks. Rural economic life remains largely agrarian although a desire for cash and increased participation in modern life is a salient dynamic in rural Buganda today. Urban life overall provides increased economic opportunities and rapid access to modern goods and services. Success in contemporary Buganda still requires considerable manipulative skill, or as one informant put it, "The gift of tongue." Whereas in the pre-modern period social skills were primarily useful in the political sphere, nowadays Baganda also aspire to success through various types of modern status, including professional, commercial, administrative, and many other urban positions. Thousands of Baganda women, for example, are employed in Kampala in various salaried occupations such as nursing, teaching, secretarial work, and banking, as well as in semi-skilled jobs such as newspaper seller, salesgirl, telephone operator, etc.

Nowadays, for both sexes, "upward mobility" provides a means for a larger income and the wherewithal to acquire modern material items. As in the past, "cleverly turned compliments," "persuasiveness," and other traditional social skills are useful and admired. Baganda respect the person who is able to successfully "convince" (*okumatiza*) others of the validity of his point of view. We have often observed Baganda extending great efforts to "persuade" peers, patrons, clients, and others for various purposes (e.g., to beg for money, to extend a loan, to conceal an adulterous affair). An act of persuasion usually elicits the admiring response *mattide* ("I am convinced"). Deception (*okulimba*), social cleverness (*mugezi*), and other manipulatory skills are also valued by Baganda. Social involvement, manipulatory or not, is the most admired personal quality. One male Muganda informant, educated in sociology, informed us that:

> Three major values characterize Baganda. We have a concern for wealth, in particular money and property. We are arrogant or like to "show oneself" to others. If I had a new car, I would like to be seen around. In Buganda, the normative layout is relational. It's all making a correct impression, greeting people, not things like "perseverance" or "being alone on an island."

Another informant, an 18-year-old girl, feels that to become a successful person one must:

> First of all be a sociable person, otherwise you will find that you have no friends; and if you don't have friends, it's quite difficult to make any progress in your work. Being sociable here in Uganda means a great deal and it's also the same as having good manners (*mpisa*).

The importance attached to being sociable is strikingly apparent in the elaborate degree to which ritualized greetings are emphasized among Baganda. One of the first things that a child learns is how to greet others properly, that is, in a high-pitched fashion considered to be respectful. There are appropriate greetings suitable for a variety of social circumstances. Propriety requires that neighbors exchange greetings when passing along the road or meeting casually in the village. These greetings can vary by the time of day, age of the participants, length of time since previous encounters, and so on. A common usage, for example, appropriate for a casual encounter some time in the early morning is: "*Wasuze otyanno?*"

meaning "How did you sleep?" One typically responds, "*bulungi*" or "fine."
When participants are not in a hurry (for example, going to visit friends),
the initial greeting is usually followed by a rather extended sequel. The
following exchange is common although it by no means limits the possibili-
ties:

Greeting	Response
Agafayo? (What happens there?)	*Ekyali* (O.K.)
Webale emirimu (Thanks for your work)	*Kale, naawe webale* (O.K., you too I appreciate your work)
Mutusinya ki? (What do you have more than us?)	*Nkuba* (rain), *Musana* (sun) or some other event
Abeeka bali otya? (How are people at home?	*Bo Balungi* (they are fine)

For individuals who have been separated for a long time, one might say
"*Olabiseeko?*" meaning "so you have appeared." A particularly delightful
surprise at seeing a returned friend or loved one is expressed by saying:
"*Ndaba ku ki?*" or "Whom do I see?"

On those occasions when city folk return to their rural villages, formal
greetings are sometimes quite lengthy. On one such occasion, we observed
a family of ten people welcoming back their urban relative with a formalized greeting sequence lasting about fifteen minutes. Urban informants
sometimes privately express annoyance about this. In the city, greetings are
far less frequent and usually shorter in duration, although such behavior is
by no means insignificant. Women in Kampala are, however, less likely to
kneel while greeting men or social superiors, a custom still widely practiced
in rural areas. In particular, urban bars where many modern Baganda
congregate provide a setting where, in addition to the standardized greetings among customers and clientele, some men jokingly and sometimes
covetously engage barmaids in standardized vulgar sexual greetings.

Occasions where one is expected to be sociable are numerous in Kiganda
society. Collective village life largely revolves around attendance at weddings and burials. During these events, a village can seem to be quite
deserted as neighbors amass for several days of feasting, drumming, and
dancing. Temporary shelters are constructed to accommodate guests, many

of whom come from afar. Extended visiting for burial of a distant kinsman is, in fact, a primary social responsibility. One male informant noted:

> Attendance at funeral is an obligatory social function in the life of a Muganda. No wonder attendances at funerals outstrip attendances at church, weddings, and public meetings. Absenteeism from office by Baganda is most of the time due to funeral attendances. Probably 90% of the total commercial advertisements on Radio Uganda is daily taken up by Luganda announcements of death and the sick.

The bar, especially for men, is another often frequented behavioral setting in Kampala, as well as in the villages. During the late afternoon and evening, Baganda enjoy gathering in bars. The bar setting, although ubiquitous throughout Buganda, varies somewhat by the degree of modernization of its location. Rural bars are often located in the homes or stores of beverage manufacturers. Traditional banana wine or distilled banana wine called *waragi* are served. The woman of the house is frequently the hostess. Bars in Kampala are on the whole much larger; customers frequently number between one and three hundred. Barmaids are uniformed, and prostitutes may also be present. A variety of iced, European drinks are served. Villages are not, however, especially cohesive social units in Buganda. Traditionally, each household head formed a client tie to a particular chief which remained intact as long as the chief proved to be a beneficial patron. Families in general moved comparatively frequently, seeking an optimum political-economic relationship with a patron-chief. Indeed, residential mobility began early. Very young children were at times sent to live temporarily with grandparents, other kinsmen, or potential benefactors. Adoption by relatives was, and still is, also common, particularly in cases of divorce, where the child is raised by his father's family since the child "belongs" to the father.

Beyond the local village, norms of sociability and hospitality are extended to others in one's clan. Most Baganda are affiliated soon after birth with the clan of their father. Kings, however, belong to their mother's clan. Each clan has a hereditary head who, with the aid of a council consisting of heads of subordinate segments, makes important decisions regarding clan affairs. Such matters as land allocation, financial assistance to members, legitimacy of claim to membership, etc., are common concerns of each clan. Due to a high degree of mobility, most Baganda do not reside in villages associated with their clans; therefore, the clan tends to "crosscut" widely dispersed local villages. Even so, the social significance of clan membership, and identification with it, remain strong. One example of this is the degree to which aspirations of men for many children are related to a concern for increasing one's clan. Adherence to clan exogamy and observance of food taboos associated with each clan remain strong in all sectors of society. It is considered proper to be hospitable and helpful to a clansman in need of assistance, such as school fees.

The emphasis on being sociable and involved with other people should not be confused with an indiscriminant, sentimental involvement with *all* other people. Quite to the contrary, although Baganda enjoy and seek out social encounters, many relationships are formal and circumspect. In-laws, for example, are to be respectfully treated or altogether avoided. Propriety requires that a son-in-law, for example, not see his mother-in-law; he must even step off a road to pass by her should this be necessary. Fathers, in Buganda, are not to be considered "buddies" as in our own culture. The relationship between brothers is also strained due to competition over succession to their father's position. A Kiganda proverb states: "Brothers are like dried gourds. They bang against each other." The need for social involvement and preference for human company versus symbolic communication with books and television or with animals is directly indicated by numerous statements of our informants. Most Baganda, for example, find it incredible that tourists rarely, if ever, return home with photographs or films of Africans, preferring instead pictures of animals. Few Baganda care to visit game parks or, with the exception of dogs, to keep or pamper pets.

Preference for social involvement is indirectly indicated by examining the content of dream narratives taken from ninety-five Baganda (Kilbride 1974). The following items appeared with decreasing frequency among these dreams: People other than dreamer (N = 68, 72%); animals (N = 11, 12%); food (N = 8, 8%). In eighty-nine of the narratives (94%), the dreamer was actively involved, usually with other people, in his dream. Common social activities experienced by these dreamers included such things as visiting, traveling afar, attending feasts or ceremonies, and farming. Some narratives, however, particularly those elicited from urban residents, involved accounts of personal disappointment, such as the death of a loved one or difficulties in interpersonal relationships.

We have considered in this ethnographic section materials which are intended to be illustrative of social relation patterns widely distributed and intensely experienced in East Africa. Our focus has been that of cultural

analysis of particular ethnic group experience but with the intended gener-
ality to the region for most patterns. We have not focused on differences of
ethnicity, culture, or social class. We believe that most East Africans would
be very much "at home" with the social relations and values described
above. Granted the Baganda were the most centralized society, for them,
the king can be best understood in a family idiom as a father figure or a
powerful clan elder who has gained much authority. Family, village, and life
and death as significant events, for instance, are ubiquitous. L. Fallers
(1964) has argued that Baganda society never developed "class" differences
in culture. Virtually all Baganda, we believe, did share a common value
orientation as outlined above irrespective of differences in quantity of
goods and services actually controlled by rank. Our ethnographic work
with people of varying wealth and education shows that differences of
"class" are now more notable than previously in Uganda and Kenya.
Nevertheless, we believe that the domain of family and childhood cultural
issues considered in the next section of this book transcend not only ethnic
groups but also class differences based on education, wealth, residence, or
whatever other social criteria. In general, the more rural and the less
educated a person, the more his or her overall participation in exclusively
African-derived practices. Unfortunately, as we shall see in section 3, some
of these practices are now present in delocalized form.

Change in Tradition: Popular Views

We turn now to the East African mass media as a source of commentary on
the modernization of tradition. Our interactive ethnography, it will be
recalled, seeks as a methodological requirement to permit members of the
host community to "speak for themselves." We cite here selected examples
to illustrate that our concern for delocalization of family as a research query
is not imposed from outside, but is, quite to the contrary, an active ongoing
aspect of East African phenomenological experience. Such changes will be
the subject of our attention in section 3. Mass media in East Africa is
nowadays a salient component of what has been elsewhere referred to as
modern "micro technology," small items used by individuals (Robbins and
Kilbride 1987). The radio has, for example, caused the following changes

as perceived by informants living along the southwestern shores of Lake Victoria in Uganda:

> We buy radios for news and announcements. When a person dies in a certain family, and a person is going to hold a succession ceremony, a twin ceremony, or a wedding party, he passes this to his relatives through the radio, so it is very helpful to householders or people who manage a house.
>
> It keeps visitors busy when one is away trying to get beer or preparing food. Also it shows that the person is rich, particularly if he owns a big radio.
>
> It makes a person get more friends than before and the neighbors come for news and announcements. When they don't, they don't because there is no music for young people.
>
> To those that are not married, the radio makes women to love the men. (Robbins and Kilbride 1987:214)

Newspapers and magazines in English and Swahili are widely available and read by people whenever possible. Nairobi has three English and one KiSwahili daily, all of which have a national distribution in Kenya. Similar to radio and TV, printed media has provided numerous reports, articles, editorials, letters to the editor, and feature stories about substantive issues of concern to us. We conclude this chapter on the modernization of tradition by letting Kenyans speak for themselves through their mass media. Our Kenyan materials are the most recent, and they are reported here.

Some topics which are commonly discussed in the English-speaking Kenyan news media in the form of journalistic accounts, editorials, letters to the editor, etc. will now be considered. The selections here are based on our impression that the topics mentioned are quite common and will also serve to illustrate our concern with moral delocalization. From among hundreds of news clippings in our notes, the subjects of polygyny, parenting, the extended family, children, and "tradition" have been selected. We provide examples of what various categories of people, particularly those in a position of social leadership, such as government officials, church leaders, and educators, believe about these concerns.

The question of polygyny (commonly referred to as polygamy in Kenya) aptly illustrates what we intend to capture with our term moral delocalization. While the question of polygyny in modern Kenyan society will be the topic of a later chapter, we introduce polygyny here as a phenomenologically salient question among our East African hosts. Western-educated, urban women frequently voice opposition to polygyny. The following account is from a prominent Kenyan politician:

> Ogot Urges Church to Back War on Polygamy," by Victoria Okumu
>
> Nominated MP, Mrs. Grace Ogot, speaking at the opening of a two-day seminar on "Women and the Church" called for an end to polygamy which she described as "more dangerous than malaria." Mrs. Ogot said that neglect by their husbands because of other women caused many women to spend their nights in tears. "It was painful for an old woman to see her 'kingdom' invaded by a girl as young as her daughter, especially since some of these young girls were very selfish. She, however, did say that women should try to understand the problem of single women who because men were fewer than women "were understandably bitter and had no alternative but to chase other people's husbands or settle as second or third wives." *Daily Nation* (May 18, 1985)

In our experience, modern educated men tend, on the whole, to support polygamy compared to their female counterparts. The following opinion will serve to illustrate this pattern:

> "Foreign Ways to Blame for Moral Decline, says Ngumba"
>
> An assistant minister for lands and settlement, and MP for Mathare, Mr. Andrew Ngumba, while addressing a fund-raising meeting in Nairobi, blamed foreign influences for the decline in African morale. As an example, he stated that "old practices like polygamy could help reduce the number of unmarried women roaming the streets as prostitutes. He stated for them that it was important for everyone in Kenya to respect the traditions of other ethnic groups. "Traditionally," he said, "a man was always buried in his home area and there is nothing wrong with modern Kenyans doing the same." *Daily Nation* (July 9, 1985)

As we mentioned earlier, women and men who are not heavily exposed to Euro-American influence tend to be much more favorable about polygyny than their educated counterparts. In a survey in Western Kenya, for example, Lwanga found that most uneducated women there (21 of 24) favored the custom, but only under the traditional obligation of wifely consultation before choosing a second wife. (See Lwanga n.d.).

Many Christian churches (unlike some of their traditional offshoots or Moslems) have moral concerns about accepting polygamy. Sometimes differences of opinion can lead to conflict, as shown in the following account.

> "Church Row in Kakamega."
>
> The Friends Church in Vokoli, Vihiga Division is facing a serious leadership crisis between the "old and monogamist founders" of the church and the "young and polygamist followers." The polygamist followers were opposed to the church's condemnation of polygamy and have vowed to oust Pastor Kadenga, who joined the church in 1902 after its arrival from the US in 1901, and his cabinet. The splinter group has called in the Southern Friends Church. *Sunday Nation* (January 6, 1985)

It is not uncommon for the "polygamy" question to arise among members of the same family. Frequently, for example, children who are opposed to the custom come themselves from polygamous houses. This is true for the Catholic Cardinal, whose opinion aptly summarizes his church's official dogmatic opposition:

> "Take Courtship Seriously—Bishop"
>
> The Catholic Archbishop of Nairobi, Maurice Cardinal Otunga, spoke at Holy Family Basilica to youths from 25 parishes participating in an event whose theme was "the sacrament of marriage." "The archbishop said young people had a duty to carry out the command given to Adam and Eve to "multiply." . . . On monogamy, Cardinal Otunga said God created one man and one woman. "God wanted one Adam and one Eve, not one Adam and three Eves nor five Adams and one Eve," he said. "Moses had granted permission to a man to divorce, but Christ came and reversed it to what was there before." The Cardinal said, Christians should not seek the wisdom of their customs but do the will of God. *Daily Nation* (February 11, 1985)

Protestant Churches have recently become more tolerant of polygamy than their more delocalized Catholic counterparts. We read in *The Weekly Review,* August 1, 1987, for example,

> In May this year, a bishop of the Anglican Church in Kenya (The Church of the Province of Kenya), Bishop Dr. David Gitari of the diocese of Mt. Kenya East, said it was time his church did away with the negative stigma it attached to polygamy. Gitari's view was that although "monogamy is God's plan for marriage," and is "the ideal relationship for the expression of love between husband and wife," he warned that the Anglican church should not incorporate this principle wholesale without giving due consideration to the various cultures in Kenya where polygamy is socially acceptable. According to Gitari, the belief that polygamy is contrary to Christianity was no longer tenable.

Churches are not "absolutely" delocalized on every issue concerning the preservation of tradition. The Catholic Church, while opposed to polygamy, often seeks to build Christian community on an African-derived community ethic. We learn, for example, that:

"Polygamy Condemned as Cause of Broken Homes"

Polygamy ruins marriages, according to the bishop of Nakura Roman Catholic Diocese, the Right Reverend Raphael S. Ndingi Mwana A'Nzeki.

Bishop Ndingi recalled that in African traditional marriages there were successive stages which were a preparation for marriage and noted that these traditional betrothal parties have largely broken down. He asked the Christian community to take the initiative to replace them adequately.

He spoke about the richness of African traditions and customs, describing them as a precious heritage to be preserved and handed on to the present generation.

The bishop advised Christians to assess their religious and cultural traditions in the light of the Gospel, and incorporate these values into culture.

He noted with regret the problems that follow due to rapid urbanisation, such as the breakdown of traditional family life, un-

> married mothers, prostitution, abortion and breakdown of family authority." *Daily Nation* (April 15, 1985)

Kenyans are currently attempting to curb their rate of population increase, which is one of the highest in the world (about 4%). Traditional ideas favoring fertility were essentially adapted to an agrarian system where human labor was significant and rates of infant mortality were high. The government and churches are, therefore, seeking to support traditional values concerned with ensuring family planning as a means of population control. While there are differences in tactics (the Catholics, for example, favor only nonmechanical means such as the Billings method or abstinence), there is consensus on objective. The majority of Kenyans are, however, suspicious of "family planning." We will consider elsewhere some of their reasons. Recently, Kenya was alive with the belief that the government had put "medicine" in beer, and later in school milk, as a means of secretly limiting fertility. In general, men are more opposed to family planning while women are more receptive (at least those who already have children). The following account refers to the vice-president's views on family planning:

> "Men 'Hindering' Family Planning"
>
> Vice-President Mwai Kibaki accused men yesterday of slowing down the family planning programme.
>
> Men's negative attitude, he said, severly hindered the implementation and popularity of the programme.
>
> Speaking shortly after a televised press conference at Broadcasting House in Nairobi, Mr. Kibaki said Kenya's fertility averaged at eight children per mother and as such it was important to match population growth with other issues like health, education, social welfare and general development. *Daily Nation* (December 5, 1984)

And he urged leaders and family-planning promoters to practise what they preached so as to be taken seriously by their audience:

> There is nothing wrong with having many wives and children as long as you are prepared to take total care of them. Fortunately, at this moment in time, the number of those who prefer to have large families is fast waning.

He dismissed suggestions that family planning could best succeed if abortion was legalized as an alternative method of curbing rapid population growth. Abortion, he said, was not an alternative to birth control.

On recent church wrangles over family planning, Mr. Kibaki said the church leaders' statements showed they accepted family planning as a fact, but differed on the methods. He said:

> We are a democratic government and we cannot force an individual to use a particular method as we shall be infringing on his/her constitutional right to choose the method preferred.

He stressed that since family planning was voluntary, the Government was not going to induce people to adopt it. He added that plans were underway to harmonize the prices of all the contraceptives so that they could be afforded by all people.

Earlier, at his Jogoo House office, Mr. Kibaki officially launched the Family Planning Private Sector Programme that is seeking to assist family planning for employees of the private sector. So far twenty-one private organizations have joined the programme, he said.

The question of parenting in the modern world is, of course, a major concern of this book. There is widespread awareness and concern for how best to resolve contradictions between traditional means and modern ends. The following is the view of one educator who believes that a cultural lag in parenting needs to be addressed so that parents become more modern.

"Parents' Mistakes"

Dr. Daniel Kabithe, of the Psychological Services Center, Nairobi, states that parenting is an art that requires mastery. Dr. Kabithe feels that African parents still cling to ideas about parenting that have been handed down from one generation to another, even though some may not be applicable to today's society. Thus, a typical African parent isn't used to dissent or even a free and frank exchange of views. Children are supposed to obey their parents and take their advice and guidance unquestioningly. In ages past, elders held the knowledge of social, economic, political and military life. Today, young people hold responsible jobs and executive positions. Single parents were a rarity in the past but not now. The problems of venereal disease, unemployment and drug abuse were unknown to the ancestors. He feels there is a "cultural lag" in parenting skills. *The Standard* (January 7, 1985)

Many educators believe that the question of "cultural lag" is positive, providing East Africans with an opportunity to preserve, before it is too late, indigenous family-based institutions. This is essentially our view, which is aptly stated by Kenyan sociologists and other intellectuals through an interview given to an American journalist. There we learn:

"Africa Struggles to be Understood in Modern World," by Robert Rosenthal, Nairobi, Kenya

Among African Intellectuals, doctors and educators, as well as many Westerners, there is the view, sometimes bitter, that Africa is too often judged by a western value system that has nothing in common with Africa's traditions and little understanding of the African mind and social values which throughout black Africa are rooted to village and rural lifestyles. Dr. Philista Onyango, a sociologist at the University of Nairobi, believes that the "greatest change that has affected black Africa is the breakdown of the extended-family tradition, which is directly linked, she said, to urbanization and the colonists' introduction of a monetary economy. *Philadelphia Inquirer* (April 14, 1984)

The extended family system in Africa was widespread and efficient and it ensured that everyone—from the very youngest to the oldest—was cared for.

Within that system were taught social, ethical, and traditional values that, Ms. Onyango said, are being swept away and confused by development and the mass movements from the rural areas to urban areas, a trend found throughout Africa.

In a later chapter, our material on the significant place of extended family ideology in contemporary community life will be explored, especially in terms of its function as a significant barrier to the practice of child abuse. At this time, two examples of "Letters to the Editor" will serve to illustrate, pro and con, popular views of the dowry (progeny price) in the context of the family. Our citation of news media data will conclude by quoting a person who believes "the old ways were better."

The first writer believes that "the dowry (progeny price) doesn't foster love." He writes:

"Dowry Doesn't Foster Love," by Willy Kipkoech arap Walei, Kapsabet

Marriage is losing its meaning and divorce is rampant. What brings all these things? Is it the dowry system?

Dowry satisfies a deep longing for justice and legality in the eyes of the families involved. In the modern society with marriage breaking down, the bride price tradition is seen as a factor that links our society to the strong moral standards of its precolonial past. It makes the wife feel that she is worth something and that her husband considers her valuable. It also enables the girl's parents to provide similar dowry to their sons.

On the way the dowry system degrades the woman to the status of a commodity being bought and sold. It makes the relationship primarily an economic one in which the choice of a wife depends on one's ability to pay rather than on mutual respect and love between bridegroom and bride.

Since the wife's motivation to be faithful and helpful to her husband is affected by the fear of her parents' inability to return the dowry if she fails as a wife, it becomes more difficult for a love relationship to develop that would make marriage truly stable because selfish economic factors do not build genuine love.

The deep need for a foundation of legality and justice in marriage is better satisfied by the public vows of love and fidelity under God, witnessed and approved by family and friends.

Here young men have been blamed for wanting people's daughters free. What infuriates most young men is not the dowry system itself, but the expense of it. As it depends from house to house, most families charge exorbitantly. *Daily Nation* (March 28, 1985)

On the other hand we read that "dowry has its merits:"

"Dowry Has Its Merits," by Patrick Butalanyi Fred, Kakamega

Most people have different views on dowry. Some say it is necessary while others say it is not. I agree with former.

Dowry is a tradition which I would hate to see die. Dowry owes its origin to the beginning of mankind. Whoever introduced dowry was not blind. Dowry was introduced following the chaos which arose from many marriages.

To begin with dowry fosters lawfulness between a husband and his wife. It minimises separation of families, which would be very common if there was no dowry. It minimises the power of women and makes them respect their husbands.

It also ensures maximum protection and care of women since they are now regarded as property of their husbands. Finally, it fosters the relationship between the two groups of parents (the man's and the girl's). *Daily Nation* (April 20, 1985)

Finally, our last quotation is drawn from one reader whose opposition to moral delocalization is aptly stated:

"The Old Ways Were Better," by William Cheruiyott, Nairobi

Our ancestors were more educated than we are. They stuck to their customs, were not easily influenced by foreigners and did what they thought was good. How many crimes unknown to our ancestors are common today—prostitution, murder and robbery!

Children nowadays don't respect their elders while adults lead children into more disrespect. You find a man and his sons in the drinking places, even behaving the same way.

People in the old days lived a simple life. They knew what was important—food, clothing, and shelter. They did not fight for high rank and fame, just lived harmoniously and hardly ever quarreled.

Today how many men wait for their fathers to tell them that they are old enough to marry? Previously, some waited until their fathers were sure they could support their families. They chose well-behaved girls for wives. Sex before marriage was not allowed.

All this was changed by the arrival of foreigners, who introduced their ways of life.

I wish fellow Africans would hold on to their beautiful customs. *Daily Nation* (July 11, 1985)

Similar family-oriented materials could be drawn from the *KiSwahili* news media, for example, *Kenya Leo (Kenya Today)*. Both the popular

English and the vernacular literature contain rich illustrative materials as well. For example, a secondary schoolbook used in secondary schools entitled *Mke Mwenza* (co-wife), is a play about the institution of polygamy. This play was staged in *KiSwahili* at the University of Nairobi where it was reviewed by a Kenyan critic, Eva Ndavu, as follows:

> *Mke Mwenza,* restaged at the University of Nairobi last week, was a resounding success, offering much-needed comic relief for students fast-approaching or already consumed in an examination schedule.
>
> The play was directed by Konga Mbandu and included a number of his faithful troupe over the years—Sam Otieno, Alan Konya, Catherine Kariuki and Jim Were.
>
> The script itself presents some difficulties, but cast and direction overcame this sufficiently to make it an entertaining evening of local theatre. The conflict is that almost universal quest for male off-spring. Chabe, the main character, was played fervently by Sam Otieno. Fairly well off financially, Chabe is fast drinking himself to death because his wife Boke has only been able to bear him many daughters, "the children of women" as he says.
>
> Otieno plays the drunken braggart and repentant husband to the hilt. Sporting a nonc-too-convincing beer-belly, he struts and stag-gers across the stage lamenting his fate, chastising Boke and her female offspring and finally proposing the African male's simplistic solution to every domestic problem: to take another wife.
>
> Number-one wife, of course, responds in a most dramatic tirade.
>
> Her fear is that if the second wife produces a son she herself will lose all claims to property. Chabe does an about-face, sheepishly asking if "she wants to get married again" and the scene ends amicably.
>
> But this is not only a play about polygamy, it is about greed and mistrust as well. And the story shifts abruptly with many matri-monial surprises. The cast took this up and shortly offered the proper transition. Even the use of the witchdoctor/soothsayer (Rufus Eshuchi) to warn, comment and predict did not break the spell of laughter and thought.
>
> Catherine Kariuki was a very convincing outraged wife. She rants one moment and is sugar and spice the next. She equals the passion of Otieno and manages a memorable death scene. Her clear under-

standing of the character resulted in a rewarding performance. *Daily Nation* (June 12, 1985)

Kenyans widely read and discuss novels concerning family life with such titles as *What a Husband, So Long a Letter, My Wife Made Me a Polygamist, What Does a Man Want,* and *Coming to Birth.* These novels are about the dilemmas and contradictions raised nowadays by barrenness, unwed motherhood, polygamy, and the growing gender gap on family life issues.

Likewise, plays and situation comedies appear on the radio, television, and national theater in which the subject of delocalization of family, marriage, and childhood receives symbolic attention. In the descriptive chapters to follow, we will refer to indigenous literature where appropriate. The above materials are offered here only as an illustration to document that our theoretical concerns are "grounded" in East African experience and cultural organization. In section 2 of this book, we will provide the reader with selected descriptions of pregnancy, childrearing, and childhood in East Africa. We consider these illustrations essential aspects of traditional Africanity as revealed through our own fieldwork. Section 3, our concluding section, will consider the delocalization of such practices as also revealed in our research.

SECTION 2

4

PARENTAL GOALS, CHILDHOOD, AND THE LIFE CYCLE

"He who has no child must get his legs to do his errands."

In the first section, we elaborated on our theoretical approach, which can be characterized as a universalistic relativistic blend as advocated by A. I. Hallowell. We accordingly spell out in this chapter some African-derived ideas about personhood and human development which are themselves "relative" when compared with "modern" notions in the West or delocalized Kenyan circles. These indigenous ideas are still widely ascribed to, often by the same person who is also quite modernized. These ideas are, on the whole, quite favorable to the status of children, adults, and both genders. The chapters in this section are devoted to the theme of "children of value" whereas the following section portends the declining value of children against a backdrop of increased powerlessness of the modern Kenyan woman, resulting in children at risk.

Our material is arranged intentionally to emphasize here the "favorable" aspects of Africanity insofar as these provide for an African empirical sense of community and a refreshingly practical or consciously "meaningful" human experience that is an alternative to the pathologies of much of the modern American experience. Some of the socially disruptive materials to be presented in the next section, such as the evil eye and witchcraft, are also derived from Africanity and therefore could be presented in this section too. Nevertheless, there is some justification to consider later such socially disruptive practices along with modern practices such as a cash economy and capitalism, unregulated polygyny, child abuse and neglect, etc. The justification is both empirical and theoretical. As we shall see, Kenyans themselves consider social conflict to be more common now than previously, particularly over issues of personhood, children, and marriage. Second, our theoretical interpretation provides a conceptual framework in which to account for increased social disharmony in the modern world. Admittedly, our history is primarily interpretive for the most part although we cite, wherever appropriate and available, early ethnographies and ethnohistorical sources. In the final analysis, it is a question of "interactive" values. While most foreign writers who share similar interests agree with us that the modern illiterate African woman in comparison to African men is relatively powerless or oppressed (e.g., Oboler 1985, Shuster 1979), most may not also believe as we do that her traditional illiterate counterpart and her children were better off than now. Most foreign writers to our knowledge believe that both modernity and Africanity have been unfavorable to women. Clearly these are all *value* statements, quite difficult to empirically demonstrate for the past involving as they do quality-of-life issues. It is for this reason, that we advocate "interactive ethnography" wherein the researcher's own values are made explicit. Our values are clearly evident in the presentation of our material in this and the next section.

Returning to our ethnographic narrative, we begin our discourse with the most meaningful aspect of life as experienced by East Africans, the joy of having children. As indicated earlier, all cultures share common parental goals. These include the physical health and survival of children and their eventual development of reproductive capacity and economic self-maintenance, among others. Each culture, however, actualizes its parental objectives in the context of particular social values, beliefs, and symbolic processes. Childhood behavioral capacities for maximizing parental goals also must be "relativized" to the moral or ethical code of each society. East Africans, as we shall see, do value their children, among other reasons, for the economic potential that interdependence with them will one day hopefully realize. This objective, a universal instrumental one, is achieved by their symbolic elaboration of the social dimension. The collectivity: family, clan, lineage, or ethnic group, takes precedence over the individual. The ideal typical *person* is one who is firmly rooted in the group with a commensurate orientation to social responsibilities. The parent, therefore, literally has children *for* the social group. Children are raised as social persons who will be properly oriented to the group, its ancestors, and the needs of their own parents. For this reason, having children and raising them as group members is a religious activity with strong spiritual overtones, not unlike a sort of mystical "chain of being" experience (the closest we came to this was when our daughter was born). African religion is, in fact, "a celebration of human life" (Booth 1977). We quote, primarily for Kenya, J. Bahemuka:

> Among the Akamba, there is a creed which summarizes the individual's self-awareness, his relationship with others and with the physical and spiritual world around him . . . I am an absolute *Mukamba (Mukamba Kivindyo),* who knows and believes in the purity of rituals, and I know that these rites can bring forth life . . . I believe that a barren woman, when treated with purifying ritual medicine . . . will bring forth offspring. (1983:40)

Such religious "creeds," common in East Africa, provide a spiritual framework for the reproduction of children, as does an understanding of time and reincarnation, as we learn from Bahemuka:

> The African has a strong belief in his past, and, while he lives, he focuses his attention on the beyond, where his future lies. He believes that after death, when he attains that life beyond, his attention will be focused on those he left behind in the world of the living, and his greatest hope is that the living will enable him to be reborn. The past, the present, and the future, therefore, intermingle in the act of procreation to produce the *now,* which is the child born to continue the family line. No individual African can ignore this truth, as it is the only way that traditionally the African could capture his lost immortality. This is one reason why marriage and procreation are so important . . . Having children is a religious duty which links not only the individual, but also the Creator, the spirit of the ancestors and the biological parents . . . in each act of procreation, the chain of humanity is perceived. (1983:101)

The East African behavioral environment is, therefore, socially constructed such that the person cannot be separated from a social context.

American rugged individualism (Hsu 1983) is quite foreign to African thought. In fact, to illustrate through a common example, our informants rarely refer to themselves in the first person, preferring instead to say "we will come and see you," even though the referent is only the speaker. That persons are linked to other persons also receives linguistic reinforcement in the "noun class" classifications. All "people" terms carry the same prefix for the singular and another for the plural (*Mu* and *Ba*). In *Luganda*, for example, the following terms will illustrate this pattern.

	Singular	Plural
boy	omulenzi	abalenzi
girl	omwala	abala
child	omwana	abaana
man	omusajja	abasajja
woman	omukazi	abakazi
person	omuntu	abantu
spirit	omuzima	abazima
chief	omwami	abwami

In the Kiganda behavioral environment, the person proceeds through stages such as *omwana* (child), *omuvubuka* (youth), *omusajja, omukazi* (man, woman), until after death one becomes an *omuzima* (spirit). The cycle of life can begin again, in principle, when a dead person's name is given to an infant.

In general, therefore, parental goals for their children include the socialization of children into the socio-religious values described here. These values also provide a context for the actualization of parental goals for the health and welfare of their children. Prayers, sacrifices, the wearing of amulets, dream prognostication, etc. are believed to be effective spiritual aids in the care and protection of one's children. Parents also teach directly by formal instruction of desired behavior *or* by reprimand of disgraced behaviors. As we shall see in a later chapter, grandparents are also effective in "parenting"; in fact, elders overall traditionally transmit considerable educational materials, especially of a moral sort. Today, of course, the school is also a significant "delocalized" institution for cultural transmission, often to the neglect of grandparents or other traditional teachers (such as funeral orators). A major idiom for cultural transmission (enculturation) was, and still is, but to a lessened degree, the proverb. The following Samia proverbs illustrate ideals about the Samia person which parents seek to inculcate in children.

> A good person walks with his neighbor; a bad person walks alone and lives with animals.
> To ignore parents results in traveling until the sun sets.
> The old one will have a chance at mealtime to reprimand you.
> A person who belongs to the group will put forth more effort than one who doesn't belong.
> If you don't respect your own mother, then you won't respect your friend's mother.
> He who competes alone praises the best runner.

We now turn to a consideration of how the enculturation process transmits, throughout the life cycle, social values that are an expression of understanding about personhood. Enculturation, as we have previously noted, is that process whereby an individual learns the standards for proper social behavior in a given society. Our discussion here will begin with childhood, and the remaining chapters of this section will be concerned specifically with an extensive examination of parenting, prenatal care, and infant development. This will serve as a socialcultural background context for the materials of section 3. Any examination of childhood and infancy, however, would be incomplete without reference to the entire life cycle of which it is a part.

Childhood

The Baganda attach considerable importance to having children. A discussion of our Baganda material will illustrate this value. We provide extensive data from one society here and in later sections because this material offers the best contextual understanding. In any case, although our own Baganda materials are richest here, the Baganda pattern is not in general terms atypical. Numerous proverbs and sayings are consistently used in everyday situations to describe the joys of having children and the sorrows of barrenness. The following Kiganda proverbs are typical:

My luck is in that child of mine: if the child is rich.

He who does a service to one's child: does better than one who merely says he loves you.

Even one you have borne: will drum for you as you dance.

An only child: is like a drop of rain in the dry season.

A barren one: has visitors as her children.

While a parent sends a messenger, the barren one has carried out the errand himself.

Children are desired by both men and women. Descent is patrilineal so that a man's offspring are affiliated with his clan. For this reason, men frequently report that they desire to produce children to increase their clan. When thirty men, for example, were asked, Why do men want children? some typical responses included: "to increase their clan; to comfort them in poverty; to provide help in old age; to serve their parents; and to be remembered through their children." Women, on the other hand, primarily wish to avoid the stigma of barrenness itself—a frequent ground for divorce. When twenty women were asked, Why do women want children? the following responses were given in addition to the desire to avoid the stigma of barrenness: "to provide company at home; to make work easier; and to alleviate loneliness."

Once the child "can understand," the Baganda believe that proper social behavior should be directly taught. Previous anthropological research on Kiganda socialization has focused on the importance of learning to be obedient (see Richards 1964:194–256). The father expects and receives gratiating deference from his children, who are required to kneel before him, as well as before visitors and superiors, while greeting him in a high-pitched voice (thought to be respectful). Baganda frequently remember their harsh obedience training in childhood. Richards (1964) reports that of sixty-five adolescent school children, 32% responding to a question about the faults for which they had most often been punished answered, simply, "disobedience"; another 27% reported that they had been punished most often for "failure to show respect" (260). Many of our informants also report remembrances of their strict authoritarian fathers and fathers' sisters (*ssenga*). One twenty-year-old Muganda woman, for example, told us that she was taught three things by her father: to be obedient (*okuba omuwul-ize*); to fear God (*okutyakatonda*); and to respect people older than yourself (*okusamu bakulu bo ekittibwa*). These qualities are part of a general idea of *mpisa* (custom, habit, conduct) which subsumes a variety of approved behaviors that children are expected to acquire. *Mpisa* includes such things as being obedient to authority figures; not interfering in adult conversation; not eating while walking on the road; greeting people properly; being amiable; sitting properly (for children and women); and many other social expectations. The content of *mpisa* constitutes a code of social etiquette on how to relate to other people. Specifically, having *mpisa* requires one to become socially involved with others in the proper way. A person who consistently avoids social interaction not only has no *mpisa* but is also likely to be thought a witch (*mulogo*) or a spy. A person who is socially involved, but who consistently commits improprieties, is not to be feared (as a witch or a spy) but is rather thought to be a *mukopi* (one with no *mpisa* or manners).

Socializing agents are concerned that children learn to be sociable in the proper way. In the past, children were sent to the *kabaka's* compound, the home of a chief or advantaged relative, to acquire *mpisa*. Nowadays, boarding schools serve a similar function although most parents train for *mpisa* in their homes. When we asked 116 Baganda adults, "What is the most important thing parents can teach their children?" eighty-one (70%) responded *mpisa*. Children learn *mpisa* through direct instruction from parents, other relatives, and caretakers; through observation of behavior; and by listening to proverbs, folktales, tribal history, songs, and gossip. These conversational episodes are frequent and intense in most Kiganda homes.

Although children eat with grown-ups, on these and other occasions when adults are present, the child is expected to be a quiet and passive listener. Children are also expected to report their offenses to adults, who may "beat" them. We once observed a five-year-old go to collect a branch to be used by his mother to punish his sibling. Parents are quite active in the formation of their child's personality in what, it is hoped, will be a positive direction. It is believed that the mother, in particular, is responsible for character formation. The belief that childhood behavior is vital to later development is symbolized in the proverb: "That which is bent at the outset of its growth is almost impossible to straighten at a later age": *Akakyama amamera: tekagololekeka.*

Children at about age seven begin to assume household responsibilities. Boys, for example, run errands, sometimes help in the garden, and watch younger siblings. Girls perform domestic duties involving sweeping the compound, washing dishes, and "babysitting" for younger siblings. Frequently young girls are required to care for infant siblings, particularly during the day when their mothers are digging, visiting, or attending market. Young siblings and children from the same locale participate in a wide variety of social games where social skills are learned and practiced in dramatic play. For example, boys play "chief" with other boys; girls play "house" or "mother" with other girls. *Okwesa* is a simplified version of the adult *omweso* game, a game of strategy involving a wooden board and stones, beads, or beans. Both boys and girls play *okwesa* while many others observe and advise the participants. One game in particular enhances the conversational ability of the participants. Talking backwards or *ludikya* is a favorite pastime of the children. The "clever" child is one who can master-fully engage his peers in a round of *ludikya*. Children report that they use *ludikya* as a means of enjoyment and/or to hide secrets from their parents, other adults, and children. There are two major forms of *ludikya* in Lu-ganda. The first is called reverse *ludikya* or *omufuulo*. For example, *omusajja* (man) becomes "jja-sa-mu-o." Words in sentences, however, appear in their same order. A second form involves inserting after each syllable containing a vowel the letter Z plus the vowel in that syllable. *Omusajja* would become "o-zo-mu-zu-sa-za-jja-za". Boys and girls up to the age of about ten or eleven often play together. Separation of the sexes begins when the girl experiences her first menses. Toddlers are also seen in play groups since they are often in the care of older siblings.

Many homes have occasions in the evening where family members par-ticipate in collective "riddling" (*okukokkya*) games. As one informant said, "A main aim of the riddler is knowledge. Because this is a type of mental competition, riddles help people to train their minds in how to think and to interpret things that are hidden or related to each other. Both young and old, men and women are seen engaged in this game." A person who successfully solves riddles is awarded "villages to rule" and assumes the role of "chief." Some examples of commonly heard riddles are:

Riddle	Answer
What did the white man for-get when he came to Af-rica?	His medicine for baldness
I lie flat facing the sky and my children suck my breasts.	Food at table
The white cow has chased a black one from the fire-place.	Grey (white) hair has chased the black one from the head (of an old man or woman).

I have a wife who looks where she is coming from and where she is going to at the same time.	A bundle of firewood (The two ends are similar)
I have a razor blade which I use to shave hills.	Fire (used to burn the grass)
When my friend went to get food for his children he never came back.	Water in a river (stream)
My man is always surrounded by spears.	The tongue (It is surrounded by teeth)

In summary, Kiganda socialization goals and experiences train children for desired personal qualities that will enhance their later success in adult Kiganda society.

Adolescence—The Traditional Ideal

Adolescence in East Africa can be mainly characterized as preparation for marriage and adulthood. We illustrate this value with a continuation of our discussion of the Baganda life cycle described above. The term "youth" (*omuvubuga*) applies equally for boys and girls, however, normative behavior is quite different during adolescence for each sex. At puberty, in traditional times, boys were expected to concern themselves with "upward mobility" and preferably to reside with a chief or advantaged relative in order to serve as court pages or servants. In contemporary Buganda, adolescent boys vigorously pursue educational opportunities to enhance their career objectives. Pubescent girls were and still are expected to prepare themselves for their adult roles as wives and mothers. Although many girls do, in fact, attend school, there is still a widespread feeling that "education is for boys" and that women should ideally perform domestic duties. Consequently, with a few exceptions to be noted later, traditional patterns of sex-role education and the like have persisted, in practice, for many girls and, in ideal terms, for most others.

Sex education for a girl is largely in the hands of her *ssenga* (father's sister) although other female relatives, particularly grandmothers, sometimes play a role too. In the past, during menstruation a girl was secluded for a short time in a separate house where she would eat and drink alone. This seclusion is now rarely practiced. Soon after menstruation, and sometimes before, she is instructed in the custom of *okukyalira ensiko* or "visiting the forest." This custom consists of manipulating the labia minora to physically elongate it. Elongation narrows the vaginal entrance and keeps it "warm and tight," an attribute highly desired by Baganda men. *Ssenga* teaches the girl specific utterances and techniques appropriate during intercourse. Traditionally, women are taught to not only desire sex but to also lead an active sex life. A woman is expected to reach orgasm several times before the man and to respond throughout intercourse with vigorous body movements. A man is evaluated by women according to the length of time coitus is maintained before his orgasm (about thirty minutes is typical). A too-rapid male ejaculation is likely to evoke female anger and comparison with, for example, a "hen" (*enkoko*) who, of course, has rapid coitus. A second erection soon after orgasm is also expected of men.

Kiganda attitudes toward public sex are quite prudish. There is no open display of sexual behavior. Holding hands, kissing, embracing, or other signs of affection are private activities. Kissing is a recent innovation. Traditionally, tickling of the hand, breasts, or stomach area by either sex was considered sensuous. Today many girls remain ignorant of expected sexual behavior due to prolonged residence at boarding schools and/or adherence to Christianity by themselves or their *bassenga*. Missionaries, for example, prohibited "visiting the forest." On the other hand, most men still state a preference for traditional sexual performance and will often refuse to court seriously a girl known to have not "visited the forest." Mere Kisekka (1973), a Ugandan sociologist, reports that a common complaint of young girls is that their *bassenga* did not teach them anything about sex. These girls, mostly secondary students and urban employees, now seek advice and sexual instruction by mail from a male "authority" who writes popular pamphlets on topics related to love, sex, and marriage.

Sexual instruction for boys is not formalized. Traditionally, they acquired experience through rather infrequent and unsystematic encounters with adolescent girls in the plantain gardens. Currently, boys still lag behind girls who prefer to, and do, go out with older boys and men. In general, young girls and older men have more sexual freedom than married women and adolescent boys.

Perhaps the most significant skill that a man can possess in the arena of courtship is the ability to convince others. It is, in fact, the case that Baganda men are well known in Uganda for their skillful verbal ability to flatter women. While Baganda women expect and desire flattery, truthful or not, women from other ethnic groups often find this frustrating. One Musoga university student, for example, commented:

> About cross-sex relations, I am sorry I had a bad upbringing because I was told never to tell a lie. Baganda will come and tell you that you have beautiful eyes and beautiful hair when you've got the ugliest eyes and hair. Flattery is part of their nature; that is why I cannot have a traditional Muganda boyfriend. I always want the truth.

The skillful use of words requires knowledge of both traditional and modern phrases of endearment. Some typical ones are "your eyes are big and shiny like a light"; "your teeth are as white as elephant tusks"; "you are as slender as a bee"; "you are my twin"; "you are worth a million dollars"; "I am losing my head over you." One informant, a particularly good raconteur, commented that "there are two kinds of girls: one type likes money, and the other wants only true love. I figure out which type she is, and then I know what to tell her." Phrases of endearment would be appropriate for the latter type, but promises of gifts or money would win over the former.

Girls, too, are verbally adroit. A girl should not flatter a man, but she is expected to deceive (*okulimba*) him into thinking that he is her only boyfriend or that she "really wanted to make her appointment with him but relatives dropped in." One eighteen-year-old girl, for example, commented:

> Men deceive most of the time in many different ways. Men deceive more than the women do. But also women do deceive when they feel they like to do it. They do it especially to men when they want to get things from them. But not all women do this. There are some who are good-mannered. When a woman is having about four men and she sees that they help her in everything, she deceives them by telling each of them how she loves him very much and nobody else. She does that just because she wants to keep them all. She doesn't want to lose them.

Modern women now often enter courtship with a considerable degree of economic independence. This can sometimes be a source of frustration for men. A woman who is independent economically can opt for selective liaisons with men of her own choosing. Should she be "on the market" for a husband, then it is important that she be seen in public, at dances, parties, weddings, etc. Public exposure will, as one twenty-year-old girl commented, "increase my market value." The contemporary world of love, sex, and courtship includes many things unknown to previous generations of Baganda. The "pill," "dates," nocturnal visits to the drive-in cinema, "parking," etc. are all current practices.

There are also traditional physical and socio-personal qualities considered desirable in members of the opposite sex. One significant dimension in physical appeal is that of moderation. Baganda, for example, consider extreme black or extreme white skin color to be unappealing. Excessive blackness may evoke comparison with a much used cooking pot: "you are as black as a cooking pot." On several occasions, women literally ran away from Philip, who is of particularly light pigmentation and has somewhat rosy cheeks, shouting: "his blood is too near the skin surface; it can be seen!" A brownish color (*katakitaki*), like brown clay, is desired. Particularly sensuous is color variation, with the breasts and thighs being comparatively browner than other parts of the body. Moderation is also important in height, hair texture, eye size, and forehead length. Tall people tend to be admired, but there is no excessive concern over "heightism." There are three types of hair texture, *Kaweke* or kinky hair is not admired nor is *muaywere* or very soft hair (like a half-caste) admired. *Massade,* or an intermediate texture between kinkiness and softness is admired. Eyes should not be too large "like a fish" nor too small "like a hole in a cow's skin." A lengthy forehead is likened after the king's palace (*lubiri,* a large palace), while one that is too short is similar to a monkey's and is therefore also undesirable. Many infants receive daily head massages designed to modify their forehead in this desirable direction. The infant's nose is also massaged to elongate it since a flat *kiganda* nose is not admired. Adult women frequently rub charcoal on their necks to accentuate the lines in the neck (*ebiseera*).

The above traits are admired for both sexes, but their presence or absence in men is rarely articulated. Women are primarily the object of concern about physical traits. Other physical traits which are especially desired in women include "a rounded gluteous maximus" (*kabina*); a small space between the upper incisor teeth (*muzigo*); horizontal lines in the neck (*ebiseera*); dimples; large breasts; and a deep, soft voice. Excessive thinness is ridiculed in both men and women. Fatness is undesirable in men.

Dressing well and looking "smartee" are also admired by men and women. As we shall discuss later, concern for good grooming and attractive clothing, especially in public situations, applies even to infants and young children. In fact, as part of a study of the recognition of facial expressions,

Kilbride and Yarczower (1976) asked Baganda first-graders to choose the "happiest girl" from schematic drawings of happy, sad, and neutral facial expressions. They found that although only 8% chose the girl with a "sad" facial expression as being the happiest of the three, 75% chose as happiest the girl with a sad expression when a red dress was added to this drawing. Furthermore, in another study, we asked our mothers what they would do with it if someone gave them 100 shillings. Sixty-seven percent responded that they would buy clothes for themselves and/or their children. A Kiganda proverb that indicates the importance of dress in Kiganda society states: "Someone who excels others in dress is a source of envy to many." Personal qualities are also an important consideration in mate selection and courtship. "Good manners" (*mpisa*) and sociability are desired in both sexes. Industriousness and hospitableness are two other personal traits admired by all Baganda. A man who "speaks well," as we have noted, is admired. Women, on the other hand, ideally are expected to be relatively shy (*nsonyi*) in comparison to men and to not "look them straight in the face." Physical appearance, personal deportment, and the like are all subsumed in the notion of "dignity" (*simbo, ekitibbwa*). How a person looks, talks, and behaves contributes to or detracts from his or her dignity. A person who is dignified is highly desired as a spouse or lover. We now consider the "adult" person, once again using our Baganda material as illustrative.

Adulthood: Marriage, Family Life, and Relatives

The ultimate course of a successful courtship leads to marriage, known in *Luganda* as *jangu enfumbire* or "come cook for me." Selection of a marital partner is based, in part, on the desired personal qualities described previously. Additionally, one should marry a person not from one's own clan (i.e., exogamy) lest clan sanction and sickness result. In the old days, Baganda men would sometimes acquire wives from neighboring tribes through military conquest of them. Conversely, however, there tends to be a stated preference for women to marry within the tribe (i.e., endogamy). One Muganda woman stated:

> Regarding marriage the man is allowed to marry a stranger because of patrilineal descent; therefore, the children will be Baganda. Outside marriages for women are considered to be a disappointment. When a wife from a foreign tribe comes into a house, she is treated as a Muganda. However, it is never forgotten that she is not a Muganda. Her children are considered to be Baganda. When Baganda women marry outside, they are likely to be mistreated because of envy.

Frequently clan exogamy and tribal endogamy continue to be the normal practices although there now tends to be relatively more intertribal marriages among educated Baganda, particularly with neighboring Bantu tribes. Marriage within one's own religion is another modern trend.

Once a decision has been made to marry, the couple's family, at least ideally, are consulted for their approval. The Baganda have a system of "bride price," although it is not nearly as elaborated as in many other African societies. A typical bride price might include 500 shillings, two large gourds of *Kiganda* beer, a basket of meat, a robe for the girl's father and one for her older brother, a dress for the girl's mother and something (often underclothes) for her *ssenga*. Soon after the "negotiations," the suitor informs, frequently by mail, the girl's parents of his decision to provide or not to provide the bride price. The girl or her parents may also refuse at this point.

After marriage a new household is established, usually in the village of the husband. It is in the home that the daily round of maintenance and social life unfolds: children are cared for, gardens cultivated, and visitors entertained. Farm work is usually completed before the noon sun, at which time food is prepared for use later in the day. In the afternoon women can be seen visiting neighbors, weaving floor mats, sewing (usually crocheting table cloths and infants' dresses), or leisurely plaiting their hair.

Traditionally, the moral order sanctioned polygyny, especially in cases where the first wife was barren. Relations among co-wives were frequently strained although cooperation was expected. In fact, the word "co-wife" (*mukazi-muggya*) is probably derived from the term "jealousy" (*buggya*). The senior wife enjoyed some privileges, but her relations with her husband were mediated by her co-wives. Roscoe states, for example:

> When a husband lost hope of having children, and the woman was pronounced to be sterile, she lost favour with him, and though he

seldom put her entirely away, yet where there was a second wife, the latter came to the front, and received the attentions and affection of her husband, while the barren wife became more and more the drudge. (Roscoe 1911:46)

Co-wives lived in separate but adjacent houses. The husband had his own house in front of the women's quarters where his wives slept with him when invited to do so. Sororal polygyny was also permitted, a practice which may have reduced potential conflict among co-wives.

Marital cooperation is normally maintained in family affairs such as division of labor, sharing of income, and raising of children. Authority patterns in the Kiganda home, as we have noted, are not egalitarian. The husband expects and receives gratiating deference from his wife and children. The husband is served food first and, in traditional homes, the wife kneels before her husband while greeting him. Husbands are addressed respectfully as *Ssebo* (sir) by their wives. Some modern marriages are egalitarian although most men prefer the traditional way. One university-educated father in our sample even participated enthusiastically in the care of his infant son. He especially enjoyed bottle-feeding him, and his wife, a primary school teacher, stated that when her son cried at night her husband was the only one who could comfort him! Traditionally, caring for the infant has been a strictly female role with men rarely taking an interest in the infant (and certainly not admitting to doing so) until the child can speak and understand.

The institution of marriage serves to widen the kinship network of the individual. Affinal relatives are now acquired in addition to those consanguineal kinsmen already recognized by "blood." We have already described the social importance of *ssenga,* about whom there is a well-known Kiganda saying: "if she was not a woman I would call her my father." Moreover, a girl calls her *ssenga's* husband "my husband" since in the past she would sometimes marry him should her *ssenga* die. These days, *Ssenga's* husband not infrequently initiates his "niece" into her first sexual experience. This is a relationship known in anthropological parlance as "privileged familiarity."

Affinal relatives (*bako*) are acquired upon marriage. A person's father and mother-in-law are accorded extreme deference and respect. In particular, one should avoid any physical contact with them or as the Baganda put it "share the same wash basin with them." A wife's sister or a husband's brother, on the other hand, do "share the same basin" and call each other "spouse." A wife's brother and husband's sister are also close and friendly, often sharing secrets with each other. They are expected to be the "peace-makers" should any marital difficulties develop between their sibling and sibling-in-law.

Old Age and Death

In Buganda, the attainment of high status or prestige is largely achieved rather than ascribed. We have seen the marked degree to which Baganda manipulate their social environment as a strategy for self-improvement and upward mobility. A cultural focus on individual merit has minimized the importance of age as a positive factor in the allocation of prestige. There-fore, the social position of old people is not as enviable as in many other East African societies, such as the Masai, where important political and religious roles are assigned to the aged. On the other hand, most Baganda would deem undesirable the American family pattern of dismissing elderly kinsmen to live in special locations, often with inadequate provisions.

The Luganda term *mukadde* (old person) is used for both men and women. An extreme or pronounced age can be signified by assigning one or more *nyo* (very) modifier, as in the case of one informant of a hundred years or so who was often referred to by others as *mukadde nyo nyo nyo*. Until recently age was not recorded in years, so many elderly Baganda do not know (or care) "how old they are." Elderly Baganda do discuss their age in terms of whatever *Kabaka* reigned during their birth. There is no social recognition of menopause, which is treated as a private personal matter. By and large, however, "being old" is largely based on one's realistic percep-tion of diminishing strength, failing health, lack of sexual desire, and other biological factors. There is no socially determined "age" at which a person becomes "old" (as 65 in our own culture). Baganda, for example, consider someone to be *mukadde* if he or she has skin wrinkles and white hair. The Baganda believe that growing old is a natural process, sometimes referred to as "God's plan." However, through too much worry, excessive drinking, or many years of hard labor, "God's plan" can be accelerated. For women, bearing many children is an additional factor considered to cause a prema-ture old age.

Since age is not an important determinant of high social status, becoming old or being old is not a particularly desired quality. In fact, many Baganda attempt to conceal their age by applying dye to eliminate white hair. Many young adults realize that to grow old without children is especially undesirable since the care of old people is largely in the hands of their children. We have seen that one of the reasons why children are desired is that they can provide help during one's old age. For those having children, old age can be a rewarding experience. Otherwise, good health is necessary for survival. A close, free relationship obtains between children and grandparents. It is believed that grandparents are likely to spoil their grandchildren. A grandson might even address his grandmother as "my wife," and she would reciprocate with "my husband." In general, then, for the aged, children are a source of instrumental satisfaction and grandchildren a source of expressive satisfaction.

One technique used to discover the "insider's" point of view of growing old was to interview a small number (N = 20) of old men and women living in a rural village near Kampala. Some common responses to the question "What do you like best about old age?" included:

Men	Women
Nothing	Good health
I have no alternative. It is better to live it and be content eating and resting.	Respectability
	My children
	Nothing
Peace in my country	
Sleeping well	
Drinking beer	
Happy remembrances	
Respect attached to my age	
Responsibility, decision-making	

Our informants gave the following statements in response to the question "What do you dislike the most about old age?":

Men	Women
Nothing	Nothing
Working, because my body is weak	Weakness; shaking; losing senses

Young people who have
    failed to keep the ways of
    our tribe
Blindness
Lack of everything; unpleas-
    ant appearance; no com-
    pany; lack of attention and
    care; being looked down
    upon
Lack of ability to help myself
Lack of strength

Nothing, because I have
    grandsons
Suffering because I can no
    longer help myself

In addition to eliciting short answers from our elderly informants, we also asked them to recount an important event in the life of any old person known to them. It was assumed that this procedure would provide a "projective" experience for the informant or indicate his or her own feelings. Overall, these narratives show considerable concern about stresses associated with being totally dependent on others. The following episodes, for example, were provided by male informants:

> When my father got old he lost sight and could not help himself. He was touchy and always ordering me about. He thought I mistreated him; I must admit I did mistreat him; but at least, for him, he was lucky he had a son to help him though I was stubborn at times. As for me I have no child; I only pray that I do not grow old as he did because he was such a pitying sight.

> I once knew an old man who was so old that he could no longer walk. He was moved about on an animal skin from the house outside. All his senses were distorted. For example, he used to quarrel with the wind about children making noise. "Cooked matooke is like flames of fire"; this old man used to think that matooke was fire when he was given food. He was very irritable. Such old age is not good; in fact many people were relieved when he finally died.

> The old man I know had five daughters and one son. All the daughters died, and he was left alone with the son. He was so grieved that he never forgot the tragedy of his daughters. He was given food by his son, but he never forgot the tragedy of his daughters. In our culture, we believe that it is a curse for your

children to die before you because some people think that a person is comforted when he has his children to bury him. Eventually this man died, but I think that grief speeded up his death.

The following situation was described by a woman:

> Somebody gave birth to children, my brother's sons. One son was taking good care of the father: giving him food, providing water, some clothing, etc. Unfortunately, the son who loved the father died before he had finished building a house for him. The man remained without help. He started begging for food. In the end the old man figured out he could not go on living by begging because no one visited him nor offered him food. So he committed suicide. People discovered that the man had died when ants were building around him.

In general, the above typical narratives indicate that old age in the absence of supporting children and good health can be quite stressful, sometimes resulting in suicide. Blindness in particular is an especially hazardous misfortune. Lack of general community concern for the condition of the elderly is also indicated. At the village level, the occasion of death, however, brings forth considerable community solidarity. It is considered proper for neighbors to dig the grave for the deceased. Relatives are expected to be grieved and therefore do not normally participate in such activities. If, however, a person is for any reason despised by the neighbors (as in the case of suicides), then they will refuse to dig a grave. On these rare occasions, next of kin do the digging.

Soon after death strikes, male neighbors congregate to dig the grave in preparation for the *kuyika* or funeral. Men take turns digging and while at rest drink *mwenge* (beer), which has been provided by the host family. Whenever possible, the *kuyika* is announced over the radio so that friends and relatives from afar can attend. On the day of burial, it is not uncommon to see hundreds of people walking or driving to the event. Money is collected at the funeral (called *mabugo*) to be used for such things as purchasing bark cloth, paying travel expenses for some visitors, and providing support for the surviving relatives of the deceased.

Ancestors or spirits of dead people (*bazimu*) are thought to play a significant role among the living. Beneficent *bazimu* can provide warnings, often through dreams, about the proper course of action to avoid difficulty or provide strength to endure laborious activities such as farming. Failing to venerate *bazimu* through prayers and sacrifices or committing breaches of conduct with the living, can, however, induce anger in a *muzimu*, who, for vengeance, will cause difficulties for the transgressor.

Baganda also believe that ancestors live on in descendants who are born after their death. When babies are named, a number of names of deceased relatives are spoken to the infant until the baby smiles. The infant is then given that name because it is thought that this ancestor elicited the smile. The living maintain "symbolic" communication with the deceased relatives through use of photographs. The "photograph" is a modern artifact of enormous saliency throughout rural East Africa. Visitors to homes are frequently shown the host's photo album which itself becomes quite a conversation item. In our own research, the giving of pictures, often taken on request, is a crucial rapport-building activity. A common request was for a photo of an elder person so that a "memory" of him could be retained after death (Robbins and Kilbride 1987). The "social-relational" pattern referred to earlier can be seen in a quote from Wober concerning the home of one of our informants:

> One notion often put forward by testers in Africa was somewhat discredited by some of Kilbride's evidence; this is, that uneducated Africans usually have no pictures in their homes. But Kilbride reports that one peasant farmer had: four photographs (of self or friends); calendar pictures of Pope Paul and another; one polychrome painting; magazine or colour cutouts of Gina Lollabrigida, a blonde girl, a black girl, the British Royal Family and a civet cat. (1975:90)

We turn our attention in chapter 5 to the infant's world, beginning with a consideration of pregnancy. This is as it should be now that we have considered the "life cycle" for which infancy is one period in a circular developmental pattern, which includes ancestor veneration and even suggestions of reincarnation. Indeed, children are the wellspring of traditional Africanity, without whom the social world has little meaning or understanding. Perhaps nowhere is the metaphorical saying, "and a little child shall lead them" more appropriate. A belief in the mystical influence of children and encouragement for the early development of their social skills are concerns that will become apparent in our discussion of pregnancy and childbirth in the next two chapters.

5

BELIEFS AND PRACTICES DURING PREGNANCY
"Something Has Caught Me"

"Luck takes you further than goodness alone."

Our information on the prenatal environment is most detailed for the Baganda; therefore, we shall refer to them for illustrative materials. It should be noted, however, that the Abaluyia (i.e., Samia) practice many similar customs during pregnancy, and some of these similarities will be mentioned where appropriate. Pregnancy is generally welcomed for both men and women. Children are a source of pride for both sexes and are considered to be a means of assistance in old age. Traditionally, the pregnant woman's body was seen as little more than a vessel in which the infant grew until ready for birth. Billington, Welbourn, Wondera, and Sengendo (1963) report that the woman's body was thought to contain a mold into which the ingredients for shaping a child were deposited. If a woman's mold was turned upside down, she would be barren. They report further that:

> The fetus was thought to sit upright in the mother's abdomen with his arms bent to feed himself. A pregnant woman always knelt while eating her meals because if she sat with her feet drawn up beside her

> in the customary way, with her trunk twisted sideways, the baby
> might come to lie transversely. (134)

It should be noted, however, that there is no *Luganda* word for fetus. The
being inside the mother was nevertheless thought to be living and separate
from the mother since, if the pregnant woman died, it was extracted from
her and buried separately. This was done because no two "people" can be
buried in the same grave. There is no word for fetus, and little, if any, talk
about the unborn child before birth for fear that it might be born a serpent
or leopard, or otherwise deformed. Indeed, the idea of pregnancy was
expressed indirectly. When a woman announced that she was pregnant she
did so by saying, for example, "syphilis has caught me," "some disorder has
caught me," or "I am not normal."

A moral code for sexual behavior during pregnancy existed. A woman
could not even sit on the same mat on which a man had sat nor use the same
cup or dish that he had used. When walking along a path, she had to push
the grass along the path aside with a stick in order to chase away any evil
spirits from a man having walked there before her. Breaking any of these
rules, which was thought to be immoral behavior, might result in prolonged labor or other delivery problems. Orley (1970), in his study of
mental illnesses among Baganda, reports the belief that committing adultery with many men (i.e., five or more) during pregnancy will result in the
illness of *amakiro,* which can cause the death of the mother or her infant at
the time of birth. Identifiable by the marks it leaves on the body, *amakiro*
most often results in the woman trying to "eat her baby" (cf. 9). It is
believed, however, that taking certain traditional medicines can prevent
this affliction.

Very little is known about current prenatal practices of the Baganda.
Ainsworth (1967) mentions pregnancy in a discussion of lactation and
weaning. Traditionally, as well as presently, should a Muganda woman
become pregnant while she is nursing her infant, she would be expected to
discontinue the nursing. Baganda believe that a pregnant woman's milk
becomes sour; therefore, breast feeding during pregnancy can make the
infant sick if he or she continues to suckle. Geber (1956) mentions the
difficulty she had in obtaining responses from Baganda women to her
questions about heredity, pregnancy, and delivery. Perhaps because of this
difficulty, she does not report her findings from these interviews. In a later
article, Geber (1958) reported that the Baganda woman is in no way upset
by her pregnancy and continues to be quite active up to the moment of

delivery. When we spoke to Geber in 1972, she expressed surprise that we had obtained any information concerning pregnancy because, as we've stated, Baganda mothers do not like to talk about their unborn child for fear of causing harm to the child. Prenatal clinics have apparently alleviated some of this fear since Janet, working in 1972–73, had little difficulty in obtaining responses to our questions concerning prenatal practices. The misgivings of some mothers were allayed by using circumlocutions; for example, instead of asking about the "baby," the mother was asked about "that thing growing inside of you." In addition, many of the questions asked indicated that the researchers were personally familiar with Kiganda practices (e.g., "Do you massage the parts of your body?"). We administered our prenatal questionnaire to fifty pregnant Baganda women (twenty-five primigravidae, twenty-five multigravidae). Mothers were interviewed in *Luganda* by Janet and her Muganda research assistant, and the mother's responses were written down during each interview. Our discussion of pregnancy among the Baganda is based mainly upon the responses of the 50 pregnant Baganda women whom we interviewed. In some cases, we will also mention the responses of 25 pregnant Baganda women (18 multi-parous, 7 primiparous) from Masaka, the rural area located 80 miles south-west of Kampala, where we did our 1967 study. Using an abbreviated form of our questionnaire, a Muganda student who resided in Masaka inter-viewed these women in 1973. For political reasons, no foreign researchers were allowed to work in the Masaka area at that time.

A narrative description of Kiganda pregnancy will be presented, realiz-ing, of course, that when the authors write "the Baganda," they are refer-ring to the 50 Baganda women who responded to their prenatal question-naire. Most pregnant Baganda women who attend prenatal clinics begin doing so somewhere between their fifth and seventh months of pregnancy. However, those who live long distances from a clinic may wait until their eighth or even ninth month. Only a few have private doctors (usually those who have had previous complications) since most deliveries are performed by midwives. If there is one near enough to home, a hospital or dispensary is often preferred for delivery. Traditional Kiganda doctors tend to be consulted only when the woman is experiencing some difficulty with her pregnancy, feels she has been bewitched, or desires herbal medicines (usu-ally mixed with clay) to ease her labor pains or shorten labor, for example.

During pregnancy many Baganda (and Abaluyia) women experience a "craving" (*okwoya*) for clay (*ebumba*). Eating *ebumba* is a practice approved of for women only. In fact, there is a Kiganda proverb which states, "a person who will eat anything is like a man who eats clay." As part of our investigation of soil eating, Philip interviewed fifteen Baganda women who ate soil regularly even when they were not pregnant. Most reported that they did so because of the soil's "good smell and taste." Some mentioned that it could become habit forming much like the habit of smoking tobacco. Through informal discussions with pregnant women, we learned that they are especially partial to eating clay because they like its taste or smell, it helps to settle the stomach, or others have recommended that they do so.

Feelings about the implications of clay-eating are mixed. None of those interviewed knew of any benefit for the fetus. Some felt that it was a harmless practice, but others insisted that eating too much clay would cause the infant to be born with poor skin color or pimples or, in extreme cases, covered with clay. Although clay is usually eaten, some women prefer to hang it over an open fire and inhale the smoke. Another type of soil (*takka Lyobudongo*) is taken from the walls of the cooking house and then eaten. This soil originally comes from termite hills. The flavoring of the smoke from the cooking fire makes it particularly tasty to many.

In addition to eating plain clay, Baganda women (as well as men) take clay mixed with Kiganda medicines (*emmumbwa*). *Emmumbwa* is comprised of various herbs mixed with soil, preferably collected from an area surrounded by a well. The clay and whatever herbs are needed are combined and baked in the sun. Each clay is made by different people and named for the content of its medicine. The mixture is taken by dissolving it in water and drinking it. There is no limit to the amount of different leaves or herbs that may be included. Thus it is thought possible for *emmumbwa* to cure any disease provided the relevant medicine is present since one kind of medicine will not stop the other from working. The most popular *emmumbwa* taken by pregnant women is *mukalakasa*. *Emmumbwa* is usually bought in the market or obtained from a relative or a friend. Abaluyia women also ingest herbs to ease the delivery at birth (*omutele*) and to induce urination to "clean the stomach" (*omusengese*).

The origin of mixing traditional medicines with clay is not clear. Some people think that the practice was brought into Buganda from other African tribes, while others say that it was started in Buganda. At any rate, it was seen as a convenient way to store medicine for future use. Another recount of the origin of *emmumbwa* goes back to the time when farmers drained water from swamps, where clay soil was found, in order to grow their crops there. When they got thirsty, they would drink some of this water which was mixed with the clay soil. They liked the taste of this water and of the food grown in such swamps because it was sweet and salty. When people found their traditional medicine to be very bitter, they mixed it with this clay to reduce the unpleasant taste of this medicine. It was such a successful blend that *emmumbwa* continues to be used today. Of the 50 pregnant women we interviewed, 36 (72.0%) had used traditional medicine sometime during their pregnancy. In our Masaka sample, 24 out of 25 (96%) reported using traditional medicine. Modern, educated Baganda also continue to use Kiganda medicine in combination with Western medicine. Mothers expecting their firstborns are particularly likely to use traditional medicines because they don't "want to take any chances." In fact, one Muganda father, a newspaper reporter who was interviewed by Philip, reported that one of his wives became quite annoyed when her baby died "as a result of his refusing to allow her to take Kiganda medicine during her pregnancy." Everyone was blaming him, so during the next pregnancy he permitted her to take the Kiganda medicine, and the baby was quite fine.

In a discussion of "custom and child health in Buganda," Billington et al. (1963) warn about the possible dangers of some Kiganda medicines. A popular traditional medicine is derived from the leaves and bark of a plant called *Albizia gummifera,* from which is extracted an alkaloid, *albitocin,* which causes severe rhythmical contractions of uterine muscle. Billington et al. stress that:

> The danger of these herbal medicines cannot be too strongly emphasized; since labour is likely to be difficult in any case because of the shape of the Baganda pelvis, the giving of uncertain quantities of powerful oxytocic drugs greatly adds to the hazards of childbirth. (135)

Nevertheless, certain traditional beliefs encourage the continuance of taking some traditional medicines which might be dangerous if taken in improper amounts. For example, Billington et al. (1963) report:

> In a difficult labour, some specially expert old woman was called in. The mother was urged to confess to immorality, and was sometimes beaten to make her do so. It was believed that failure to deliver a child within six hours of the onset of labour was a certain sign of marital infidelity, and therefore herbal medicines were frequently used with the intention of accelerating labour. (135)

While most pregnant women do not eat any special foods during pregnancy, some reported difficulty eating matooke, cassava, and sweet potatoes, so they avoided eating these staples. Traditionally, women were deprived of high-protein foods such as mutton, eggs, chicken, and fish. Ojiambo (1967) reports for the Abasamia that there are a number of food taboos surrounding pregnancy. In addition, our Abasamia informants told us that salt should not be taken during pregnancy or the baby will have a rash. Rib meat of any kind will cause the infant to develop sinewy skin. Similarly, Billington et al. (1963) report for the Baganda that:

> Salt was not eaten during pregnancy because it caused the child to have sores or swelling of the arms after birth. Hemorrhage from the cord was also said to be due to "*munnyo*"—salt. Other foods were avoided, for example, sugar-cane, onions, "*gonja*" (sweet plaintain) and "*enswa*" (white ants). If they were eaten the child would die at an early age. (134)

When the pregnant women we interviewed were asked whether there were any foods they were not eating because they were pregnant, only 13 out of 50 (26.0%) mentioned avoiding any foods (i.e., cassava, sweet potatoes, plantain). When asked whether they were eating any special foods because they were pregnant, nine women (18.0%) stated that they were (i.e., plantain, white potatoes, milk, clay, fish, eggs). Twenty-three women (46.0%) reported that they experienced a general lack of appetite at some time during their pregnancy while 32 women (64.0%) experienced a lack of appetite for a particular food. A majority said they no longer desired to eat sweet potatoes. Twenty-eight women (56%) had strong desires or cravings for particular foods, especially fish.

Traditionally, the Muganda woman engaged in various strengthening activities to prepare her for labor and a successful delivery. Billington et al. (1963) give the following account of traditional practices which can be compared with our findings concerning contemporary Kiganda prenatal practices:

> Women were encouraged to dig, lift burdens and go up and down hills; at dawn they would go out and stand in the morning air with few clothes on to cool the body (which also served to lessen the effect of "heat" during pregnancy). About ten days before delivery, a woman would sit in a bath, made from a herbal brew, in which she

stretched her legs out straight. This practice was called "breaking the bones" ("*okumenya amagumba*") and was intended to make the thigh muscles and pelvic joints supple and mobile. Just before delivery, the woman's friends massaged the abdomen with butter containing herbs, working from back to front and also giving a rocking movement to the abdomen. This was supposed to straighten the baby in the birth canal and to strengthen the abdominal muscles. (135)

Today both Baganda and Abaluyia pregnant women still believe that they should remain active and exercise during pregnancy. An Abaluyia expectant mother is told to sit with straight extended legs so the fetus's head will remain straight down in the proper position for birth. Older Abaluyia women advise pregnant women to remain physically active. Therefore, many pregnant women exercise by running around the compound, for example, several times a day. When asked whether they did any exercise during pregnancy, 14 (28%) of our Kampala area Baganda mothers reported that they did so. (Running was the most preferred activity.) When their responses to this question were combined with their responses to the question of whether they were working in their garden during pregnancy, the number "exercising" increased to 29 (58%). Among our Masaka respondents, who interpreted the question on exercise to include "work not games," 80% reported that they did so during pregnancy. Including their responses to the working-in-the-garden question increased the percentage to 88. Women were also asked, "Do you carry anything on your back when you are pregnant?" Looking only at those mothers who were not expecting their first child, we find that all (100%) of the Masaka mothers, but only eight (16%) of the Kampala mothers, reported that they carry their youngest babies on their backs. None reported carrying anything else in this manner. If there is no one else to help with the work, pregnant women will continue to carry food, water, or firewood on their heads. Pregnant women are encouraged to work hard so that they will build up strength for delivery. They are also warned not to sleep too much lest they become lazy and lose strength.

Contemporary Baganda still engage in traditional bathing practices. In fact, these practices have been extended from the traditional last weeks of pregnancy to as early as the fourth or fifth months of pregnancy. Herbal baths are composed of *cold* water and special Kiganda plants, the favorite being *Kiralan Kuba*. Only three mothers out of 75 admitted to ever using hot water, and then only on cold nights. Reasons given for this practice were: to get strength; to ease the delivery and to cool the "heat" of the body. Seven primiparous women, who were also very young, said they did so because a mother, mother-in-law, or father's sister (*ssenga*) told them to do so although they did not know why. One woman said she bathed with *amalagala y'alumonde* (sweet potato leaves) so that she would not "eat her baby." Most bathe the entire body except the head; others exclude the head or bathe only the vaginal areas with the herbal mixture.

A pregnant woman also massages her stomach and vaginal areas with vaseline or oil and various Kiganda medicines such as *ekigogi* and *esonko*. Women report doing the massaging themselves rather than having someone else do so. Most massage themselves once a day after bathing in the evening. Sixty-eight percent of our 50 Kampala area mothers reported massaging themselves, and all 25 of our Masaka mothers reported doing so. Massaging isn't begun until the seventh or eighth month of pregnancy. Reasons for massaging include: "to shape the tummy; to remove dead skin and soften the skin; to ease the bones; to keep the baby together or make it feel better." Abaluyia also practice stomach and breast massaging during pregnancy.

The idea that Baganda mothers joyfully accept motherhood and are very relaxed during pregnancy (Geber 1958) is only partially true today and may have been so in the past also. While most Baganda women (72%) like being pregnant because they want the baby, many of them (48%) fear the pain associated with giving birth—not an unusual concern since anesthesia is rarely given at delivery. Every mother in our longitudinal sample had a normal delivery, and only two of these twelve mothers had any anesthesia during delivery. When asked what they liked least about pregnancy most said, "when the baby dies." In addition, a majority of Baganda women felt that their pregnancy was giving them difficulties (e.g., vomiting, headaches, dizziness, lack of appetite, food cravings, fevers, backaches). An overwhelming majority of Baganda (86%)—stop sleeping with a man (usually the father of the child) for some length of time during the pregnancy. This is especially true during the last few months of the pregnancy. Most expressed a dislike of or discomfort from intercourse at this time. Similarly, among the Abaluyia, intercourse is usually terminated after six months of pregnancy. Regarding traditional methods of birth control, Kisekka (1973) reports that Baganda used only abstinence and certain "magical cures." An unwanted pregnancy, for example, could be magically "tied" (*kulusiba*) so that it "disappears on the back" (55). Abortion was known to be brought about by inserting slimy weed (*ennanda*) into the vagina and piercing the uterus with oxytocic plants like *oluwoko*. Only four mothers out of the 50 we questioned stated that they had planned their pregnancies. Since having children is extremely desirable, most rural non-working women have as many children as they can. Fifty-eight percent of the Kampala area pregnant women we interviewed said they were preparing nappies (diapers), cot sheets, and/or dresses for their babies. Seventeen (34%) women said that they would return to their jobs or seek employment after delivery. Maternity leaves are usually about six weeks.

Thus we see that pregnancy is a welcome event surrounded by many traditional African practices such as clay eating, herbal medicines, herbal baths, massaging, and exercise. Even Western-educated East Africans engage in such activities along with modern medical practices in order to ensure the health and survival of the unborn child, a child of value and the subject of our next chapter.

6

CHILDREN OF VALUE

"An only child is like a drop of rain in the dry season."

Birth and Infant Mortality

As we saw in the previous chapter, pregnancy is filled not only with the joy of having a child but with fear and apprehension concerning the pains of childbirth and the survival of the infant. Much care, therefore, is taken during pregnancy to ensure the strength of the woman and the well-being of the expected infant. The delivery of the infant traditionally occurred in the "shamba" (banana plantation) during the day or in the home at night. Women were typically assisted by female relatives. Nowadays most women deliver in hospitals, dispensaries, or maternity centers under the care of midwives. Kisekka, a Muganda sociologist, reports that:

> Even when delivery takes place in the maternity hospital, Baganda are still inclined to give medicinal herbs for chewing . . . Some of these medicines are strong and cause tonic contractions during delivery. . . . In child labor a woman is caused much exhaustion for she is told not to sleep or turn her neck from side to side. She is also not given food or drinks. Child labor pains are not borne in silence; out-loud cries are not discouraged. (1973:53–54)

During normal hospital deliveries, no anesthesia is administered. The mother usually spends two or three days in the hospital or maternity center with her newborn, who is placed at the foot of her bed. Men are not supposed to witness childbirth. Kisekka (1973) recounts that the emphasis on secrecy concerning matters of childbirth is exemplified in the Kiganda admonition to a talkative child:

> *Mwana wange oyogera nnyo olyogera n'eby'omuzzaliro.* (My dear child you are so talkative you might reveal what goes on in the delivery room.) (53)

Upon returning home, the new mother receives much care and attention from relatives and friends. In fact, she is now addressed as *Nakawere,* that is, mother of a newborn. Kisekka (1973) writes that

> . . . this is the time when she receives most attention from all around her as they go to great lengths to please her by preparing her favorite dishes . . . Usually during this period some elderly relative, her mother or mother-in-law *Nyazaala* will come to stay with her, bathe her, wash and change the baby's soiled clothes, and do all the household chores while all she does is sleep and suckle the baby (56). Our materials show that the range of relatives who were coming to help after delivery included: mother, grandmother, mother-in-law, father's sister, sister, and co-wife. Sometimes housegirls were employed in this capacity. Of fifty women who were questioned, forty-two (84%) stated that they would receive assistance with the newborn.

Traditionally, the placenta was buried in the mother's compound to protect the child from witchcraft. The umbilical cord was (and still is) retained for use in a ceremony (*Kwalula Abaana*) in which the child is seated on a mat along with other members of the father's clan who are to receive their clan names. First, however, it is required that the infant's legitimacy be established. The paternal grandmother fills a chosen basket with water and Kiganda medicine. Each mother then brings her child's umbilical cord (which she has saved sometimes for years) to the grandmother, who drops it in the water. Previous to this, the mother has put cow's butter (*muziigo*) on the cord. If the cord floats (an occurrence helped by the buoyancy of the butter), the child belongs to the family and will be given a clan name chosen by the grandparents. If, however, it sinks, the child is not considered to be a member of the family and is not given a clan name. The mother is asked to name the real father of the child. Those children to be named sit naked on a bark cloth. The ceremony symbolizes a "rebirth," and even an adult can be named; the adult is naked above the waist only.

The birth of twins (*balongo*) is considered to be of importance and a cause for ceremonial observances. Honorific terms are taken by the parents; thereafter, the mother is called *Naalongo,* the father *Saalongo.* Among the Abaluyia twins were called *Amakhwana* and the mother of twins was nicknamed *Abakhwana* or *Balongo.* Among the Baganda, when the twins are girls, the firstborn is called *Babirye;* the second born *Nakato.* In the case of boys, the first is named *Wasswa;* the second is known as *Kato.* Soon after the birth of twins, a special ceremony is held at the mother's home. Drinking, feasting, and somewhat lewd dancing occur at this time. There are many observances which must be followed by parents of twins since twins can be dangerous to other people. Should they, for example, be incorporated (by mistaken paternity) into the wrong clan, then many people in that clan might die or suffer skin disorders.

In the case of the Abaluyia, the firstborn boy twin may be called *Opiyo* and the firstborn girl called *Apiyo.* If the twin born second is a boy, he is called *Odongo* while a girl is called *Adongo.* Rituals and ceremonies are particularly important during the first months of the twins' lives. Traditionally, the husband and wife remain in their hut for at least a month before the twins are "exposed" to society.

Although much care and attention are given to the mother and her newborn, various diseases and nutritional deficiencies too often result in the death of the neonate. Carolie Rendle Short (1962), then Professor of Obstetrics at Makerere Medical School, reported that at Mulago Hospital in Kampala there were about 80 stillborns per 1000 newborns. She states further that:

> The most common causes of maternal death in Uganda are obstructed labour resulting in ruptured uterus (34 per cent of all deaths), or exhaustion, sepsis, or shock (32 per cent of all deaths). Preeclamptic toxaemia and eclampsia, which are one of the main causes of maternal and perinatal mortality in Europe, are relatively rare and account for only eight per cent of maternal deaths. (14)

According to Jelliffe (1963), then professor of Pediatrics and Child Health at Makerere University College Medical School in Kampala, there is also a high rate of sickness and mortality among children. During a similar time period, mortality in the United States (1960) averaged 26.0, with 22.9 for whites and 43.2 for non-whites (Harms 1962); the Baganda rate was about

160 (Jelliffe 1963). Illness and death in the "toddler" age group are also very high. Jelliffe (1963) reports:

> The common types of disease in children admitted to hospital are diarrhoeal infections (18 percent) and protein-calorie malnutrition (14 percent), Kwashiorkor (10 percent), nutritional marasmus (4 percent), followed by malaria, pneumonia, anaemia, intestinal worms and accidents, especially burns and scalds. Many of these conditions are, in the Baganda context, unnecessary and to a considerable extent preventable. (122)

Of the 25 multiparous mothers (those having more than one birth) from the Kampala area that we interviewed, five (20%) reported that one or more of their children had died either shortly after birth or within the first few years of life. Four women reported having had miscarriages. Thus we can see that infant mortality is still a major problem among the Baganda. Traditionally, the death of an infant was interpreted as a curse from the spirits of the dead. Infant mortality presents a similar problem for the Abaluyia (see P. Kilbride 1980).

Baganda women seem to prefer female infants, at least as their first child, because of the help they give the mother in housework and caring for younger siblings. Other reasons for preferring girls include: they are easier to raise, they know their mother's problems, and they are girls like their mothers. Out of the 50 women questioned, 32 said that they wanted to have a girl, 15 wanted a boy, and 3 had no preference. Those that wanted boys had already given birth to all or mostly all girls. Among the Abaluyia both boys and girls are desired; girls as firstborns are especially useful as sources of labor and bride wealth. Boys will inherit their fathers' land and property and through their offspring increase the size of their family and clan. Both sexes are hoped to be a help during one's old age.

The Infant's Home Environment

Infants experience their most intense and significant interactions within the maternal and social confines of the household. What is the home into which the infant is born most typically like? We will describe the Kiganda home for descriptive purposes. Rural homes, located among banana groves, and *shambas* or gardens are usually made of waddle-and-daub and have thatched or corrugated iron roofs. Most homes are rectangular in shape and contain several rooms. (Among the Abaluyia circular homes are also popular.) The homes of more affluent farmers are constructed of cement and have tile roofs. Some homes have electricity and running water, but most rural homes have no electricity, and water must be fetched from a well or collected when it rains. There is commonly a separate cooking house, and cooking is done on an open wood fire although some affluent farmers have Primus stoves. When windows are present, they usually contain no glass nor screens but have solid wooden shutters which are closed at night or whenever no one is at home. A latrine is located behind the house in the "shamba" or garden. Young children have their own latrines since they might fall into the adult latrine. Separate latrines also protect them from sickness which, Baganda believe, may occur if children's and adults' feces are mixed. Furniture usually consists of a wooden platform bed with a mattress, a table, and a few wooden chairs for the use of men and an occasional "European" (i.e., white or *muzungu*) researcher. On hand-woven straw mats, women and children sit modestly with their knees together and bent to one side in the case of the former, and bent underneath the buttocks, in the case of young children. (For the Abaluyia, it is appropriate to sit with legs extended, however.) Only a few rural homes have Western-style sofas and armchairs. Because homes contain so few breakable objects, a toddler can explore the surroundings freely without frequent admonitions from adults. Urban homes are typically of concrete with corrugated iron or tiled roofs and have glass windows. They contain electricity, indoor plumbing, an indoor kitchen, and toilet facilities. In general, the homes are much like any modern-style homes and contain Western-type furniture, including radios, televisions, phonographs, and baby cribs among the more affluent.

The human composition of households in the area varies, as a social survey of 109 randomly selected households (519 individuals) in the rural area near Masaka demonstrated (see P. Kilbride 1970:31–32). Thirty-three households were "nuclear" (a marital couple with or without children); 36 were "expanded" (a nuclear family and other people who may or may not be relatives); and 40 households were "atomistic" (e.g., lone women or men, fathers and their children, mothers and their children). There were no reported instances of polygyny in this sample. (As suggested previously [see chapter 3], Abaluyia homes are often multi-family units, and polygyny is more commonly practiced.)

Kiganda Clothing

The Baganda are quite concerned with personal cleanliness. A daily bath is routine for adults, and hands are washed before meals. Infants are frequently washed two or three times a day. A concern for a favorable personal appearance also includes being well-dressed. The rural Muganda women typically wears a *busuuti*, a floor-length, brightly colored cloth dress with a square neckline and short puffed sleeves. The garment is fastened with a sash placed just below the waist over the top of the hips and by two buttons on the left side of the neckline. It can be worn throughout pregnancy by simply loosening the sash since the skirt portion consists of several yards of material. The dress is also conducive to breast feeding because its two front buttons allow easy access to the breasts. Traditionally, the busuuti was strapless and made from barkcloth. Breasts could or could not be exposed since they were not considered to be erotic symbols before Westernization and the introduction of Christianity (cf. Kisekka 1973:35). The traditional dress of the Muganda man is a *kanzu*—a long, white, cotton robe. At present, on special occasions, it is worn over trousers with a Western-style sport jacket over it. Young children and adolescents usually wear Western-style clothing. No distinction is made between the dress of male and female infants since both wear long dresses. Toddlers who are being toilet-trained will be seen with their dresses tied above their waists. Male toddlers sometimes wear shirts instead of dresses. Because of the warm climate (mean temperature = 70° F), infants at home can often be seen wearing only colored, plastic beads around their ankles, wrists, and/or waists. These are worn "for decoration," "to keep the body parts slim," and/or "to prevent diseases." A red string tied around the wrist is thought to ward off measles. Anklets of brass and aluminum bells are worn by older infants who are being trained to walk; the ringing of the bells is thought to encourage the toddler to walk.

Urban adults and children usually wear Western-style clothing although the busuuti is still popular with married women, especially for occasions such as funerals, weddings, church services, etc. The more Westernized Baganda dress their infants in sex-typed, Western-style clothing, including rubber pants, bibs, booties, and hats of the appropriate pink or blue color. Men wear Western-style slacks, shirts, sport jackets, suits, ties, etc., as well as African-styled "Kitangi" shirts. In Kampala, clothes are a major part of the Kiganda budget. Robbins, Thompson, and Bukenya (1974) report that "both men and women strive to look 'smarti' and 'omulembe' (or up-to-date) by emulating Western European and Central and West African dress styles" (12). Western-style clothing covered by a colorful cloth (e.g., *Kanga*), from waist to ankles in the case of women, is popular among the Abaluyia.

Kiganda Food Practices

Food is another large portion of the budget for most Baganda living in Kampala. Many complain of the high cost of food in comparison to its abundance and inexpensiveness in the rural areas from which most of the food is transported. The staple food of the Baganda is *matooke*, a plantain which is steamed or boiled and served with ground nut sauce or meat soups. The Abaluyia staple has been sorghum or millet, now unfortunately replaced by the easier-to-prepare maize meal, *ugali*. Sweet potatoes, yams, rice, cassava, and English (white) potatoes are also popular. Because of the year-round growing season, there is no shortage of vegetables and fruits for any period of the year (not as in Western Kenya, where there is a "hunger time"). Sources of protein include eggs, fish, beans, ground nuts, beef, chicken, and goat as well as termites and grasshoppers in season. The most common vegetables are cabbage, beans, mushrooms, lettuce, string beans, carrots, onions, and various types of greens. Fruits containing vitamin C that are available include sweet bananas, oranges, pineapples, tomatoes, passion fruit, and papaya. Margarine and "kimbo," which are used in cooking, provide a source of fats and oils. Typical beverages include tea, coffee, milk, diluted fruit juices, and beer (traditional or modern), as well as other alcoholic beverages and occasionally soda (e.g., "Pepsi," "Orange Crush"). Although the Baganda have an adequate variety of foods available to them, the diet of children is high in carbohydrates. Infants, young children, and women have traditionally been deprived of high-protein foods which were usually reserved for men. Adults did not realize that children needed special diets or that food supplied the necessities for growth and development. Dean (1961) reports that children in Uganda who have been treated for protein-calorie malnutrition (e.g., kwashiorkor, marasmus) often come from Baganda families who adhere strongly to traditional practices and are not necessarily the poorest families. Kilbride (1977) reports for the Samia a similar problem with infant malnutrition, often thought to be the result of a child being bewitched.

Infant Care Practices

The earliest ethnographic description of the Baganda (Roscoe 1911) tends to be somewhat biased by the author's missionary background and the *Zeitgeist* of his time. He says ethnocentrically of the Muganda infant, "It was not trained in habits of cleanliness, and it grew up more like an animal than a human being" (60). Mair (1934) and Southwold (1965) also give brief descriptions of Baganda childhood. The most comprehensive description of infant care among the Baganda, to date, is Ainsworth's (1967) *Infancy in Uganda*. Her work was done in *1954–55* in six villages about 15 miles from Kampala, and it is based on a combined cross-sectional and longitudinal observational-interview study of 28 Baganda mothers and infants. As mentioned previously, we questioned 50 pregnant Baganda women (the same 50 as previously described) in *1972–73* concerning their childrearing expectations. We will describe some Kiganda infant care practices as they are today—a combination of the modern and the traditional. Comments on Abaluyia infant care will also be made where appropriate.

During the first week after delivery, most Baganda mothers receive help from a relative (e.g., grandmother, mother, mother-in-law, sister, sister-in-law, *ssenga* [father's sister] or a hired housegirl.) In fact, many Baganda mothers have help in caring for their infants. If no older siblings are available, a young relative may be brought from another household to stay with the mother. In some cases, "Ayahs" or babysitters are hired, although the major responsibility for the care of the infant still rests with the mother. From the very beginning, both Muganda and Luyia infants experience a great deal of physical and social stimulation. Typically, the Muganda infant receives a warm, herbal bath (Kiganda medicine used to prevent *nnoga* or rash) two or three times a day. For the first two to four months the forehead and nose are gently "shaped" and limbs and fingers are massaged. Soon after birth, for about a week, the Luyia infant's head is washed with *endulandula* leaves to remove facial hairs. No attempt is made to shape facial features.

Infants are breast-fed on demand, although employed mothers combine breast with bottle- or cup-feeding. Other mothers bottle-feed (a practice becoming more prevalent than in the past), feeling their milk supply is insufficient. The overwhelming majority of Baganda and Abaluyia mothers agree, however, that breast milk is best for the baby. The breast is often used as a pacifier, and most mothers are quick to pick up a crying infant.

More modern mothers, nevertheless, express the opinion that the infant should not be picked up immediately if there is nothing wrong and he is only crying for attention. In the past, the nursing infant slept with her mother; currently, many mothers prefer to place baskets, shaped like the body of a baby carriage, next to their beds. More affluent mothers and typically the more Westernized or educated prefer only baby cribs. The father has a separate bed which may or may not be in the same room, and the infant is placed next to the father during a nap or in the morning. Although traditionally the father rarely expressed any interest in playing with or helping in the care of any child less than a year old, some fathers, perhaps influenced by modern education, are becoming more directly involved in the care of their infants. Some of the fathers in our Baganda sample, for example, bottle- or cup-fed their infants, rocked their infants to stop them from crying, helped put them to sleep, and even helped in the training of motor skills such as sitting.

Infants are very much the center of attention. Even the newborn is given to visitors to hold, as propriety requires, and the older infant is seated on the mother's lap facing toward the visitors. The infant, in turn, is expected to be happy and sociable in responding to all this attention. Indeed, we found that Baganda infants are advanced in their social responses to persons and a mirror image of themselves. (This finding will be discussed in detail later.) Before the infant can sit alone, he or she is usually held in some way (on the lap, at the shoulder, on the back, or on the hip) by his mother or someone else most of the time that he or she is awake. Both Baganda and Abaluyia infants are trained to sit, an important motor and social skill for them. The infant is usually held on the lap or at the shoulder when she is very young and as she gets older she is held on the hip or on the back mostly when the mother is traveling or working.

Among the Baganda, an infant up to about three or four months of age is called an *omwana omuwesi* but thereafter is referred to as an *omwana*. Although the boundary is not sharp or based on a specific age, some informants report that an infant who can sit is no longer an *omwana omuwesi*.

The most apparent difference in child-care practices between Baganda and American mothers is carrying the infant on the back. (The recent U.S. adoption of cloth baby carriers and metal-and-cloth backpacks is an obvious imitation.) The infant is secured to his mother's back by one piece of cloth which covers his buttocks and his back up to his neck; the cloth is tied above and below the mother's breasts. His feet straddle his mother's waist, sticking out at the sides and his head is free to turn. There are three main variations used to put the infant on one's back. Traditionally, the infant was lifted by one arm and swung over onto the back. Nowadays, most mothers use two hands to lift the infant then swing her onto the back with one hand. Still others lift the infant onto the hip with a hand under each of her shoulders and then slide her around to the back. Traditionally, the infant was put on the back when she was one or two months old; at present, she is more likely to be between two and four months of age. Some mothers try to wait even longer for fear that the infant will fall off their backs or become bowlegged. If the infant is one who cries a lot, however, they will usually put him on the back as early as possible in order to quiet him. While the infant usually cries the first time he is put on the back, he quickly learns to adapt to this and seems quite content and often falls asleep there. When awake, his position on the back allows him much visual and tactile stimulation. Most mothers stop carrying their infants by the time they are two or three years old, but some continue until the child is as old as six years. While the infant was traditionally lifted by one arm to be fed or held, most mothers who have attended prenatal or child welfare clinics pick up the child by two hands under his arms at the shoulder. A few also support the child's head, but most do not find it necessary to do so. Geber and Dean's (1957) findings of remarkable head control among Baganda newborns are in agreement with our observations of sixty-two Baganda newborns (see Kilbride 1974).

Baganda mothers, and the Abaluyia as well, have a relatively relaxed and permissive attitude toward their infants. The only things that most mothers must keep their babies away from are the cooking fire or other hot things or anything which might harm the child. Most mothers report that they protect their infants by keeping harmful things away from the baby rather than keeping the baby away from harmful things by reprimanding him or curtailing his movements. "Toilet training" occurs gradually and casually, although it may be begun as early as two or three months of age. Whenever a mother senses that her infant is about to urinate, she will "hold him out" in the air and or with his feet touching the ground. This is not supposed to be done quickly or suddenly and, often, if the infant has already begun to urinate, he will be left seated on the lap. He is held in a squatting position with his feet touching the ground in order to defecate. Children are usually not taught to excrete outside the house until they are old enough to understand (i.e., when they can speak). Until then, the child's excretia is wiped up with a banana leaf and deposited in his latrine. Most children are "toilet trained" and use their own latrine by the time they are three years old. Many urban mothers use diapers, but because they are expensive, they have few of them; therefore, they are likely to remove the diaper and squat the child if they anticipate an elimination.

Traditionally, toys were made for the infant out of banana fiber (e.g., balls, dolls, rattles). Most urban mothers, however, purchase toys for their infants. The most popular are balls, dolls, rattles and motor cars. Dolls are considered to be most suitable for girls while balls and cars are best for boys. Toys, nevertheless, are usually few, and the contact between mother and infant is predominantly visual and tactile and rarely mediated by objects.

Our studies of infant-care practices and sensorimotor development best exemplify the positive environment experienced by the much-valued East African infant. For this reason, we will conclude this chapter with some of these findings.

Infant Sensorimotor Development

Our first field trip to Uganda involved, among other studies, an assessment of the motor development of Baganda infants. Using the Bayley Scales of Infant Development (Bayley 1969) for this cross-sectional study (and a later longitudinal one), Janet Kilbride tested 163 Baganda infants (71 males, 92 females). They ranged in age from one month to two years and lived in villages in the vicinity of our field home in Kako, which is about eight miles from Masaka, Uganda. The results of this study have been published elsewhere (e.g., Kilbride, Robbins, and Kilbride 1970; J. Kilbride, 1973). The main purpose of this study was to verify the reliability of the finding of advanced motor development of Ugandan infants (e.g., Geber 1958) using a more homogeneous population and a better standardized testing instrument. Overall, the motor development of our sample of Baganda infants was found to be significantly in advance of United States infants. Their mean, median, and mode Bayley motor-development indexes were 123 (SD = 15.54), 123, and 124, respectively.

Our second study was undertaken in order to investigate whether any socioenvironmental factors might be affecting this advancement. A research design with a longitudinal-cross-sectional mix was employed. In order to obtain information concerning prenatal and childrearing customs, 50 pregnant Baganda women (25 primiparous, 25 multiparous), attending prenatal clinics in Kampala, Uganda, and within 40 miles of Kampala, were interviewed in *Luganda* by Janet Kilbride and a female Muganda research assistant who was trained as a nurse and midwife. The women were told that the researcher was interested in learning how Baganda mothers care for their infants because she had heard that they were very good at this. Mothers were asked, therefore, if the researcher and her assistant could visit with them in their homes after the birth of their babies. All but one of the expectant mothers, the co-wife of a chief, agreed to the visits. From this larger group, 12 mothers were selected for intensive observations. Selection was based mainly on interview responses that indicated some individual variation in child-care practices hypothesized to be relevant for infant sensorimotor development. The sample, though small, represented variation in residence, education, marital status, religion, and occupation. (See Table 2.) Three households were located in the city of Kampala, and nine households were situated in four villages located two, fifteen, seventeen, and thirty miles from Kampala. Table 3 presents a description of the homes of our infants.

The age at which a mother expects her infant to accomplish certain skills or the age at which he will develop certain capabilities may influence the way she interacts with him. For example, most Baganda mothers believe that a child does not begin to hear sounds until she is about three months old. Interestingly, most mothers do not begin singing to their infants until they are at least three months old. The median ages when the fifty expectant mothers judged that an infant would acquire certain skills or that their own infant would be able to do certain sensorimotor skills are presented in Table 4.

Mothers were then asked whether they would teach their baby to do any of the sensorimotor skills listed in Table 4. All fifty mothers replied that they would. When asked which things they would train their infants to do, they stated that they would teach their infants to sit, to stand, to crawl, and to walk. In addition, if their infants were slow at learning any of these skills, most mothers said that they would increase their efforts so that he would learn more quickly. Fewer mothers mentioned that they would try to teach their infants to talk. The two methods used for the latter are to "make" the infant talk after the mother or name things for the infant while pointing to them. A Muganda infant is taught to stand by being leaned against a wall or anything firm, or less frequently, by being held by the hands in a standing position. Walking is encouraged by holding the child's two hands and walking backwards. A variant of this is to stand the child facing you with his feet on top of yours while you walk backwards. A more traditional method is to have the child hold onto a wall with one hand while you hold the other hand and walk him. Only half the mothers reported that they would train their infants to crawl. All but one stated that they would do this by putting something attractive just out of the child's reach. One mother suggested pushing the infant from behind while he was lying on his stomach. Baganda infants are rarely seen on their stomachs; the preferred method of lying the infant down is on his side.

Both Baganda and Abaluyia mothers consider sitting to be an important landmark in the infant's development during his first six months of life and are quite conscientious about training their infants to sit (See Kilbride & Kilbride 1975, P. Kilbride 1980.) Beginning sometime between one and three months of age, the infant is set on the lap with one arm around his waist and no support for his head (lap training). At three or four months of age, the infant is placed on a mat in a sitting position with his knees bent and his heels almost touching each other. Cloths are wrapped around him up to his waist for support. Traditionally, the infant was placed in a hole dug in the ground and bark cloth was wrapped around him. A modern adaptation of this is to sit the infant in a small, round, plastic wash basin (with or without cloths). The infant's hands are placed on either side of the basin. Ideally, the first time a Muganda infant is seated on the ground is at his "sitting ceremony," *kukuza omwana*. Roscoe (1911) reported, "until this ceremony of placing the child to sit had been accomplished, the nurse, or the mother, had to carry the child about, or to put it to lie down on its back" (58). The mother of the infant's father sits the child on a mat with cloths around him or in a hole and proclaims, "Now you are a man (woman)." That evening, the father of the baby jumps over the mother of the baby (a symbol of intercourse) in order to strengthen the infant. Traditionally, the importance of sitting may be related to the *kwalula abaana* or clan-naming ceremony in which the child is seated on a mat along with other members of the father's clan who are to receive their clan names. For those infants who cannot sit alone, their mothers sit on the bark cloth and hold them. The usual procedure is for the mother of the person being named to sit behind her child. The father may sit anywhere he chooses. All members of the family on the father's side may attend the ceremony. (A child belongs to the father's family, and in case of a divorce they may claim the child.) No ceremonial complex appears to be associated

Table 2 Demographic Description of the Research Sample

Background Variable	Case Number					
	1	2	3	4	5	6
		Mother's				
Age	15	17	18	15	21	27
Education	9	9	2	7	10	3
Married	No	No	Yes	No	Yes	Yes
Occupation	student	student	farmer	farmer	teacher	teacher
Religion	Protestant	Protestant	Catholic	Protestant	Catholic	Muslim
Residence[a]	vnk	vnk	vfk	vtk	K	vtk
		Father's				
Age	18	24	19	20	25	40
Education	11	16	7	11	M.A.	7
Married	No	No	Yes	Yes	Yes	Yes
Occupation	typist	student	salaried	farmer	teacher	shop owner
Religion	Catholic	Protestant	Catholic	Muslim	Catholic	Muslim
Residence[b]	different	different	same	different	same	same
		Infant's				
Sex	m	f	f	f	m	f
Birth order	1	1	1	1	1	7
Number living in household	9	11	3	7	4	10
Head of house (relation to mother)	aunt	great-grandmother	husband	aunt	husband	husband

Table 2 (*continued*)

Background Variable	Case Number					
	7	8	9	10	11	12
Mother's						
Age	24	26	20	21	31	26
Education	6	6	8	12	9	7
Married	Yes	Yes	Yes	Yes	Yes	Yes
Occupation	farmer	farmer	farmer	stenographer	nurse	farmer
Religion	Catholic	Protestant	Protestant	Adventist	Catholic	Catholic
Residence[a]	vfk	vsk	vfk	K	K	vsk
Father's						
Age	29	40	24	27	36	38
Education	8	11	9	B.S.	13	9
Married	Yes	Yes	Yes	Yes	Yes	Yes
Occupation	truck driver	projectionist	salaried farmer	accountant	clerk	driver
Religion	Catholic	Catholic	Protestant	Adventist	Catholic	Catholic
Residence[b]	same	same	same	same	same	same
Infant's						
Sex	f	f	f	m	f	f/m
Birth order	5	5	1	1	5	4/5
Number living in household	7	8	3	5	10	8
Head of house (relation to mother)	husband	husband	husband	husband	husband	husband

[a] vnk = village near Kampala; vfk = village 15 miles from Kampala; vsk = village 17 miles from Kampala; vtk = village 30 miles from Kampala; K = Kampala

[b] same = lives with mother of infant; different = does not live with mother of infant

Table 3   Description of Homes of the Sample

Object	Case Number											
	1	2	3	4	5	6	7	8	9	10[a]	11	12
Glass windows (#)	7	0	0	7	4	0	0	0	0	m	0	0
(m = many)												
Shutters (#)	0	m	0	0	0	0	3	2	0	0	6	2
Opening near roof (#)	0	0	1	0	0	0	0	0	1	0	0	2
Tin roof	Y	Y	Y	Y	Y	Y	Y	Y	Y	—	Y	Y
(y = yes; n = no)												
Concrete walls	Y	Y	N	Y	Y	N	N	N	N	Y	Y	N
Waddle-and-daub walls	N	N	Y	N	N	Y	Y	Y	Y	N	N	Y
Electricity	N	N	N	N	Y	N	N	N	N	Y	Y	N
Outbuildings (#)	3	—	0	4	0	2	1	3	0	—	2	2
Rooms in house (#)	6	6	1	8	5	3	4	4	1	7	4	4
Water supply	W	F	W	W	F	W	W	W	W	F	F	W
(w = well; f = faucet)												
Distance from home	.5	0	.5	.25	0	n	.25	.5	n	0	0	.25
(miles) (n = near)												
Couch and armchairs	Y	Y	N	Y	Y	N	N	N	N	Y	Y	N

[a]Case No. 10 lived in a modern apartment building in Kampala.

with infant sitting among the Abaluyia. Sitting is seen as a means of freeing the mother for work activities.

We hypothesized that the practice of "training" the infant to sit is positively related to the early performance of sitting behavior. Ideally, half of the mothers in our sample would have trained their infants to sit while the other half would not have done so. This, however, was not a naturally occurring possibility due to the importance of sitting in Kiganda society (see Kilbride and Kilbride 1975). Only one of the 12 Baganda mothers in our sample reported that she was not going to train her infant to sit and had not done so by the time he was 4 months old, the length of time he was observed. This infant did not "sit with slight support" until he was 4 months old, which is similar to the Bayley U.S. median of 3.8 months for this item but later than the Baganda median of 3.0 months. "Training" to sit means that each day the infant is seated on the caretaker's lap beginning at 1 or 2 months of age. At 3 to 4 months of age, the infant is seated on a mat with cloths wrapped around the body for support. Those Baganda infants who were both trained to sit and also tested on all eight of the sitting

Table 4   Maternal Expectations of Age of Attaining Selected
Sensorimotor Skills

Question	Median (months)	Range (months)
At what age does a child:		
start to hear sounds?	3.0	1–6
begin to see?	2.0	.25–8
start to understand what is said to him?	15.0	5–60
begin to speak?	18.0	8–42
At what age do you expect your baby to:		
keep his own head steady?	4.0	2–8
sit supported?	3.5	2–8
sit with no support?	6.0	3–12
stand supported?	8.0	3–18
stand with no support?	10.0	5–24
crawl?	6.0	3–10
walk?	12.0	8–18

Note   Mothers were also asked at what age they expected their babies to
learn, but this question was misunderstood by most mothers to mean formal
learning between 4 and 6 years when the child enters school. Other mothers
reported about 3 months of age.

items obtained a mean sitting score that is significantly in advance of the
computed Bayley mean score for these same items $t(7) = 9.925, p < .001$.
On the average, Baganda infants are 1 month advanced on each of the
sitting items (range = .8—1.6 months). Thus it is tentatively suggested
that a positive relationship exists between the Kiganda practice of training
the infant to sit and the advanced sitting behaviors of Baganda infants. (See
Table 5 for ages at which Baganda and United States infants performed
various sitting skills.) Similarly, Super (1980, 1981) found that Kipsigis
infants, who are also trained to sit, are likewise about 1 month advanced in
sitting skills in comparison to Bayley's American norms. "Training" is
similar to the traditional Baganda method in which the infant is seated in a
hole in the ground with cloths around him for support. A sample of urban
Kipsigis (Kalenjin), half of whom still trained their infants to sit, had
infants who were able to "sit alone momentarily" about two weeks after
their rural counterparts, but three weeks before Bayley's American norm.

Super (1980) also reports that Kipsigis infants in traditional or rural
environments spend over 60% of their waking time in the sitting position

Table 5   Comparison of Sitting Behavior of United States and Baganda Infants as Measured by the Bayley Scales

Item	United States (Bayley)		Baganda[a] (Kilbride)	
	Median	Range	Median	Range
	(months)		(months)	
Sits with support	2.3	1–5	2.0	1–3
Sits with slight support	3.8	2–6	3.0	1–4
Sits alone momentarily	5.3	4–8	4.0	4–5
Sits alone 30 seconds or more	6.0	5–8	5.0	4–5
Sits alone steadily	6.6	5–9	5.5	5–6
Sits alone with good coordination	6.9	5–10	6.0	5–7

[a]$N = 7–10$ due to illness of infant at monthly testing or infant being too young or too old to be scored on some of the items.

during the course of their daily existence (cf. 58). Sayegh and Dennis (1965) provided experience in sitting with support to five infants from The Creche, an institution for infants in Beirut, Lebanon. Three infants were 7.2, 7.4 and 10.3 months of age but had a four-month developmental age on the Cattell infant scale. Two infants, aged 14.5 and 18.1 months, were included in the experimental group since they were also unable to sit alone unaided. The eight control infants, aged between 7.6 and 18.7 months, were all unable to sit alone. The experimental infants were carried to a room and seated in a chair with a tray and then placed sometimes prone and sometimes supine on a thick foam-rubber pad. The infants were first placed in a sitting position on the pad on the second day of training. All toppled over on the first trial. The next day they were given several trials; whenever a child fell over he was returned to the sitting position. Sessions lasted for one hour a day for five days a week for three weeks. By the end of the seventh training day, four of the five "trained" infants could sit on the pad without using their hands for as long as they wished. They were not, however, able to attain the sitting position by themselves, but no experience designed to train for this skill was presented. Unfortunately no mention is made of the sitting behavior of the control infants during this time, but the researchers do state that the improvement in developmental age of the control group was not statistically significant. It does appear, however, that providing an infant with experience in sitting helps to develop this skill.

Baganda infants were also found to be about one month advanced in their performance of social behaviors as measured by the Bayley scales. No significant relationship was found between either physical contact between caretaker and infant or the frequency of infant-initiated social vocalizations and infant social behaviors. Physical contact alone is apparently insufficient for predicting early sociability. Infant social vocalizations comprise only one aspect of sociability since social behaviors, as they have been categorized in this study, involve a complex set of responses which include the social smile, visual recognition of the mother, vocalizing to a social smile and talk, reacting to the disappearance of a face, and social interaction with a mirror image. A combination of factors are perhaps needed to understand the advanced sociability of Baganda infants. In the next chapter, we will describe sociocultural factors which may be related to the early manifestation of sociability behavior among Baganda infants. Among these are an adult society that places much value on being sociable; a social structure which allows for upward mobility through being socially skillful at manipulating others, and child-care practices which encourage sociability. As we have seen, the Muganda infant receives much physical and social stimulation beginning as early as his first week of life. He receives twice daily during his first few months a warm herbal bath during which his head, hands, arms, and legs are gently massaged. He is typically breast-fed on demand and is the center of attention and conversation right from the beginning since propriety requires that the Muganda mother give her infant to visitors to hold and, when seated on her own lap, that she sit the infant facing out towards the visitors. Sitting is considered to be a social skill among the Baganda, and the infant receives a great deal of positive attention and encouragement while he is being trained to sit. He is also in frequent social interaction with adults and other children who try to coax the infant to smile. In general, then, the Muganda infant experiences much social attention and is highly valued by his society.

It has been suggested that the Baganda infant's advanced rate of sensorimotor development might, in part, be related to the large amount of physical contact between caretaker and infant (e.g., Ainsworth 1977). In our sample of Baganda infants, the mean percentage of physical contact between caretakers and infants is 52.7% ($SD = 8.4$). Moss (1967) reports that American infants at three weeks of age are held 49.3% of the time observed, but by 3 months of age this has declined to 33.4%. Baganda infants show a similar, but lesser decline from approximately 58.0% to 46.0%. It should be noted, however, that at each age physical contact is greater for the Baganda. These figures suggest that Baganda infants receive more physical contact than American infants. Konner (1977) reports that the !Kung San of northwestern Botswana, who are advanced in certain motor skills, also receive relatively much physical contact with their caretakers. He also presents examples from other cultures and suggests that physical contact may be a phenomenon more characteristic of nonindustrialized than industrialized societies. Super (1980), in comparing the amount of physical contact between Kokwet infants in Kenya and infants from Cambridge, Massachusetts, found these Kenya infants receiving two to three times as much as the United States infants.

If we accept these differences in amount of physical contact, then the question arises as to whether there is any evidence that physical contact between caretaker and infant has a faciliatory effect on sensorimotor development. Looking at mean percentages of physical contact and mean development quotients, one finds that a high frequency of physical contact is positively and significantly related to both advanced motor development and advanced mental development. Similarly, Yarrow, Pederson, and Rubenstein (1977), in their observations of five- to six-month-old American black infants, found that the amount of kinesthetic stimulation the infant received was significantly correlated with the Bayley Psychomotor Development Index ($r = .36$) and the Mental Development Index ($r = .41$). The findings of our study provide further evidence, in a naturalistic setting from another culture, of the importance of physical contact to infant sensorimotor development. It also should be noted that the daily massaging of the Muganda infant during and after bathing may also be a factor in enhancing motor development as Hopkins (1976) suggests.

In this book and elsewhere (1974), the authors have suggested that the advanced sociability of Baganda infants is best understood by a combination of factors, including an adult society that places much value on being sociable, a social structure which allows for upward mobility through being socially skillful at manipulating others, and child-care practices which encourage sociability. (See table 6 for ages at which Baganda and United States infants performed various social skills.) Looking at table 6, we see that there were few, if any, differences between Baganda and United States infants in early social skills. There were, however, striking differences in the age at which a mirror image elicited social responses. Baganda infants "socialized" with their images from 1.9 to 3.2 months earlier than their United States counterparts.

In 1976–77, P. Kilbride undertook a study of Samia infants. As part of this study, he investigated the rate of development of Samia infants on selected social skills. Table 7 presents the median ages at which Samia,

Table 6[a] Social Responses to Persons and Mirror Image

	Median (months)	
Item	United States	Uganda
Regards person momentarily	.2	.2
Eyes follow moving person	.7	.2
Responds to voice	.7	.3
Social smile: E talks and smiles	1.5	1.5
Visually recognizes mother	2.0	2.0
Social smile: E smiles, quiet	2.1	2.0
Vocalized to E's social smile and talk	2.1	2.0
Reacts to disappearance of face	2.4	1.0
Mirror-image approach	4.4	2.5
Smiles at mirror image	5.4	3.0
Playful response to mirror	6.2	3.0

[a]Adapted from Kilbride and Kilbride 1974, Table 2, 308.

Table 7 Rate of Social Development of United States, Samia, and Baganda Infants

	United States		Samia		Baganda	
Test Item	Median	Range	Median	Range	Median	Range
Social smile: E talks and smiles	1.5	.5–4	1.7	1.0–2.5	1.5	1–2
Social smile: E smiles quietly	2.1	.7–6	1.9	1.5–3.0	2.0	1–2
Vocalizing to E's smile and talk	2.1	1–6	2.5	1.7–3.0	2.0	1–2
Mirror-image approach	4.4	2–7	3.1	1.7–6.0	2.5	2–5
Smiles at mirror image	5.4	2–12	3.1	1.7–8.0	3.0	2–7
Playful response to mirror	6.2	4–12	4.9	3.0–8.0	3.0	2–6
Mean social score	3.61		2.86		2.33	
Standard deviation	1.97		1.15		.60	
t*	1.740		1.821			
p	$.05 < p < .10$		$.05 < p < .10$			

*One-tailed tests were used since it was predicted that the Samia infants would be more advanced than the Americans and less advanced than the Baganda.

Baganda, and United States infants achieved the various social skills. It is interesting to note that the initial social-smile items are achieved at about the same age among all three groups. Responses to the mirror image, however, show differences among the three groups with the Samia, as predicted, tending to be more advanced than the United States infants but less advanced than the Baganda infants.

Three major conclusions can be derived from our findings concerning Baganda infant sensorimotor development. First of all, Baganda infants are advanced in their rate of both mental and motor development in comparison to American infants. The advancement is greater for Bayley's motor skills than for her mental skills. A previous cross-sectional study by Janet Kilbride (1969) of 53 Baganda infants, aged 2 to 8 months, reported a mean developmental motor index of 128 ($SD = 11.33$). This is remarkably similar to the mean PDI of 130 ($SD = 11.45$) obtained in our longitudinal sample of Baganda coevals. Secondly, it was discovered that precocity is not equally evident in all sensorimotor areas. Instead, there is a pattern to the Baganda infants' sensorimotor development, with some areas of behavior advanced and others similar to American infants in rate of development. Baganda infants are advanced in sitting skills, visual skills, social skills, grasping and manipulative skills, prewalking skills, and auditory skills. No significant differences exist in: vocalization, prone behavior, supine behavior, fine-prehension skills, cause-effect exploratory behavior, and object permanence. Postural and head control showed a marginally significant difference; however, Baganda infants were not tested until 1 month of age, and three of the six head-control items have age placement norms below 1 month. The rate of development for head control was therefore probably underestimated since the author's observations of Baganda infants showed good head control as early as the first week of life. In addition, the remarkable head control of Baganda infants has been reported by both Geber (1958) and Warren (1973). Thus it is possible that prenatal and/or genetic factors may be important for understanding this particular area of advancement.

Finally, an examination of intracultural variation in child-care practices and caretaker-infant interaction patterns suggests that the observed differences in rates of development for the various sensorimotor behaviors are predominantly related to socio-environmental factors. Although the clinical assessments by Geber and Dean (1957) had suggested remarkable advancement from birth, the findings of Warren and Parkin (1974) reveal that very few behavioral differences were found between African and European newborns tested in Kampala. They conclude:

African and European newborns differ in the external physical characteristics normally used to assess gestational age and on a modest number of neurological and behavioral measures. These differences are small and not clinically obvious. On available evidence, they provide only poor and internally inconsistent indications of the relative maturity, in neurological and behavioral terms, of one or the other group, and thus cannot support a claim of precocity at birth of either group. (1974:971)

Thus the advancement appears best explained by predominantly cultural factors. Those favoring a genetic explanation of this precocity (e.g., Jensen 1969) should be asked to explain why the pattern of precocity appears to match the cultural practices. Adult values and child-care practices most certainly play an important role in infant development.

The sensorimotor precocity of Baganda and Samia infants which we have described has also been documented in our previous publications (e.g., J. Kilbride 1973, 1976; P. Kilbride 1977, 1980; Kilbride & Kilbride 1975, 1983). The interested reader can refer to these publications for further details of our methodology and findings. For our purposes here, we have presented selected examples of infant development that serve to illustrate our conviction that certain traditional child-care practices should be retained and not discarded during the ongoing process of modernization and delocalization. In the next chapter we will discuss the close affective relationship between mother and child as exemplified by the traditional African mother and her infant.

7

MOTHERING AND AFFECTIVE EXPERIENCES
High Positive Affect

"He who does not respect one's father and mother may have to walk until dawn without assistance."

W e provide in this chapter a discussion of "high positive" maternal affect, itself an adaptive outcome, especially in a context where children are so vital to family and community economic interests. Some breakdown of traditionally derived affective states can be observed in the contemporary experience, for example, of extreme co-wife conflict and child abuse to be presented in section 3. The final chapter of this book will argue that a "genuine emotional experience," following Sapir (1962), can still be observed in East Africa, but it is under peril as modern forces transform society into a "spurious" one, particularly for women.

The people of East Africa nowadays experience affective states in the context of the full range of modern experiences. In the next section, we shall specifically encounter some of the "negative" emotions which are the cost of such practices as the evil eye, witchcraft accusation, marital conflict, and child abuse. Social life in the past certainly contained an affective underpinning that also involved such negative emotions as fear, sadness, and anger. The positive affects associated with happiness are richly represented in both traditional and modern life. What is problematic for interactive ethnographers and others who seek understanding of the "interior feeling" of another society is that such states are "relativized," "masked" or otherwise made difficult for the outsider to detect, let alone to interpret. We will not here fully consider this problem, but will briefly provide a few general remarks to set the table for our more complete discussion of "maternal affect," a necessary topic for the present book.

East Africans in general believe, along with the Baganda, that "the heart is thought not only to be the centre of emotions such as fear, anger, joy and jealousy, but in the past, it was also considered the place where wisdom and memory reside" (Orley 1970:2). In our own research in Kenya, we experienced renewed difficulty in translating the meaning of the English verb "to feel" into vernacular languages. Generally, the attribution of affect to another person is linked to how they "look" rather than to the western assumption of an "internal state" residing "inside the individual who is responsible for his feelings." This is also true for the Baganda about whom Orley writes:

> The verb *okuwulira* is usually translated 'to feel,' but encompasses hearing, smelling, touching as well as understanding and obeying. It does not express the feeling of emotions, which are thought to be *possessed* rather than *felt*. A person may have anger, sorrow, or happiness in his heart, or he might be caught by anger or sorrow. The difference between anger and sorrow is not stressed to the same extent as in English. (1970:3)

In general, a relativistic, phenomenological assumption is necessary when one attempts to describe the emotional landscape of East African people. We will consider how this is accomplished below. First, however, it is important to emphasize that extreme relativism is not appropriate for emotional states or any other areas of East African cultural experience. We will show below that most African mothers, as do all mothers everywhere according to adaptive functional theory (Izard 1983), experience positive affect for their children. In fact, the recognition of most Western scientifically described emotions is quite possible in East Africa, in spite of numerous methodological problems (Kilbride and Yarczower 1980). Working in Uganda, Kilbride and Yarczower report that, "in general the present study found cross-cultural agreement between American children and Baganda children and adults on the recognition of happy and sad expression" (1976:188).

We now turn specifically to the issue of "maternal affect" as it emerges from a consideration of our Baganda material. Our experiences with other societies in Western Kenya are in general agreement with our Baganda work. The materials to follow are informed by a relativizing universalism of the functional sort described previously in this work and now applied to affect. Our method once again is one of interactive ethnography.

Robert LeVine (1970) has suggested that the following combination of affective traits may be typical of sub-Saharan African agricultural societies:

1. social distance of individuals differing in age and sex
2. emphasis on material transactions in interpersonal relations
3. functional diffuseness of authority relations
4. tendency to blame and fear others when under stress
5. relative absence of separation anxiety and related affects.

In general, and here we disagree with LeVine, he describes a comparative lack of intimacy in interpersonal relationships, including the mother-infant relationship. He states:

> In public, African mothers rarely lavish on their infants the kind of verbal and physical affection that we think of as "instinctively maternal" behavior, and they are capable not only of carrying on conversations or tasks like trading while nursing their infants but also of inflicting necessary pain on them (in force-feeding and bathing) without hesitation and without concern over their crying. (1970:295)

Elsewhere, LeVine (1977) views this lack of affective involvement as part of an adaptive pattern of child-care practices that have evolved in order to ensure the health and physical survival of offspring in societies characterized by high infant mortality. The pattern of infant care he describes is one that attempts to meet the infant's physical needs but one that provides "relatively little treatment of him as an emotionally responsive individual" (1977:23). For example, the infant is in frequent physical contact with a caretaker's body, feeding is on demand, and crying is attended to quickly. LeVine, however, contends that in this pattern of infant care:

> We find a certain pattern of bodily proximity, feeding, responsiveness to crying, and absence of disciplinary training that looks "in-

dulgent" to us, but without the equally "indulgent" maternal behaviors of smiling, eye contact, face-to-face smile elicitation, chatting, cooing, and kissing, that usually supply the psychological context in which we interpret a Western mother's "indulgent" behavior. (1977:23)

LeVine's observation of what might be termed "low positive affect" in the maternal-infant relationship is based primarily on his reading of the literature and his own excellent studies of the Gusii of Kenya. In particular, he makes reference to Ainsworth's study, *Infancy in Uganda,* where she reports:

> In our American households the parents, loving relatives, and interested visitors alike bend over the baby as he lies in his crib, presenting him a smiling face, and waggle their heads and talk to the baby in an effort to coax a smile. This kind of face-to-face confrontation was not observed to occur in this Ganda sample. Indeed it was rare for an adult even to hold a baby so that there could be a face-to-face confrontation. . . . (1967:334)

LeVine's view about low affect is also seemingly grounded in two principles outlined earlier in our discussion about "interactive ethnography." LeVine, of course, cannot be faulted for not practicing interactive ethnography, as here construed, nor can Ainsworth, who preceded him. Nevertheless, they seek specific localized understanding for which we think such an ethnographic approach is a requirement. First, as we shall show below, positive affect is demonstrated somewhat differently in East Africa, and to get at this, one must experience private domains of social life. Second, a reflexive attitude would require one to question even the assumption that Africans, or any other population for that matter, could have, even "in theory," a patterned profile of low emotional affect. The psychiatrist Orley, after many years living and working among Baganda, writes, "in fact, of course, life in a rural community in an underdeveloped country is fraught with danger, with grief because of high infant mortality (unless one cares to believe another myth that African mothers do not grieve over the death of their children as much as European mothers do—*our aside*) and with worries over the possibility of crop failures (1970:51).

The case for African fathers is also in need of reflexive analysis. John Demos notes that a common scholarly view about the father in colonial

America is that he underinvested in children whose survival was doubtful. He writes,

> Yet fragmentary evidence suggests otherwise. An occasional diarist or correspondent can be glimpsed in postures of extreme parental concern . . . The depositional records of local courts afford scattered impressions of the same phenomenon: for example, a village craftsman who remembered that 'when his child was sick, and likely to die, he ran barefoot and barelegged, and with tears . . . ' [S]uch materials raise, but not resolve, important questions about the *interior* dimension of colonial fatherhood. (1982:430)

While LeVine argues that low affect is typical among African agricultural societies, he also is aware that variations in this pattern do exist. In fact, in his study of Yoruba children in Nigeria, he found that urban Yoruba children and adults are much more gregarious than Gusii children and adults; Yoruba sociability is "deep-seated" and expresses itself in many domains of their life (cf. LeVine 1970:298).

Super and Harkness (1974), in response to LeVine's reviews, take specific issue with his description of the mother-child relationship. They cite literature such as Laye's *The African Child* (1954) which shows maternal sentiments of love and affection for children and unhappiness at being separated from one's children. Moreover, in their own study of Kipsigis infants in Kenya, Super and Harkness found affectionate attention by mother to infant, as measured by looking and face-to-face interaction, to be slightly more than that reported for American infants. See also Munroe and Munroe (1980) for a relevant discussion of these materials.

The Baganda and Maternal Affect

Until quite recently, the Baganda were organized into a state structure with a king at the apex of a pyramid of territorial chiefs who served at his pleasure. Social mobility was common as individuals maneuvered for personal advantage through strategic interaction with others above and below themselves in the sociopolitical hierarchy. In this tightly organized state, children were, unsurprisingly, socialized for obedience which was sometimes quite severe (see Richards 1964). Breaches of conduct on occasion resulted in harsh punishment such as caning, being deprived of food, or being locked inside a room. Authority relations in the nuclear family to some extent "mirrored" the wider society's hierarchical structure. For example, the father, like the king, was perceived as an object of fear and respect. He expected and received gratiating deference from his wife and children. The mother, on the other hand, was a source of affection for both boys and girls. Richards, who studied Baganda children's attitudes toward their parents in the late 1950s reports:

> None of the boys in our school sample spoke of having been afraid of their mother, and many told of their kindness, their constant forgiveness and the protection they gave from the father's anger. Of the girls, over half expressed nothing but love for their mother. . . . (1964:267)

Moreover, emotional states were often intensely experienced by children. Richards, for example, notes that when speaking of their fathers, girls used such phrases as "when I saw him I felt like bursting into tears," or "when he spoke to me I had no courage to answer," or "his prestige made me tremble."

In the wider society, as in the family, affective states are varied and, depending on the social relationship or situation, intensely experienced. When Kabaka Mutesa II, for example, returned from exile in the mid-1950s, drumming, dancing, singing, laughter, tears of joy, etc., abounded in Buganda for many days. We have observed Baganda women crying at airports over the departure of loved ones for trips abroad or for loved ones at funerals. Emotional experience such as joy, fear, and jealousy is situationally structured such that no single emotional state can be said to characterize all or even most relationships, although a specific social relationship does to some extent determine emotional experience. For example, brothers as well as co-wives are often "jealous" of each other; fathers and fathers' sisters are "feared"; and friends returning after a long time away are a source of joy. Emotional states are, moreover, quite varied. Luganda has hundreds of words and phrases which convey affectional meaning and also has a folk theory which recognizes "character type," which assigns responsibility to the mother for shaping character in a positive direction and designates the heart as the seat of one's emotions.

Baganda attitudes toward emotional experience recognize a sharp distinction between public and private expression. Baganda are well-known by ethnographers for their ability to "mask" true feelings in public, a skill that is, no doubt, adaptive in the context of a political system where "singing the praises" of a despised chief or modern head of state has considerable survival value. Similarly, public expressions of affection in heterosexual friendships are strongly discouraged. In private, however, a Muganda woman is socialized by older women to engage ideally in pleasurable sexual relations for herself and her partner. This is achieved through the use of sexual conversation to stimulate her mate and the expectation of orgasm by women (Kisekka 1973). In principle, therefore, private heterosexuality is one relationship where intense emotional feelings are expected to be overtly expressed.

To conclude, in attempting to evaluate the emotional feelings of Baganda women for their children it is important (1) to differentiate between private and public situations; (2) to consider that intense feelings of joy, warmth, and fondness, or "high" positive affect, are in fact experienced by Baganda in certain situations or relationships; and (3) to note that in Buganda, the mother herself is the recipient of high positive affect from her children. Thus it should come as no surprise if analysis in relatively private situations of mother-child relations should show high positive affect of mothers for their infants and children, a pattern not discovered by Ainsworth in Uganda.

To demonstrate the presence of behavior that can be interpreted as high positive affect, we now turn to our infant-mother interaction data. There were thirteen infants in our sample since one mother had dizygotic (fraternal) twins. There were four boys and nine girls: seven were first-borns and six were later-borns. An average of one hour-long continuous observation was recorded weekly or bi-weekly for each mother-infant dyad in their own home by J. Kilbride and a Muganda research assistant concurrently. Overall, there was a total of 107 hours of observations made, beginning, in most cases, during the infant's first week of life and continuing for six to eight months. Observations were made at different times during the day between 8:00 A.M. and 6:00 P.M. in order to limit any bias which might be caused by observing an infant at only one particular time in his or her daily routine. Each hour of observation was divided into 12 five-minute periods. For purposes of the present study, however, only those observation periods during which the infant was awake and the mother was present, that is, the total number of periods when interaction could have been possible, were used in our analyses. If positive affective behaviors by mothers to their infants were observed during a five-minute observation period, a score of one was given for each of these periods, regardless of the number of times a behavior occurred during each period. Thus the percentage of positive affect by mothers to their infants was determined by dividing the number of observation periods in which positive affect occurred by the total number of observation periods during which the mother was present and the infant was awake. Similar calculations were also made for each type of positive affect coded, namely hug/cuddle, kiss, stroke or pat, smile, gaze or look at, and face-to-face position.

For our total sample, out of 547 five-minute observation periods during the first eight months of life in which positive affect was possible, it was observed in 310 of these, or 56.7% of the time (S_E = 2.1%). Table 8 presents the percent frequency of occurrence of the various types of positive affect observed during 526 five-minute observation periods during the first six months of life, beginning at five days of age. For this analysis, the first six months were used because data were available for only three infants beyond six months. If each type of positive affect were equally likely to occur, one might expect to observe each of the six behaviors one-sixth, or 16.7%, of the time. Computation of tests for the significance of a proportion (see Bruning and Kintz 1977:220–21), however, revealed that the observed affective behaviors were not equally distributed. Thus hug, kiss, and smile were significantly less likely to occur, and stroke, face-to-face, and looking behaviors were significantly more likely to occur (p's < .001) than one might expect by chance.

Given the above fact, one may ask whether the six types of positive affect differ significantly from each other in the likelihood of their occurrence. Table 9 presents the results of a Z-test for the significance of the difference between two proportions (see Bruning and Kintz 1977:222–24). As stated previously, Baganda mothers have been described by Ainsworth as showing little, if any, positive affect toward their infants through hugging and kissing. A comparison of these behaviors with the other types of positive affect showed that while some hugging and kissing was observed, the combined percentage of maternal hugs and kisses (7%) was significantly less than each of the other behaviors, as was, of course, the frequency of hugs and kisses taken separately. Thus relatively little hugging and kissing of babies by mothers has been observed for the Baganda in comparison to other modes of affective expression. The most frequently observed type of positive affect was looking, which occurred significantly more than face-to-face interactions between mothers and infants. The latter

Table 8   Percent Frequency of Positive Affect Behaviors

Behavior Observed	Frequency (%)*
Hug-cuddle	2.5
Kissing	4.4
Smiling at infant	11.0
Patting-stroking	22.6
Face-to-face	31.2
Looking at infant	35.4

*Percentages do not add up to 100 because more than one of the above behaviors could have occurred during the same five-minute observation period.

Table 9   Differences between Proportion of Occurrence of Affective Behaviors*

Affective Behavior	H + K	Sm	St	F-F	L
Hug and Kiss	—	.003	.001	.001	.001
Smile		—	.001	.001	.001
Stroke			—	.001	.001
Face-to-face				—	.038
Look at					—

*p-values for two-tailed Z tests.

was significantly more frequently displayed than stroking, which occurred significantly more than smiling. The pattern of positive affect that emerges, then, is one in which the Muganda mother holds her baby facing her while looking at, stroking, and smiling at the baby, but rarely demonstrates affection by means of hugging or kissing.

The present data overall suggest that Baganda mothers display high positive affect towards their infants. There are, of course, individual differences among mothers; however, this is to be expected to some extent in any society. These findings are particularly noteworthy given Ainsworth's

(1967) widely cited study in which she reports comparatively low displays of affect among Baganda mothers. She nevertheless discovered that Baganda mothers overall spent relatively much time engaged in what she labels as "mothering" behaviors. That is, mothers rather than other caretakers were mainly responsible for the baby's care, which typically involved, for example, frequent attention to his bodily needs. Mothering, however, did not typically involve displays of affection such as kissing, hugging, or nuzzling. Additionally, she reports that her notes contained only one observation of a mother holding her baby so that there was a face-to-face confrontation (cf. 1967:93). Although she does not state explicitly that Baganda mothers do not feel positive affect, this could be inferred from her material. The present study, in agreement with Ainsworth, also found comparatively little hugging and kissing. This finding is not surprising given the ethnographic fact that traditionally Baganda do not "kiss" in adult life. We found, however, much stronger evidence for positive affect than did Ainsworth, especially in the area of face-to-face interaction. Several reasons can be tentatively offered to account for differences between the two studies. First, our study occurred about 15 years later than Ainsworth's fieldwork. Over this time, some changes have occurred in Kiganda society, including, apparently, a more widespread practice of kissing in private sexual life along with the continuing acceptance of romantic love and related affects. On the whole, however, no striking changes in Kiganda life have ensued which could conceivably account for a reorientation of affective feelings.

It seems far more likely that differences between the two studies can be accounted for, in part, by the domain of methodology. Ainsworth conducted her research in the context of what she calls a "social visit," thus very likely eliciting from mothers more "public" than private behavior which is more likely to involve displays of affect. The Baganda typically do not display affection physically in public. Additionally, her perceived role as an "authority" figure, particularly one who was introduced via local government officials, also may have contributed a more public atmosphere to her observational settings. She herself reports that Baganda mothers in her presence regularly "hold out" their babies, facing the group and away from the mother. This is, in fact, customarily done on social visits so that all visitors can enjoy the baby. Thus Ainsworth's informants did in fact seemingly share her own self-perception of being a visitor. The methodology of the present study, which purposely attempted to establish informality through participant observation, use of Luganda, and so on, may be better suited to detect affective domains than was Ainsworth's style. Ainsworth and her assistant also conducted interviews with mothers during their visits to Kiganda homes, thus lessening the likelihood of mother and infant interacting playfully or affectionately. Along with observing Baganda in a variety of private circumstances in our attempt to conduct emic-oriented ethnography, we also asked a small number of men and women to indicate reasons why women wanted to have children. One-third of the women, but none of the men, explicitly stated that children were desired for affective reasons such as providing joy and alleviating loneliness, in addition to instrumental reasons such as taking care of them in their old age. Ainsworth's excellent and pioneering research, itself an impressive landmark in cross-cultural child development, tells us less about the mother's attachment to her infant than about the infant's attachment to her, which was, after all, the primary focus of her work.

To summarize, any generalization about affective states in East Africa must view the pattern of socialization for affect among the Baganda, and also other ethnic groups where we have worked, as having the following features:

1. a rich and strong emotional life among adults but one that is highly sensitive to situation, context, and social relationships
2. high positive affect of mothers for their infants
3. the development, in response to mothers' stimulation, of an alert, socially precocious infant, as demonstrated by our previous studies of Baganda and Samia infancy (see P. Kilbride and J. Kilbride 1974, J. Kilbride and P. Kilbride 1975, P. Kilbride 1980)
4. a persistent affective bond with the mother throughout the life cycle

In section 2, we have described the social-emotional climate into which the East African infant is born as one typically involving a joyful acceptance of motherhood because of the high value placed on having children. There is also a realistic concern for the well-being of both mother and infant. The anxieties of pregnancy and birth are alleviated by seeking the help of both western and traditional doctors and their medicines. Once the infant is born, the proud parents share their happiness with relatives and friends (and even an occasional researcher), who are offered the baby to hold. Thus, from the very beginning of his life, the infant becomes a part of the social group and is, indeed, the center of attention. In section 3 we will discuss some problematic aspects of child care in East Africa today, using mainly our Kenyan materials as illustrations. East African encounters with modernity have brought with them increased risks of economic delocalization resulting frequently in female powerlessness, as we argue in the next chapter. Following this, we will address issues of concern to modern-day East Africans, namely premarital pregnancies, polygyny, and child abuse and neglect.

SECTION 3

8

ECONOMIC DELOCALIZATION AND FEMALE POWERLESSNESS

"He who provides for you, controls you."

The previous section has provided a holistic descriptive account of present cultural practices which are essentially derived from "tradition" or Africanity. We have emphasized in these materials essentially "positive" domains of life and related practices that regretably are showing signs of becoming delocalized in history and cultural meaning. In this section, we also will concentrate on contemporary life, but here our focus will be on some recently derived negative consequences of a "delocalized modernity." Such forces as industrialism, nationalism, missionary activity, formal education, and a monetized economy will be examined in the context of their current influence on marriage and family life. We will consider in this chapter the essential facts of economic delocalization, a theoretically assumed primary antecedent for the related processes of cultural and moral delocalization. Gender relations will be emphasized as a means of concretizing our thesis of a growing power disparity between men and women as modernization has proceeded. Men and women are both, of course, comparatively "powerless" in a delocalized economy compared to previous times, but the modern situation has become particularly acute for women. We show this effect on women in the next three chapters by dealing with teenage pregnancy, delocalized polygyny, and child abuse and neglect.

Economic delocalization is derived from a colonial heritage throughout East Africa. Pre-colonial social formations were, as we previously pointed out, predominantly agrarian in subsistence type. In these farming populations, a woman had access to land in her capacity as daughter, wife, and later on in life, as mother (of sons). A man inherited land directly from his father or through his father's wives in polygynous homes. In the colonial era, however, land began to become scarce due in large part to the usurpation of land by Europeans. Africans in colonial Kenya became essentially "squatters" living on European farms, many of which were as large as hundreds of thousands of acres. The acceleration of population growth in the post-modern era is another major factor contributing to today's land scarcity. With the evolution of modern devices such as the "deed" and "private" ownership, land usually is registered by the male "head" of the household who becomes the "owner."

The colonial era also saw the Hut Tax (1901 in Kenya), an obligation which prompted men to migrate from rural areas to towns in search of monetary employment. The city of Nairobi, numbering now over a million, did not even exist less than a century ago! This out-migration has had drastic effects on rural social life, particularly its economic structure. We will summarize from the work of Kayere (1980) to illustrate the influence of male migration on female social roles in rural Kenya. Not all of the changes have been disruptive, but some have been so.

Kayere reports that fifty percent of the jobs in the modern economic sector are in the cities of Nairobi or Mombasa. She continues, "the migrants are predominantly young adult males with some form of education; conversely, those who are left behind are predominantly females, children, and old people with hardly any formal education or skills. Thus an estimated 1/3 (or 400,000) of all rural households in Kenya are headed by females" (1980:2). One of the consequences of male migration is the fact that women are now the primary source of rural labor in food production, encompassing work done previously by men. Women now do, for example, pre-planting land preparation, ploughing, planting, etc. for both subsistence and commercial crops. On the positive side, many women now participate with authority in commercial agriculture and trading, or in religious and secular associations. On the negative side, we quote Kayere (1980:4):

Though the current female participation covers a wider sphere, there are some pitfalls relating to its efficiency. These are mostly noted through the decreasing agricultural productivity in rural areas, explained by the ever growing urban centres and the accompanying drain on rural labor (particularly male labor) . . . While this assertion may to some extent hold, the fact of low agricultural productivity in the rural areas may be reflective of the failure to recognize women's traditional role in agricultural production by agricultural extension officers . . . the neglect of women in the delivery of services has also been noted by K. Standt (1975) among the Idakh of western Kenya.

The delocalization process has indeed, among other consequences, rendered rural Kenyan agriculture dependent on external forces which are far more numerous than can be handled by overburdened agricultural extension officers. We will now consider some of these forces based on our own research work in western Kenya. Following this, we will discuss the Ugandan situation where, there too, delocalization has had a negative consequence for women even though in Uganda there were fewer European settlers, and the British ruled by indirect rule. For this reason, migration and urbanization were not as intensive or as disruptive as in Kenya; nevertheless cash crops became controlled by men in Uganda also.

In 1985, Philip Kilbride surveyed residents of a western Kenyan location to ascertain some of the economic problems which they perceived to be troublesome in their lives. As it turned out, their problems could be linked directly to the delocalization process. The respondents were living in the areas around Matunda and came from two quite different "social classes." The first group included large farmsteads with an orientation to the Kenya market for their dairy products and grain. The area also included much smaller farms where subsistence needs dominated, although maize is an important commercial crop. The entire region is now occupied by African migrants who "immigrated" there to reoccupy lands in the so-called "White Highlands" after independence. Both men and women living in these two areas were asked, as part of a general survey, to indicate some of the things they believed to be "desirable" and "undesirable" in their residential areas. Table 10 shows the most frequent responses by area but not by gender since their answers did not systematically vary along this dimension.

On the whole, these people, who have all migrated primarily from areas

Table 10   Residential Survey in Western Kenya

Desirable	Undesirable
Large Farms (Schemes)	
—primary schools are near	—few taxis to Eldoret
—maize, beans, and coffee do well here	—no adult education
—few farm disputes because land is more plentiful	—tap water is not regular
	—no films for the people
—large harvests to feed ourselves and to sell	—infrequent visits from agricultural officers
—social relations are good because our relatives are not here to backbite	—irregular water during the dry season
	—too far from relatives
—abundant wealth here frees one from envy and witchcraft from relatives at home	—soil requires expensive fertilizers
	—hospitals are far away
Small Farms (Sisal)	
—children don't get as sick here	—hard to get firewood
—dispensary is near	—tap water is not adequate in dry season
—climate is good	
—children survive better (common)	—farm too small (common)
—neighbors friendlier than elsewhere (common)	—bad roads
	—insufficient money for fertilizer and pesticides
—food is cheaper here (common)	

further west with land shortages, describe themselves as "better off" than previously. They view their present location as a social environment which is relatively free of envy and jealousy. It is also seen as one affording the opportunity to engage in a cash economy for profit for one's family along with the opportunity for education and health services for one's children. Their concerns are primarily utilitarian ones, as are their perceived problems in local life. The small-farm (sisal) community members are overall much more preoccupied with fundamental *subsistence* issues such as water problems, insufficient land, and money for school fees and other needs. The large-farm group (schemes), having a common cultural background and utilitarian orientation, appears to be comparatively more "delocalized" than their less wealthy counterpart in terms of both economic and cultural concerns. The schemes group more frequently expressed desires for services needed for success in "large-scale" farming such as transportation, roads, farming specialists, etc. (Such concerns, while not absent among small-scale farmers, are voiced to a lesser degree.) Significantly, the large-scale farmers, on the whole more educated and cosmopolitan than their counterparts, also showed a stronger sense of perceived cultural delocalization. Taxis to bring in newspapers or to transport one to a city for entertainment (not just for marketing), adult education, a local cinema, etc., all capture the de-localized needs of these farmers. It is presently this sort of delocalization that East African regional planners and politicians must address if "rural" living is to be encouraged as development policy. Rural-to-rural migration itself is significant since virtually all of the Matunda area farmers come from elsewhere. On the whole, they seemingly favor their improved position vis-à-vis previous homes in more severely economically delocalized areas, par-ticularly evidenced by land shortage.

The domain of cultural delocalization is, of course, a major focus of this book. Ethical standards are also an important component. As we shall show shortly, previous cultural standards about proper behavior no longer work as smoothly in regulating sexuality and family life, for example. Neverthe-less, the cultural lives of the farmers mentioned above are still very "tradi-tional." Residents' lives are dominated by a "people-oriented" ethos replete with regular attendance at funerals, weddings, circumcision ceremonies, and "holidays" (e.g., Christmas is lively in rural areas since *everybody* comes home from the cities). Economic delocalization resulting in "poverty" for many residents presses in on what is otherwise a robust social life and a general search for regularity and security. The famine season is particularly depressing for all concerned, a time when many people, especially children, go hungry. For this reason, many people migrate to cities and towns in hopes of a better economic fate.

The modern East African experience is most intensive in the city environ-ment (cf. Robbins and Kilbride 1974). It is here that the overall most wealthy, educated, and cosmopolitan people reside. Cultural paradoxes in the delocalization process are most acutely observed in this environment although they are not, of course, absent in rural areas. Such paradoxes or dilemmas include such things as monogamy versus polygyny, acceptance of "illegitimate" children, birth control versus child bearing, self-interest ver-sus communal responsibility, and love versus money, to mention only a few here. These are particularly acute for women, who must encounter them against a backdrop of social powerlessness and economic difficulties.

We will consider in detail teen pregnancies, unwanted children, and the role of grandmothers as problems facing the contemporary East African woman. Before turning to these materials, however, we will describe the urban context in which modern East Africans most intensively grapple with modernity's paradoxes. The report of urban barmaids in Kampala, Uganda, done by Philip Kilbride, will be reproduced in part here as an example, albeit in extreme form, of the problems of modern women in a delocalized environment (see P. Kilbride 1979). This fate is not entirely without some advantages, as we shall see. Nairobi and other Kenyan towns do not generally have "barmaids." Instead, prostitutes seem to be more common in Kenya. This is probably due to the large European communities and greater number of tourists when compared to Uganda.

Position of Women in Traditional Kiganda Society

The Baganda are a well-described population numbering around two million people (e.g., Roscoe 1911; L. A. Fallers 1964). Most Baganda are rural, peasant cultivators, although many reside in Kampala-Mengo where they constitute the majority group. They enjoy a privileged economic and social position due to the fact that the city grew up on several hills where the Baganda kings resided in the late 1800s. Until 1966, the Baganda were organized into a political kingdom with the kabaka (king) serving at the apex of a complex bureaucratic structure. The system permitted considerable political skill in the verbal arts or "the art of being ruled," as the Baganda phrase it (Kilbride and Kilbride 1974). Women were particularly admired for their verbal expertise in riddling and storytelling. Additionally, they were able to "move up" by attracting the eye of a powerful chief. A woman's overall deportment and physical beauty were, therefore, important assets in contracting a desired marriage to a powerful man. (As we shall see, the modern barmaid combines verbal skills with physical attractiveness to enhance her success in contemporary Kampala.)

The traditional subsistence base was agrarian, with some men specializing in fishing or such industries as ironworking, canoe-building, pottery-making, and beer-brewing. Farming was the married woman's domain irrespective of her rank. Roscoe states:

> Princesses and peasant women alike looked upon cultivation as their special work; the garden with its produce was essentially the wife's domain, and she would under no circumstances allow her husband

to do any digging or sowing in it. No woman would remain with a man who did not give her a garden and a hoe to dig it with. (1911:426)

Women grew such staples as plantain, cassava, and sweet potatoes. Men, however, retained control over the growth of bark cloth, which, along with beer, was a primary object of taxation given to chiefs and the king. A prosperous household was one with multiple wives, their gardens, and their children. Offspring were highly valued, particularly as a potential means of upward mobility for the family. Some children, for example, were frequently sent to the king's palace, where a successful political career was commonly available for an ambitious boy. Young girls could win economic favors for their families through judicious marriages to men of rank. In general, a married woman enjoyed a symmetrical economic relationship to her spouse. Her roles as gardener and childbearer were vital to the success of the domestic unit. Importantly, a woman who did not bear children was the subject of considerable ridicule. Roscoe writes on the stigmatized plight of the barren woman: "Every married woman was anxious to become a mother, and expected to show signs of maternity within a few weeks of her marriage. A woman who had no children was despised and soon became the slave and drudge of the household" (1911:46). Both men and women enjoyed prestigious economic roles in traditional Buganda.

Divorce, which was often due to barrenness, was common. Romantic ties between spouses were not emphasized, although a satisfying emotional and sexual life for both husband and wife was expected. Women were admired for their physical beauty and were trained in adolescence by older women to gratify themselves and their husbands in conjugal sex (cf. Kisekka 1973). A double standard existed; married men could acquire additional wives, but married women ideally were not expected to commit adultery. Authority patterns in the home were a mini-replica of a large social order. The husband was addressed as *seebo* (sir), and women and children were expected to kneel in his presence. In conclusion, the position of women in traditional Kiganda society did have its unfavorable aspects. Co-wives were often competitive with each other, and a barren woman possessed an unenviable status. In particular, a barren woman was not a contributing member of her household's economic enhancement because she had no children who would be a source of labor and a potential means of material gratification, should they contract important marriages or political offices.

The position of women was modified with the advent of the colonial era, which began in 1890 and extended to independence in 1962. The British colonial policy was motivated by a concern to maintain law and order, to create a source for taxation, and to facilitate the development of cash crops (M. Fallers 1960:40). During this period, many Baganda became wealthy through the farming of cotton, Robusta coffee, and tea. It is significant for our purposes that these cash crops were owned, cultivated, and sold by men. Women continued to cultivate subsistence crops as in traditional times. The development of skilled white-collar occupations was supported by the establishment of institutions of formal education, including the first university in East Africa. As elsewhere in the Western world (and in colonies), men received favored educational opportunities; few Baganda women entered the professions until recently. Women who did receive an education were commonly expected to enter the convent or do primary school teaching, nursing, or secretarial work. Importantly, Christianity became the dominant religion during the colonial era although a smaller proportion, about 10%, of the population embraced Islam. Urbanization, monetization, and Christian values combined to render the traditional polygynous household dysfunctional and in general to lower the status of women. On this point Fallers (1960:57) states, "Formal monogamy is becoming more and more the practice, but many marriages break up and there are as yet few modern 'companionate' marriages to form an influence toward an ideal of loyalty to one person—affairs outside marriage increase."

Position of Women in Modern Kiganda Society

The post-independence period (1962 to present) has seen increased urbanization and industrialization in Uganda. Even remote areas of the country have become increasingly more interdependent with international capital networks. Rural economic life remains largely agrarian, although a desire for cash and increased participation in modern life is a salient dynamic in rural Buganda (Robbins and Kilbride 1974). Urban life overall provides increased economic opportunities and rapid access to modern goods and services. Baganda in Kampala-Mengo are distributed among housing estates, low-income temporary settlements, and middle- to upper-class residential areas on the city's periphery. Thousands of Baganda women are employed in Kampala in various salaried occupations such as nursing, teaching, secretarial work, and banking, as well as in semiskilled jobs such as newspaper seller, sales girl, telephone operator, and the like. A large number of younger women also reside in Kampala during their schooling. Economic life in the city is characterized by financial uncertainties affecting women to a greater extent than men. Robbins, Thompson, and Bukenya, who have researched economic matters in urban Kampala, report that:

> At any time a large portion of the urban population is permanently or temporarily unemployed, and of these, women are the most numerous. . . . The high cost of living in the city is further aggravated by a high rate of inflation. Between 1966 and 1971, the overall cost of living rose 29 percent. The price increase in necessities has been even greater. For example, food and clothing increased 47 percent and 64 percent respectively. (1974:12)

Men in Kampala have greater economic power than women by virtue of their over-representation in the higher-paying occupations and professions. In rural areas, males continue to maintain their control over cash crops, which are the major source of income in these areas. In general, the colonial and modern eras have been characterized by an asymmetrical economic relationship between the sexes, compared to the more symmetrical one described previously for traditional times.

The modern woman faces somewhat of a paradox. On the one hand, monetization of the economy with some access for women has meant comparatively more freedom and independence for the employed and more educated woman. She potentially remains relatively free of economic dependence on a man, although there are considerable uncertainties and risks associated with such independence given the overall unfavorable economic position of women in modern society. On the other hand, marriage to a successful man continues to provide an avenue for economic security as it did in traditional times, but often at a loss of personal independence and freedom. Many women try to resolve this contradiction by choosing to form relationships with married men who can provide money and economic opportunities in exchange for sexual favors. Modern Luganda terms such as "sugar daddy" and "tycoon" symbolize this phenomenon. The barmaid, as we shall see, has become a kind of scapegoat for the overt pursuit of this type of relationship with men although many young women engage in this behavior more covertly and with fewer men.

For a society with a "double standard," married women are generally comparatively tolerant of male sexual transgressions. What is despised, however, is public impropriety and parenting children outside of marriage. Women who take money from the family are particularly troublesome. The married woman, therefore, sees the barmaid as one who does not contribute to her household (as the co-wife did) but instead as one who serves as a drain on it. Since the moral order no longer clearly sanctions polygyny, the barmaid serves as a kind of "functional" co-wife for men in that she serves sexual and often affectional needs for them.

Nowadays the ideal, particularly for the educated, urban, middle, and upper classes, is to have a "ring" marriage (*obufumbo bw'e mpita*). Marital cooperation is maintained typically in matters involving the division of labor and the raising of children. Some modern urban marriages are, however, more egalitarian than they have been in the past. One hears, for example, some women using their husbands' first names in public and sees some husbands lighting their wives' cigarettes or opening their car doors for them. Nevertheless, marital discord and separation are not uncommon. The most serious problems revolve around infidelity and barrenness. An unfaithful wife, for example, is likely to be beaten, divorced, or abandoned. Male infidelity is more frequent, and some men "move" in public places with their girlfriends. Children born "outside" are sometimes a source of strain in the home. Popular songs, for example, heard on radios and on juke boxes in bars extol the advantages of marital faithfulness and warn against the dangers of unfaithfulness. One Luganda song, for instance, includes the following lyrics (loosely translated by M. C. Robbins and J. Bukenya, personal communication):

> God gave all women a gift:
> Even when you lie to them they discover it right away.
> When you think of a clever plan, your wife will sense it.
> Say you tell her that your bike had a puncture, and you had to walk home;
> She will know it is a trick.
> I do indeed marvel at women.
> We should learn what makes women angry;
> They don't like their husbands to engage in affairs.
> To love Mere and Lucy gets women upset and will cause them to pack up and leave you.
> If you are faithful, the woman is happy and makes your bed quite comfortable.

She cleans your shirts and does every other job contentedly because
you are faithful to her.

Married couples in Kampala usually maintain independent circles of male
and female friends. Most men, for example, visit bars after work, returning
home in the late evening for their dinner. Many wives find this pattern less
than ideal, as the following Luganda song illustrates:

> Speaking on behalf of married women
> Who show their husbands good manners and patience,
> I want to say that we do all that because of devotion.
> So, we are begging you to show us good manners in turn.
> Leaving us alone in the houses will make us disgusted.
> Dear husband, I am fed up with your ways, leaving me alone in the
> house.
> I did not marry to eat alone, stay alone, for in my home
> I had plenty of food, drinks, and clothes;
> Sure you give me nice food, but I get tired of eating alone.
> I hate to embarrass you in front of your friends;
> Therefore, husband, pray change your ways.
>
> (trans. Robbins and Bukenya)

The barmaid, as will be later described, is often one who has herself fled the
unfavorable aspects of married life but who, paradoxically, is seen to serve
to perpetuate this condition for married women.

The Bar Setting

Kampala-Mengo has numerous high-rise tourist hotels, banks, a modern
university, large markets and shops, and several night clubs. One of the
most conspicuous visual physical features in Kampala-Mengo is the number and density of bars. By the 1950s, beer-selling, barmaiding, and prostitution were significant female occupations in the Kampala-Mengo area of
Kisenyi studied by Southall and Gutkind (1957). They state:

> There are at least five or six dozen beersellers, three-quarters of them
> women, concentrated here in an area of not more than fifty acres, and

> beersellers are scattered in large numbers everywhere throughout the greater Kampala area. . . . Together with prostitution in its varied forms, beer selling is one of the main foundations of the new-found economic independence of African women . . . landless women divorced from their husbands, and girls who fail to marry . . . rely more vitally on beer selling to maintain their independence. (Southall and Gutkind 1957:60–61)

Nowadays the majority of urban Baganda do not live in Kisenyi, and most regard it as a "slum." "White collar" Baganda, for example, patronize bars that are more modern than those of Kisenyi, ones where bottled beverages are available. Parkin (1969), for example, in the context of his post-independence research in East Kampala, reports that in Upper Kisiwa there are many 'European' bottle beer bars. He states:

> This beer is, of course, far more expensive than 'African' beer. The bars are semi-permanent dwellings, seemingly modeled on the European-type clubs. The proprietor employs a woman as a barmaid and no more . . . As a place of recreation offering the most expensive bottle-beer bars and women, Upper Kisiwa attracts a clientele of higher than average socio-economic status who are themselves not residents. (Parkin 1969:15)

The present research was conducted in residential areas similar to Upper Kisiwa (Bwaiise, Natete, Nakulabye, Wandageya). Barmaids in this study are, accordingly, ones who normally encounter men who are employed in white-collar and professional occupations. Bars in the research locations vary in size, and it is common to find several hundred customers patronizing the larger ones. Each bar typically possesses one or more juke boxes, a refrigerator, a bar, and a wide variety of local and European beverages. Furniture in the form of stools, easy chairs, sofas, and tables are also present. Each bar employs many uniformed barmaids, sometimes numbering as many as thirty in the larger bars. Each bar has its own color of uniform although the style is similar among bars. The uniforms are tailored blouses and skirts of the appropriate fashionable length. Men alone or in groups constitute the major clientele, although women do frequent bars. Individuals from different tribal groups and social classes sometimes drink in the same place (Robbins and Pollnac 1969).

Upon entering a bar, a client may choose to sit at the bar and order his drink directly from a cashier who is usually a female. Most, however, proceed to a table (perhaps in another room, in the larger bars) where a barmaid has been assigned to serve them. Propriety requires that the barmaid properly greet her client (using extended and standard phrases) and engage in conversation with him before asking for his order. Her duties mainly involve serving several tables and, when invited, having a drink with whichever customer offers to buy her one. Barmaids may also be asked to run errands to nearby stores for cigarettes and coffee beans (a delicacy) or to select records on the juke box. Clients patronize a bar primarily to drink, to forget their problems, or simply to socialize (Robbins and Pollnac 1969). Many patrons, however, particularly married men, wish to attract a barmaid as a potential lover. So an important dynamic in the client-barmaid relationship involves, on the one hand, strategies for keeping all men interested but only a few satisfied. Expertise in sexual conversation (*okuwemula*), deception (*okulimba*), and other manipulatory verbal strategies are things that a barmaid must master in order to please clients and avoid conflict with fellow barmaids, thereby being successful in her occupation. Several examples will serve to illustrate the importance of social manipulation in the work lives of barmaids. One barmaid made the following comment:

> The important thing is to never tell a man you don't love him or don't want to go with him. She can pretend she is sick and can make the appointment another day . . . Sometimes this reaches an extent of telling him to buy aspro (a common medicine for headache). Another trick is to say you can't go with him because your relatives have come for a visit so the appointment will have to be on another day. Sometimes there is a man who buys a barmaid drinks all of the time but then she will never want to sleep with him. You must give him excuses every day until he finds out you are deceiving him and he loses interest.

Another barmaid notes that:

> When a barmaid has several boyfriends she must cleverly deceive them all so that each one thinks that he is the only one. If two come to a bar, a barmaid will keep very busy until one leaves or she will stay with the one who gives her the most. Most people think that barmaids are bad and I agree. They always deceive.

The following observations on deception and cleverness were offered by a third barmaid:

> One must be a very clever girl to work in a bar. A barmaid will deceive a man by accepting a drink and then taking it back for the money when the man isn't looking. Sometimes she can take money from a man who buys her a drink and go and collect a bottle from another table which a man has bought for her there and bring it back and say that it was obtained from the bar with the money given her. Barmaids take advantage of a drunk man, bringing him bills twice and not giving him receipts.

Barmaiding and Social Stigma

Barmaids are thought by most Baganda to possess a number of undesirable qualities, including public rowdiness, sexual promiscuity, and heavy drinking. These negative qualities are frequently commented on in editorials in Ugandan newspapers. One typical editorial, for example, reported the following:

> The scenario: Three different places in and around Kampala, but all of them connected with bars. The theme: free love and free drinks. A barmaid in one of the Kampala bars learned that her boy friend was with another good-time-girl in a bar on the outskirts of the city. She took a French leave and hired a taxi to investigate further. As soon as she entered the bar she saw her boy friend with a girl—incidentally also a barmaid. She looked at them fiercely but the boy did not budge and the apparently innocent girl did not care. As the barmaid said later, she could not "stomach it." As a punishment for the "scornful couple" she filled her glass with beer, strutted to the boy friend and asked him what he was up to. Before he could answer she poured the drink over his head. She then dashed out, caught a taxi and went back to duty. (*Voice of Uganda* January 8, 1973)

Encounters such as the one described above frequently involve physical violence between barmaids fighting over a man, or, at times, men fighting over a barmaid. After closing hours, around midnight, men can be seen cruising about in cars searching for barmaids on the streets while barmaids can be observed "running away" from those whom they do not wish to see. In fact, appointments with men provide the best opportunity for income in the form of gifts of clothing, food, or rent. Barmaids are in fact quite poorly paid for their work, averaging about 80–150 shillings (7 shillings/dollar) a month, thereby falling in the "low income," unskilled-worker category enumerated in the 1971 *Statistical Abstract* of Uganda. On this point an editorialist noted:

> If there is any miserable employee in this country, it is the barmaid. Apart from being misused and insulted, barmaids are exploited by their employers. I have discovered to my astonishment that these girls or women are underpaid. The proprietors do not pay them the legal wages. For example in Kampala it should be 150 shillings a month. Instead of 150 shillings they are paid 80 shillings. (*Uganda Argus,* August 10, 1972)

Many Baganda have informally commented to us on undesirable qualities attributed to barmaids. These conversations revealed that married women are particularly hostile to them. One married woman, for example, aged about twenty-five, made the following lengthy commentary when specifically asked about her view on barmaids:

> Most barmaids are crooks. They are the snatchers of husbands. Wives stay home crying for their husbands. Barmaids are very active. They snatch men like beer. They keep on talking about silly stories; what type of man took her the last; how they slept; and how much she got from him. They are sure to look for men who have got money and wait in the evening to convince them. So many men are away from their homes because they wait for barmaids after twelve and go stay with them. If a man wants a quick service, he just goes in a bar and picks one girl, and they enjoy the evening. Barmaids have spread a lot of diseases in countries. They never stay with one man because they are paid very little; they want to look attractive all the time. Some barmaids put on dresses of 200 shillings while they get only 60 shillings a month, and they rent houses of 150 shillings a month. So if a barmaid is not active in attracting men, she cannot manage all these expenses a month. In fact, barmaids are not good

people to befriend. They always cause trouble. When men meet they start to fight. Some lose their eyes, and others get serious wounds. If a husband avoids barmaids, he is one of the best and a wife is proud of him because barmaids are the worst people in the country. Their way of behaving towards men is not good at all, and men must avoid them.

Upon hearing the above comments, one of our married research assistants, herself a nurse, commented that she fully agreed with this informant's opinion of barmaids. The above narrative aptly illustrates the degree to which married women view barmaids as women who take away from the household both the husband and his economic resources. The barmaid is viewed as someone who lives beyond her means and must, therefore, acquire additional money from men. Men also consider barmaids to be lacking in self-respect and a potential drain on their economic resources. In contrast to women, however, men directly interact with barmaids and are thus in a position of being directly deceived by them. The following narrative by a male informant illustrates the major male complaint of not having much control over a barmaid. Even after having spent a considerable sum of money on her, he may receive little in return.

She sits comfortable and accepts anything you may wish to offer her. Such things as this happen with four or five other people in the same bar, and she will never be worried. You may suggest going with her to your place if you feel safe, and she will not refuse but will just ask you to wait until work is finished. Some sincere and honest barmaids (who are very few) may discourage the idea at once and perhaps try to date you on some other time but, in the majority of cases, you do not get them but you just find yourself alone after the close of business, and the girl is taken by someone else.

The above editorials and informant interviews stress the undesirable characteristics of barmaids. An occupational card-sort procedure (P. L. Kilbride, 1979) more completely revealed the range of social characteristics, both negative and positive, attributed to barmaids by other Baganda. Data from the card sort (N = 41) were combined for males (N = 12) and females (N = 29) since males (75%) and females (75%) equally chose barmaiding as one of the two least desirable occupations. Table 11 lists, for each occupation, the number of times an informant grouped it with bar-

Table 11 Female Occupation, Occupational Prestige, and Frequency of
Association with Barmaiding by Occupation

Occupation*	Least Desired (N)**	Most Desired (N)	Grouped with Barmaid (N)
Teacher	2	12	2
Nurse	1	12	2
Farmer	0	19	3
Secretary	0	7	4
Tailor	1	1	3
Midwife	1	5	2
Nun	1	0	1
Hair cleaner	0	0	7
Beautician	0	5	9
Receptionist	0	1	11
Cashier	0	3	5
Salesgirl	0	1	5
Telephone operator	0	2	5
Newspaper seller	2	0	10
National lottery seller	3	0	8
Curer	0	0	0
Kiganda dancer	0	1	0
Petrol attendant	0	0	10
Airline stewardess	4	7	12
Barmaid	29	0	—
Prostitute	30	1	21

*Although informants were asked to name the 2 most desired and the 2 least desired
occupations, some named only one occupation. Thus, total responses do not add up to 82 in
each case.
**Total N (respondents) = 41

maiding. The only two occupations never associated with barmaids by any
informant were those of the curer and the Kiganda dancer. Interestingly,
these are the most traditional roles represented in the present study. Barmaiding and prostitution were the most strongly associated occupations
and were overwhelmingly considered to be the least desirable female occupations. Table 12 presents types of reasons given for grouping barmaids
and prostitutes in a single category. All reasons appear to have negative
connotations. These two occupations also made up the most frequent
grouping, with 21 people combining the two into a single category. Two

Table 12   Respondents' Reasons for Grouping Barmaids and Prostitutes in a Single Category

Responses
These two are equal because they are after men and money.
These two are all the same and are very bad people; they do not have one man.
The least important jobs of all.
Everyone enjoys on them; they don't respect themselves as a woman should.
These people are after men and money.
Most of the time they are found in the same place (bars).
Usually put together by most people—barmaids are thought to be prostitutes.
They almost behave in the same way and almost do the same things.
They are concerned with attracting men.
These serve fools and high people in the same way.
Usually found in bars and hotels and both want things for nothing.

individuals preferred not to group barmaiding with any other occupation but considered it a separate category. These people noted about barmaids that "they are very drunken people" and that "barmaids are not good, but they get money from that." A third respondent, who preferred not to group barmaiding with any other occupation and who was herself a barmaid, stated about her occupation: "I like this because one gets money from this." Significantly, some respondents (N = 9) did not combine barmaiding with prostitution, either singularly or in combination with other occupations. Instead, their groupings elicited criteria Baganda consider to be positive ones such as sociability, being well-mannered, or being concerned with beauty in clothing and personal appearance.

The Insider's View

Many barmaids do not share the wider society's feelings of stigma attached to their occupation. For example, when five barmaids were asked to rank female occupations, none included barmaiding as among the two least desirable occupations. Nevertheless, only one of them listed barmaiding as among the two most desired occupations. The interview material also revealed variation among barmaids in their view of barmaiding as a career.

Some barmaids would prefer another job if an opportunity for one were available to them. This viewpoint is illustrated in the following statement:

> I have just started working in a bar and have been here for only one month. I became a barmaid as a last resort after seeking employment in a number of factories. I don't like the job at all since barmaiding is generally despised as a low type of occupation. I lived in Masaka as a child, but I returned to Kampala when I was fifteen. I had a child a few years ago. I work at this bar because the owner is a relative of mine.

At the other extreme is the following case:

> I have always wanted to be a barmaid since I was a young girl. Being a barmaid is like being a prostitute because they get things for nothing. I once went to Kololo club where I was going to be a prostitute. They told me to sit and wait for men, and they would pay me. I just couldn't do it, and that is when I went to work as a barmaid.

Many barmaids view their job in a very pragmatic way, seeing very little cause for the negative label attached to them. Those having this opinion, for example, often note similarities among all female occupations. The following two narratives serve to illustrate this commonly held viewpoint.

> Many people think that barmaids are prostitutes, but this is unfair. Some barmaids do have many boyfriends, but most women in fact do. For example, some secretaries have as many as ten boyfriends while some barmaids have only one or are even married. One friend who is married has just left work to go and see her husband in Jinja.

> Some barmaids really like their jobs. They get everything from it. Others don't like to be a barmaid but are forced to work in bars because they can't get other jobs and want money. Some people think bar girls are prostitutes. I would never tell my parents I work in a bar because I would be accused of being a prostitute and a drunkard and would be beaten. This is not true. A barmaid has a job; a prostitute does not have one. She just dresses up and goes to find men to sleep with her for money. A barmaid is just like any other girl employed in firms who can sometimes accept a man's

money for sleeping with him. In fact, some barmaids stay with only one man. She goes to work and comes back home to her man like any other girl who works in an office.

It is pertinent to note here that there are, in fact, hundreds of prostitutes (*balaya*) in Kampala and that these women do not work in bars, although they may frequent them. Baganda men rarely hire a prostitute and consider them to be primarily for Europeans and tourists. Moreover, barmaids and prostitutes rarely befriend one another. Ugandan barmaids are typically not engaged in prostitution if by prostitute one means "a woman whose livelihood over a period of time depends wholly on the sale of sexual services and whose relationship with the customer does not extend beyond the sexual act" (Little 1973:14). In modern times prostitutes do exist, according to this definition, in Uganda and elsewhere in Africa. The reader is referred to Little (1973) and Cohen (1969) for a discussion of prostitution in Africa and an analysis of prostitution in a West African society, respectively.

Barmaids sometimes live together in rented rooms owned by the bar owner and located near their place of work. Close friendships are frequently maintained between barmaids, and on occasion several barmaids may collectively seek employment together at another bar. Barmaids commonly spend their free time drinking or visiting other bars where relatives or friends work as barmaids. Friendship patterns among barmaids serve as a buffer against the wider society and better enable them to manage their social stigma.

In the agrarian past and what is still prevalent in the rural areas, as we have seen, is that women, although deferential to men, enjoy full economic rights in their own somewhat separate sphere of agricultural activity. The production of food for consumption in the past was largely their responsibility. Today, however, many urban women, especially barmaids, find themselves seeking participation in a monetized economy where the rules of the game are more heavily weighted in favor of men. The barmaid serves to symbolize the wider society's discomfort with the major means whereby modern women become successful by manipulating men for economic reward.

Finally, it is clear that in Uganda the emergence of monogamy as the valued marital form closely parallels the emergence of barmaiding and prostitution as stigmatized roles (see Davis 1971, for a discussion of the relationship between monogamy and prostitution in Western society). It would appear, for example, that many married women and others who have a vested interest in monogamy feel particularly threatened by barmaids. It is not a *fait accompli* that barmaiding will lose its stigmatization in Uganda should polygyny be reinstated as a cultural idea. Importantly, this study argues that the presence in modern times of a stigmatized female role, such as the barmaid, will persist until economic conditions and related power interactions are reconstituted to be more symmetrical between men and women. Another increasing problem for women in non-marital relationships is that of undesired pregnancies and unwanted children—an issue to be discussed in our next chapter. As we shall see, increased moral delocalization, along with the lessening economic benefit of having children, present modern-day challenges to the traditional support network of the extended family, especially in the cases of single parenthood.

9

PREMARITAL PREGNANCY
A Challenge to Extended Family Ideology

"Reliance on a brother's wealth can lead to failure to marry."

Kenya currently has the highest birthrate in the world. Improved medical care and a high rate of adolescent pregnancies contribute to this. Increasingly, premarital pregnancies are becoming a problem, especially for unmarried mothers. In this chapter, we will discuss this issue in the context of our modernization and delocalization perspective. An orienting principle of "pragmatism" can be clearly seen in traditional beliefs and practices concerning family life, sexuality, and reproduction. Practical education in proverbs and folktales, social consensus, and contextual consideration by elders of moral rule violation are being replaced by Western colonial-derived standards of "right" and "wrong." One of the consequences of such moral delocalization is, in our opinion, an increase of premarital pregnancies and without doubt the now-common and largely undesired social situation of raising children out of wedlock by parents and grandparents. Modern Kenya now has the "illegitimate" child, the "outside" child, the "unwanted" child. There is commonly a parental and grandparental dilemma of managing the "stigma," "shame," and economic problems associated with these "unwanted" children. This is the personal side of what in Kenya is widely considered to be a national social problem of countless children living in the streets of Nairobi "working" as "bus-boys" (parked-car "guards"), or child prostitutes. In a later chapter we will consider the problem of physical child abuse and neglect as a further consequence of stress associated with unwanted children. Here we concentrate on premarital pregnancies, one of the main causes of child abuse and neglect in Kenya.

Moral delocalization and associated modern sexual ignorance by the young is seen in the work of the Ugandan sociologist M. Kisekka (1976). She has documented the great extent to which Uganda news media's "advice letters" are now concerned with matters of sexual instruction; whereas, traditionally such matters were in the hands of "grannies" who imparted practical knowledge of sexual practices, family responsibilities, and domestic skills in the cultural experience of "visiting the forest." This educational function was typical of grannies throughout the East African region. Nowadays, however, the "love advice" column scenario is norma-tive, largely since schools and churches have not included sexual education in their province of educational responsibility. Rather, typically they have simply condemned many aspects of traditional sexual belief without offer-ing instruction in any alternative belief system. We have seen in chapter 1, for example, how the Kikuyu practice of *ngweko* was associated with sexual restraint and how this custom has been eroded through delocalized con-demnation by church authority. In fact, frequently the school is nowadays a major setting for the first experience of "true love," something idealized in the mass media, cinemas, and churches in contemporary East Africa. Our own female informants report having had their first sex with an older "school mate" with whom they were "in love," but whom subsequently bitterly disappointed them. The world of the school and "true love" are clearly quite foreign to the experience of most grannies who had quite practical and pragmatic issues in mind when they were in control of the curriculum (such as how to cook food, raise children, enjoy sex for one's self and one's partner, or other things faced by people who are expected to marry).

The modern courtship and marriage scene, compared to the past, in-cludes the following: delay of marriage in pursuit of work and education; lack of personal constraint in sexuality, particularly by boys; lessened moral influence of moralnets of home and family; and the cultural appearance of moral "absolutes" such as "abortion (and infanticide) are always wrong"; "true love is the best criterion for marriage"; and "polygamy is sinful."

The modernist in Kenya usually argues that monogamy must be the only marital form, whereas the less absolutist "traditionalist" opinion is that monogamy and polygyny can coexist. Persistence of traditional emphasis on fertility for personal self-actualization is still pronounced. Sexuality as something to be enjoyed but under the right circumstances remains a banner belief. Traditional life viewed sexuality as primarily directed toward reproduction of *social* persons meant to fit into family and community social structures. Responsible or "right" sexual behavior was expected at all times throughout the life cycle for males and females. Constraint for women for several years after the birth of a child was not uncommon since it was believed that harm could come to the child whose mother had sex before completing breast-feeding. Polygyny was one way to diffuse a husband's sexual attention to another wife who was not breast-feeding. We have seen previously that some ethnic groups permitted infanticide on occasions when the child's mother died in childbirth. In general, the African view is concerned with "quality of life" issues, but this ideal is evaluated according to social context in a pragmatic style. Human action is also governed by a belief that events are influenced by human practice such that one can through self actions bring about or prevent good or evil for desired ends. Overall, the traditional "action oriented" pragmatic orientation to life largely persists at the popular level, although it is now less functional since quite different "absolutistic" or "fatalistic" (everything is in "God's" hands) worldview constructions from outside have been forcefully imposed on local views.

What is particularly problematic is that the "absolute" moral standards are themselves derived from elsewhere where social values are quite dissimilar from those in East Africa. Mob justice provides a good example to illustrate our point. Stealing is strongly negatively sanctioned in past and present East African society. Individuals "caught in the act" run considerable risk of being stoned or beaten to death. This traditional form of justice can on occasion be observed in locations all over East Africa, including downtown Nairobi. The "practical" side of mob justice is easy to understand. The thief is caught in the act by a public audience so his guilt is clear to them. In addition, such a horrendous action can be stamped out now and a lesson made to others. Should the "thief" escape, he will soon be home where his actions may be defined as "understandable," as pillage from rich "outsiders," or acquisition of needed material goods. Moreover, at home his social role is now "multiple." Thus the "thief" is also a kinsmen or friend or has some other functional role in the community. Conversely, in the West and in modern Kenya where absolute labels and norms prevail, the "thief" has broken a universalistic social rule or committed an illegal action. His rule violation will be treated in a nonrelativistic fashion. He will be considered a "thief" by segments of society not even familiar with the case. In fact, so absolute is the label that even many of his relatives will consider him to be primarily a thief. For this reason having a "jail record" is difficult to forget once a "thief" has left prison. Such universalistic labeling is rare in small-scale pre-literate societies such as traditional Kenya (cf. Selby 1974).

In our research on premarital pregnancy, S. Nangendo, a Kenyan Bryn Mawr graduate student, elicited the views of twenty rural Abaluyia men on the subject of premarital sex and pregnancies. We were interested to discover ideological and cultural factors in such things as contraceptive use, abortion, and reproductive philosophy. One of the men interviewed felt that God was involved in creating or permitting the premarital pregnancy whereas most of the others believed that it was due to the "fault" of the girl. A few thought she was "unlucky." There was, therefore, no clear-cut consensus on fatalism (God's plan or "luck") or human action as the locus of control. Nevertheless, contraceptive use is mostly disapproved for unmarried people. Some (Christians) believed that they should have no sex and, therefore, to provide birth control is either not necessary or an ideological contradiction. Others thought more pragmatically, but sometimes erroneously, that such things as the pill, condoms, and all other contraceptives should be avoided because they will harm the reproductive system, cause sterility, or even prevent a chance to get pregnant ever. Several approved of family planning for the unmarried, though none of the twenty men had themselves used it. The idea of pragmatism can be most clearly seen in their opinion about abortion, something that is illegal in East Africa. Five felt that an unmarried woman who did not want to be pregnant should terminate through abortion. Most of the others disapproved the practice but gave *only* practical concerns against it such as its being "illegal" or "dangerous." These materials are overall not inconsistent with our historical view that at the village level relativistic, pragmatic, functional ideas about premarital sexuality do, in fact, exist simultaneously with more modern and recent absolutistic-universalistic norms, such as Euro-Christian morality and British-derived jurisprudence. We turn now to some case materials which will serve to illustrate how an "absolutizing" ethical tendency in sexual morality works to render women who do get pregnant before marriage quite vulnerable, powerless, and scapegoated. That "absolute" standards are directed primarily at women and less so at men is, we argue, best understood as a consequence of women's decline in relative economic power compared to the past when children, for example, were rarely not valued as economic assets.

Teenage Pregnancy: Cases

Our first case will serve to illustrate the male perspective on current sexual practices in Western Kenya. Philip Kilbride's informant, a twenty-three-year-old unmarried male, and he sat drinking Kwete, a local fermented beverage, while they chatted about matters of interest to them. A visitor, a twenty-one-year-old unmarried male who had been searching unsuccessfully for employment, joined them. The visitor is called *Mutua,* a name for the lastborn child (male or female) or "one who closes the mother's womb." Mutua had always received special treatment such as the best food served to him alone at the table. Ideally, he should also be the last sibling to get married with the firstborn son followed by the firstborn daughter, etc., going before him. During his visit, Mutua began to discuss (at Philip Kilbride's prompting) the "sexual life" of men in their early twenties. Both companions commented that typically girls are obtained from "anywhere" and brought home for several days. Such girls, who are between fifteen and nineteen years of age, stay in the men's cottages with their lovers. Both of these young men were around fifteen when they began "playing sex." Neither practices "birth control" for several reasons. First, they want to have children, and second, as Catholics, using condoms is "just like abortion." Girls, they report, are the ones who often try to give condoms, but boys fear the practice since these condoms are often "reused" and could contain "charms" from her previous lover.

Our premarital survey mentioned above revealed that these men were not unusual. The mid-teens for first sex is typical of that group, as is having sex in the family compound area or somewhere in the bush for the *first* encounter. Mutua has, in fact, already had a child which he originally denied was his although he knew he was the father. He "disappeared" for three months, but when he came home, he found his nineteen-year-old girlfriend at his home and pregnant. He refused to give her child support, so she went to the assistant chief and then to court. He has now "accepted to marry her" if he gets a job, although he has not seen his two-month-old daughter since the hospital. The girlfriend's parents are taking care of their daughter and granddaughter. His own parents are not annoyed because they know he has no money. He believes it can even happen again. The mother of his child is now nineteen. She left high school at Form 2 (ninth grade) because she had "no fees." In contrast to his own, her parents were angry with her.

Many girls who are impregnated report that their parents are angry with them. In one case that we know of, the girl was heavily "caned" (beaten with a stick). The latter was the daughter of a "Christian" father. School regulations require that girls who get pregnant must leave and for most readmission is precluded. Some of our female informants stated that after marriage they would "just leave" their child with their mothers. It is also believed that an illegitimate daughter has a better chance of later being accepted by her mother's future husband since she can bring bridewealth, whereas a boy, who will need to be given a *shamba* (land) may be less welcome in today's lessening land situation.

The following interview was obtained from a girl of nineteen who lives in Kakamega, Kenya, and, when interviewed, was visiting her two-year-old daughter and her mother. Her child was conceived with a fellow student when she was in Form 2 (ninth grade). She was not using birth control because "she did not understand then." She was "in love," and he was her first boyfriend. He refused to accept the pregnancy. The headmaster called his parents, but they also refused to accept the pregnancy since he was "still young" and would not agree that he was the father. She plans to marry one day, but her daughter will stay with her mother if her future husband refuses the child. Her father died in 1980; but there are about ten acres of land, and the home is a relatively prosperous one. Nevertheless, the grandmother is worried about her ability to support her granddaughter, particularly if she should die. The girl's brother lives here with his wife's son of one year. He has agreed to keep this boy for several more years after which the owner (maternal grandmother) will take him. The biological father does not want him because he is still in school. He has also denied paternity. Traditionally, such a child would have been typically accepted and raised by the paternal grandparents and/or their son and his future wife.

In the next section of this chapter, we will consider the situation of grandparents, particularly grandmothers, on whose shoulders the often economic burden of grandchild care resides. First, however, we conclude our discussion of teen pregnancy with an extended discussion of how one modern girl, sold on the idea of "true love," was shattered by an experience referred to as "my disappointment." The following case of "disappointment" should not be construed as a process of bitterness or "toughening up" (as argued for Zambia by Shuster 1979) as much as a sort of lessening of enthusiasm and what we might call the gaining of "street sense." Nevertheless, many East African women fall into the "disappointed" category although most do not experience the "disappointment": an experience where belief in "true love" combines with male deception to cause personal grief.

Traditionally, the male had less of an opportunity to deceive a prospective marital partner since both his and the girl's family were heavily involved in marital arrangements. Thus the psychological experience of "the disappointment" is probably entirely modern in its occurrence and is therefore one of numerous such negative experiences which combine to constitute what we consider a more spurious culture compared to the more traditional one.

The following case is presented in the words of our informant. She grew up in North Central Uganda, where she attended school as far as the secondary level before leaving to receive nurse's training in Kampala. Jane (a pseudonym) comes from a polygynous home and describes her relations with her father and eldest brother in very positive terms. She was a "virgin," as is ideal for Langi girls, until about age nineteen. At the time, she was working in a bank after leaving nurses training. Jane characterized herself as "cheeky" as a child. She recalls with laughter running away from home and hiding sweets from her elder sister. When we met, Jane was a very attractive woman in her early twenties who had suffered much due to the Amin regime's policy of liquidating Langi people. Her baby son was at that time living at "home" with her elder sister. We turn now to directly consider Jane's "disappointment," picking up her narration where it occurred in the urban location of Kampala.

> I told them I would like to be a secretary; I would like to go to U.C.C., do shorthand and typing and other business. So after a week a prominent man, my brother-in-law, took me to U.C.C. We looked for my sister so she could explain things to us. Unfortunately, it was Saturday. We didn't find her in the school compound. Then my brother-in-law said that *Argus* (a national newspaper) had said that Bank of Uganda needed banking assistants. We went there. It was at Liverpool Building. We went to the Secretary; he gave us forms. We had tea at 10:00 AM. In those days after duty, people just rushed to drink at the bars or hotels. All of us decided to go to St.

Joseph Hotel, a German hotel near the bank. We started drinking. Big people started coming, like government ministers, chairman of boards (names deleted by us). The chairman of————and so many big people! Then I met them. I was only a young girl, no woman. I was seventeen years old. We drank. I was drinking Fanta and Pepsi-Cola. They had a lot of money. Everyone wanted to show off, to buy the drinks. They told me not to take soft drinks. If I wasn't taking beer, I would take something else, whiskey or Baby Cham. I took Baby Cham.

On Monday, my brother-in-law drove me to U.E.B.; I filled the form. It was complicated, but the interview was not complicated. They wanted me to work in Sulu, then to Lira, then Saroti, then to go and study in England. When I wrote my boyfriend, he told me not to go away. He was coming back from America soon, and he wanted to settle down; we would get married. He wanted me to join the bank. I also liked banking so I decided to join the bank. I was accepted by letter at the bank.

On December 5, 1967, I went to work. I moved to my "uncle's" house at Nakasero. My uncle was the chairman of a Public Service Commission, having two wives. I stayed with the first wife at his government house. His second wife was staying in a flat near the International Hotel. I liked the bank so much! By then the staff was very small. People would work up to 10:00 or 11:00 PM. We could claim overtime. I had to walk to Nakasero, my uncle's home. There was a girl who stayed at Y.W.C.A.; I used to walk with her. She told me not to walk at night. We would get lifts from the officers; they could claim mileage. The pressure of work was so much, even on Sunday. The Governor was so good and kind. He would invite us to his bar where we ate chicken and drank. He paid, then claimed general ledger. Still we were paid overtime. I was working so hard; I started smoking a lot.

When my boyfriend returned, his mother and father went to meet him at Entebbe. I couldn't go; I was too busy at the bank. Later, I went to see him. He gave me a small gift from the U.S., a necklace. He wanted to bring earrings, but he didn't know if I pierced my ears. The necklace was so good! It was made from something like precious stones. He brought to his sister-in-law a present. He brought gifts to all he knows. So I started going with him; I introduced him to my uncle. My uncle said, "You are lucky to have this boy; he is so good; we know his parents. This is your future, I am sure. You two will make housewife and husband." My uncle liked him so much! He would collect me from my uncle's house. We would go to films, take a walk, drive around. We were planning to marry. My mother already knew him because he would go to my home a long time ago with my brother. When my mother heard about him, she said, "This boy is so good." But I did not introduce him officially to my parents, like taking him to my mother with me. We were going to do that later on. He introduced me to all his relatives; they liked me so much. So we were planning to get married.

I still continued with this boy. One day he was supposed to see me after duty at 5:00 PM. He was going to collect me from the bank; I told him no, I would just walk home. On the way with the other girls, a minister of the government's car passed by. We exchanged waves. The other girls branched off near Grand Hotel; I was still going to uncle's when this M.P. sent his bodyguard to come and collect me. I said no I'm not going. He said you have to come. The Big Man knows you. I said no, how does he know me, I haven't met him in person. Bodyguard said the sister of Mrs.———? I said yes. This man was a member of Parliament; he had married my sister, but unfortunately he died. So I had met all these people, but I didn't know this M.P. knew me. They took me to M.P.'s house. I was asked if I wanted drinks. I said no so they gave me Fanta. Even this M.P. used to have girlfriends. But I thought if he asked me anything of nonsense I was going to tell him off, that I am loving your cousin that I'm not going to do anything with you, and I don't love you. Fortunately, he never told me something like that, as though he knew what was in my mind. We were just talking but I was so frightened. The bodyguard and driver took me back to my uncle's place. I was lucky my uncle was not at home. He was with the second wife at the flat. The first wife never told me that my boyfriend was there looking for me.

Next day, the house girl said your husband came here looking for you about five times. He rang me at the office. He asked me where I was last evening. I couldn't explain on the telephone. Later, I told him. He was so cross with me! He had gone to my sister staying at Park Hotel; I was not there. He had rang to Jinja. He knew all my relatives. He couldn't find me. He thought I went with a man somewhere. So when I explained he felt so jealous though they were his relatives, but he was so jealous. He said he cried, maybe I was loving this M.P. I told him how I had planned to answer the M.P. Still he couldn't believe.

Later we were taking coffee at the Uganda Club when a certain man came. He was just joking when he said he knew me. When a man says he knows somebody, it means you have been a girlfriend or dating. That made the problem worse! Again there was conflict. I felt so bad I cried. He was so cross with me. Then he forgave me. He said anyway, I was wrong. I haven't introduced you to that M.P. personally, that I am going to marry you, that you are my girl. From there we planned how we were going to have children, how we were going to get married. He asked me whether I liked going to court or a wedding. I said I just liked going to church, so we were planning a church wedding and everything. He wanted ten children because his mother had ten, seven boys and three girls. For me we are also ten, seven girls and three boys. I wanted only four, two boys and two girls if G-d can give me what I want. He got annoyed. As we were planning everything he told me not to use birth control, no family-planning tablets or something like that.

Not long later, they threw a big homecoming party for him near the M.P.'s house. That party was to introduce me to the M.P. and some other ministers. By then, I was already three months pregnant. The boy knew about it. That day I didn't go to work. I was sick, vomiting. He said you must come, I will send a car to collect you from your uncle's because I must introduce you to the Big Man. He sent a car. I went to the party. It was so big. He made introductions, I said hello to the M.P. My brother was also invited, my relatives also. My brother by then rang him and said he couldn't come; he was having a party in Jinja for the birthday of one of his children. My sister came, uncles with their wives came. I was supposed to open a dance with the chairman of————.

After the introduction, the M.P. made a very good speech, "that he didn't know that his young cousin, such a good boy, had a nice fiancée. Although he was abroad in the U.S., his girl was here. She is so nice. At home, she will be a good housewife. Because during those days, it was difficult to get a girl to be a housewife. They like sitting in the Speke Hotel waiting for men to come and pick them with Mercedes Benz, take them to night club, but my cousin made a good choice, he didn't know where he got me from." He gave the speech, yet he also was interested in me!

From there we opened a dance. We danced, I was so young. I was eighteen. I didn't know what to do whenever my boyfriend wanted to dance. He was such a good man, he could come and ask me politely, "Can I go and dance with so and so?" I said, "Oh, yes, you go and enjoy yourself," because I was a bit sick, expecting. I didn't know I was giving my man to somebody else! I wished I had known; I would have refused, but I didn't, maybe G-d arranged it like that. He danced with a woman older than him. When people were leaving, I asked his cousin to go tell him I wanted to go home. He told him I should wait, he will be taking some other people home then he will return and collect me. I waited, the boy never turned up. One of his cousins took me home. It was about four in the morning. I was so disappointed in my life! I felt so bad. It was Sunday, I never slept because this boy never disappointed me before.

I went to a dispensary with a girlfriend of mine from the bank. I found out I was four months pregnant. That day my boyfriend promised to ring me on the telephone by eleven. He didn't. After examination, we stopped at a bar on the way to the bank. We wanted cold drink. He came with two girls and found me there. He tried to introduce them to me. He wanted to buy me a soft drink. I refused. I said I was going back to work. He told me in our language that he would see me later. I said O.K.

On the way back, I told my friend that he was my fiancé now I don't even know those girls. She said, "Tell me, that boy is so handsome, is he really your fiancé?" I said, "Oh yes, we are planning to get married. Now I saw him with those two girls, I don't know them." She said you are deceiving; I said I was not. She said he looks like a nice boy. I said I am not sure after seeing him with those girls. Men when they come from abroad, they keep on changing; you never know. Next day he rang and said I am sure you are annoyed; you saw those girls. They are not my girlfriends. I just met them. I said it was all right. I was so young I didn't know what love is. That was my first experience with men. After that woman took him from the party; he used to tell me he was so busy doing his study. I said he could continue his studies.

By then my stomach was getting bigger and bigger. I said now I am praying, though I introduced this boy to my uncle, he told me not to keep going out so much with this boy. He didn't mean I shouldn't go out with him, he was meaning I shouldn't be playing sex with this man so much; my uncle is a man who knows everything. I was having trouble drinking tea. Whenever I smelled it I would run and vomit without his wife's knowledge. His wife being a nurse knew everything. She didn't want to tell me. One day my uncle went abroad to interview doctors to come to Uganda. He went to Korea, China, and Britain. Then I came from duty and was sitting outside with his wife. I said these days I don't like beer and so on. She said, "Oh yes, I can see your skin, there is a change." The following time I did not come home to sleep. I used to sleep with the other wife at her flat. I worked there, did my packing slowly by slowly.

So, I went to Bukoto to live. I met so many men of my tribe staying there. Most of them liars. They used to give me a lift to work. They could give us lifts to lunch. My boyfriend was so engaged with that girl. Unfortunately, she was also staying at Bukoto. He used to ring and find out how I was. One day I got so mad. I went to Mulago hospital for examination. Everything was private. He came to see me. That girl had gone to England for shorthand. I made food. We ate together. He said don't listen to people, I'm not interested in any other girl. I love you so much. He said this because people were saying that he would lose me; he would regret that because he was going with other people he would never be happy in life. And it is true. So, I said you can continue, I don't mind. I showed him my card from Mulago; he never spoke a word. He went back. Then he never rang me the following morning so I rang him and asked, why are you so quiet? He asked why did you write my name at Mulago, private wing? You know I am not entitled for that thing, I said. Was that the reason you didn't ring?

That is so simple. Your name can be taken off, I don't mind that. I said bye bye to him. I went home early. I was so mad. This boy who I never thought had disappointed me. To make the matter worse my stomach was getting bigger. I never explained everything to my cousin, but she knew everything. She said never shame us, don't do abortion. Have your baby. She gave me some money.

I went, locked myself in my room and wrote this boy a letter. I said from today, I'm sorry we are going to wind up everything because it seems you are no longer interested in me; you have got another woman, I wish you luck. She will make you a good house-wife for your future, for your children. Maybe G-d didn't prepare me to be your wife. Maybe I wasn't going to be a good housewife. Maybe I wasn't going to make you happy. But I wish you well. I'm telling you that in my family this has never happened. No girl has ever had a child without a father. All my sisters went to church; they married well. They are all happy with their husbands. I'm the youngest, you know me well. You gave me four things why you wanted to marry me. You know my family, I'm beautiful, and the other two you know very well. But I'm telling you today, I'm sorry you are going to cancel everything, but I will say that if I have this child, a girl or a boy, I will kill him or her. But if it will be a dog or a pussy-cat I will be happy because I am sure it will just go to the bush. Forget about me from today, never dream or think about me. We shall not be sharing anything, only water from Kampala city. I wish you well in your future happiness. Then I signed my name.

When I posted I was mad, mentally sick, so instead of writing box number, I wrote telephone number. He got the letter anyway. He kept quiet. Then I decided to ring and check on this boy. Because according to our customs, whenever they are expecting the change (pregnant), women become so cool and bad. So I thought let me sympathize with this boy. I rang. He said he was so quiet because of my letter which was so bad. I said forget about the letter if it was so bad; you know what you did to me. What you told me hurt me because as an expectant mother I can even kill myself! Since I worked at hospital I know what to take to kill myself. It will be your fault. But it is better when I blow out my feelings to you. It helps me. But if I didn't write to you I would have been dead. You should know that all expectant mothers are angry, they want happiness, they don't want something which hurts their feelings. Any small person can hurt the feeling of one who is expecting. That's why most of the men when their wives are expecting keep on running away from home because any small thing will bring a quarrel. So you will have to forgive me or forget it.

One of the girls from our place found me in a party. Those days, though this boy started neglecting me, some of our men liked me because I'm so jolly and happy. I didn't care; I was all the time laughing, though I had problems I liked to forget, and think of the future only. I like to make people happy. I like happiness though I'm poor. So these people used to give me a good time, though I was expecting and this boy was neglecting me. Other men of my tribe used to collect me with other girls. We go for parties in their houses. They made me happy, to forget and dance. They said you forget about that man, he will not be happy. They talked to me so nicely. They were all educated so they knew what sort of a person I am.

We can observe in Jane's "disappointment" most of the prevailing social, economic, and cultural components of modern premarital gender relations. Jane was quite dependent on men for her procurement of a good high-status job. City life for her, away from community and immediate family conceived as a moralnet, resulted in smoking, drinking, and visiting bars. She was the object of sexual attraction for powerfully placed men, often commonly seen in Uganda as "Sugar Daddies." She nevertheless was concerned with "true love" and was eventually deceived by the one that she loved. She concealed her pregnancy through fear of retribution but did not attempt abortion (not itself uncommon in Kampala in the 1970s). Instead she had her son but sent her child to the rural area to be raised by an elder sister. Nevertheless, she is now stigmatized, particularly by her boyfriend, who showed no interest in the "parental" role, itself now so unreasonable to assume in modern life without strong kinsmen and the community sanction of the past to compel men to provide support or at least show why they should not be responsible for this support (Haley 1940). His opposition to birth control is an African value that persists without the supporting moralnets that make such a value workable. We turn now to the men and women who nowadays assume the burden of the parenting role for illegitimate children, the grandparents.

Grandparents

There is considerable information in the ethnographic literature which highlights the important role played by grandparents in the educational and affective development of their grandchildren. Through folk stories, tales, and just plain "advice" the grandparent serves as "confidant-friend" for their younger kinsmen, sometimes even engaging in "free" conversation containing "lewd" language. This "privileged familiarity" between alternating generations is a sharp contrast to the restraint, decorum, and avoidance variously found in parent or parent-in-law relationships. At the community level, grandparents or "elders" played important roles as "wise" counselors in affairs of family, clan, and community. We learn, for example, from H. Aswani that "Abanyore literature is full of folk tales because of the old woman's love of pleasing children. Old women . . . would sit down by the fireside and tell as many stories as they could think of before the children became sleepy" (1972:1). Stories told to children were concerned with pending adolescent life and were for entertainment. Aswani continues:

> Sometimes stories were about domestic life, with married women and their husbands as the major characters. Stories of this type were told to the adolescent and adult audiences. They were meant to warn both boys and girls what they were to expect of their respective partners when they married . . . The stories were also meant to teach the young men how to behave in crises which might arise in family life. (1972:2)

Idealized themes in these stories stressed morals concerning, for example, sincere love, avoidance of pride, caution, and avoidance of laziness.

When we arrived in Kenya in 1984 for a year of study of the "family," members of the community emphasized to us the need to look into the extent to which grandparents were nowadays involved in basic parenting responsibilities. Our subsequent discussions with American friends about their own grandparents evoked strong personal feelings of love and personal longing for their grandparents who, like their African counterparts, gave them gifts, love, and the feeling that they were important. In East Africa, the grandparent gives eggs or chickens as special treats in much the same way as our own grandparents would offer "lots of candy." In one of our survey attempts to gather systematic information about Kenyan grandparents, we asked, with the help of our research assistants, respondents in Nzoia and Samia locations to provide their ideal beliefs about the three most important characteristics of a good grandmother and a good grandfather. Since the second and third characteristics were quite similar in kind to the characteristics mentioned first in importance, only the latter have been included in Table 13. As we can see from these data, the grandparent

Table 13   Characteristics of Good Grandparents

Characteristics	Grandfather	Grandmother
Samia (N = 62)		
Storyteller, teacher, advisor, transmitter of custom	22	26
Takes care of grandchildren	2	8
Gives presents to grandchildren	3	10
Settles family disputes, especially land disputes	9	1
Loves grandchildren	5	4
Peace-loving, not quarrelsome; helpful, kind	8	5
Sociable, friendly, cheerful, free, trusted	3	4
Good Christian	2	1
Curer, magician	3	2
Miscellaneous	5	1
Nzoia (N = 69)		
Storyteller, teacher, advisor, transmitter of custom	13	13
Takes care of grandchildren	0	5
Gives presents to grandchildren	2	1
Settles family disputes, especially land	4	0
Loves grandchildren	20	29
Peace-loving, helpful, etc.	14	7
Sociable, friendly, trusted, etc.	9	12
Miscellaneous	6	1
No response	1	1

ideal as described above is still very much in place. In the more traditional Samia areas, grandfathers even at present play a significant role in land-dispute resolution. The expectation is common that grandparents are and should be properly involved in cultural transmission through storytelling, teaching, and advising. In so doing, they should be sociable, friendly, loving, helpful, and not quarrelsome—in short, the type of person one can enjoy being with and with whom one can feel close and free to discuss life's joys and sorrows. Interestingly, the less traditional areas of Nzoia mention love in the abstract devoid of deeds more frequently for both grandmothers and grandfathers in comparison to the more traditional Samia area.

There are numerous proverbs concerning the expectation that elders should instruct and be treated with "respect-fear" (*kutya*). This educational role can even be performed despite the infirmities of age. The Samia proverb *omukofu adirira khu sikaye*, translated as "an old person will get hold of you when you go for food which is kept where you eat," means, according to our informants, "If you make a mistake the old one will have a chance to ultimately catch you at mealtime, even though he is too old to chase after you."

It is not believed that grandparents should ideally assume total *economic* support for grandchildren, but there is idealized support for the notion that grandparents are and should be involved in "asymmetrical" exchanges with grandchildren. Grandparents should ideally "give" presents, food, and goodwill (traditionally grandchildren sometimes sleep at the house of grandparents, where they can be "spoiled"). In part, however, the major "provider" role was, as we will see later, that of the father. Due to delocalization of economy, many fathers are now unavailable, unable, or unwilling to provide for their children, and this responsibility is falling too often on the shoulders of caring grandparents. To refuse a grandchild is, in East Africa, to go against both convention and psychological sentiment.

We have seen in a previous chapter the extent to which the "resident grandchildren" category has come to typify homes in the Nzoia area. We conclude this section with two local residents who will serve as our spokespersons for the sort of negative consequences that are now felt by many elderly individuals, particularly grandmothers. Our first informant is not unrepresentative of the grandparent situation:

A fifty-two-year-old man lives with his wife, six sons, and a daughter. Two other sons and two other daughters have married and live elsewhere, but one daughter-in-law lives at his home with her three children. Two children of his other daughters-in-law also live with him. He has, however, a total of seven grandchildren living with him because each of the two daughters who have married out left behind a child obtained before their marriages. These two grandchildren were not accepted by their mothers' husbands. In each case, the alleged father denied in court his paternity. One was fined 3000 shillings, but he never paid. These two children often call their grandfather "father" and he loves them as his own children. One of these grandchildren is in Form 3 (tenth grade), and the other grandson is in Primary 5 (fifth grade). He is concerned, however, because his wife does not love these two children. She gives them less food and lots of work to do. He has told his wife to treat them better, but he feels that most grandmothers are like that and look down on such unwanted grandchildren. It should be noted that these grandparents still have seven of their own children living with them. Nevertheless, they do not appear to be experiencing financial hardships in that they are not among the poorer residents of the community.

Our second case will serve to illustrate the dilemma of many grand-mothers in the Nzoia area:

A woman in her fifties is one of three wives. She lives on several acres along with her co-wives. Still living at home are a total of twenty-four children among the three of them. Two sons live in the compound with their own families. Problems associated with school fees and clothing are acute in this compound since the husband is not a wealthy person. Our informant, in addition to her nine resident children, also supports two grandsons of eight and ten years of age. Her daughter left them behind when she married out. She had been made pregnant by two different men, one a teacher. These men "disappeared" long ago, the daughter's husband has forbidden her to visit these sons, and she sends no help. She has had three children with her present husband. Her father, already hard-pressed, has paid school fees for these grandchildren (now in Primary 4 and Primary 2), but clothing and bedding are a big problem.

The significance of grandparents can only be interpreted within the context of the importance of the extended family through consanguineous kinship and the ideal of large households further augmented by marriage ties, including polygyny. This ideal of grandparental guidance of grand-children persists, as does the custom of polygyny. This persistence is, however, delocalized and is often incompatible with contemporary eco-nomic and social circumstances, especially for grandparents and the illegiti-mate grandchildren in their care. Thus, as we have seen, the problem of teenage pregnancy and illegitimate children is a challenge to extended-family ideology, becoming, in large part, a difficult responsibility for the grandparents caring for these children. At the same time, the extended family on the whole continues to constitute for most East Africans a meaningful support group and a firm symbolic anchor for numerous cere-monial, ritual, and other culturally meaningful events and activities. The stresses and strains associated with the maintenance of extended family ideology in modern East African society provide a challenging contradic-tion now faced in the development process.

Extended Family

East African society has traditionally been organized into groups primarily on the basis of kinship, age, and gender. The idiom of kinship was the most important of these factors. In the past, ethnic groups typically maintained a "clan" or "lineage" corporate entity based on descent traced through either the father (patrilineal) or the mother (matrilineal). This principle of unilineal descent permitted large numbers of individuals to have memberships in the social group (unlike the U.S. system where descent is traced through both parents, thereby resulting in kin groups which are shared only by siblings). Large clans or lineages thus exist before and after the death of any individual, whereas a kindred spans the lives of individuals only (e.g., one's mother's kindred is not the same as one's own, which, unlike hers, includes one's father). If a person traces descent through his mother, however, then that person, his mother, his sister, and her children, for example, all belong to the same kin group which exists after his death. Clans are more inclusive than lineages, sometimes including constituent lineage by descent or incorporating individuals or groups by conquest or marriage. Lineages and clans controlled property, regulated marriage (people married outside of the clan), and regulated the moral behavior of members.

Modern society has witnessed an erosion of clan or lineage authority as land has passed from collective to private ownership (Moody 1961). Schools, law courts, and churches have eroded clan social authority, whereas, migration, urbanization, and other modern forces have lessened the moralnet functions of concern or help for another person who is simply a clan member or distant lineage mate. Nevertheless, "clans" are not without salience, particularly at a symbolic-cultural level. Most East Africans today do not wish to marry a clansman or eat certain foods tabooed by one's clan. In fact, the delocalization process has just recently resulted in a court case in Kenya concerning the rights of a widow to bury her husband versus the claims of his clan to bury him. The fact that his clan instead of his widow was awarded custody over the deceased's body clearly illustrates the degree to which clan organization and identity is retained at a cultural level. Where one's body and spirit are to be buried is a key symbol of identity since one's place of burial is what East Africans consider their "home." The city is often not "home" but simply where one keeps a "house" for purposes of residence to earn a living. Indeed, Nairobi is virtually empty at Christmas, for example, when most Kenyans go "home." In January, 1987, the nation of Kenya was captivated by a court case initiated by the death of a prominent attorney named Otieno. From the *Daily Nation* we learn:

> He was a Luo by tribe, educated in Nakesene and India and had a very substantial and varied legal practice in Nairobi. He married the plaintiff, a Kikuyu lady of one of Kenya's leading Kikuyu families,

and numbered among his clients people of all tribes and races. He
was a metropolitan and a cosmopolitan, and though he undoubt-
edly honoured the tradition of his ancestors, it is hard to envisage
such a person as subject to African customary law and in particular
to the custom of a rural community. (Egan 1987:6)

His wife is also "delocalized" in her belief that a Christian burial in their
urban residence is her exclusive right to determine since she is the wife in
their monogamous marriage legally sanctioned through their marriage at
the District Commissioner's office. Members of her husband's *umira kager*
clan, however, claimed the right of burial in their ancestral lands in Western
Kenya. While the body remained in the mortuary, the courts considered
this dramatic case. Thousands of clansmen and others waited around the
court chamber on a daily basis; sometimes it required tanks to control the
crowd. In the words of the *Daily Nation,* this case

raised many issues of wide interest to many people: The role of the
law and the family, customary law versus common law, the role of
women in the family, different ethnic traditions and their place in
Kenya society as a whole. The whole issue evoked strong feelings,
emotions, and debate. For newspapers it was a bestseller. . . . For let
there be no mistake about it, the Otieno case may be closed but the
debate it gave rise to about many issues has only just begun. (Egan
1987:7)

The practical day-by-day concerns of life, if not the dramatic symbolic sort
described above for clans, are the affairs of one's extended family based on
bilateral descent. In the past, one's kindred was important (see Wagner
1949, 1956), but the modern era has seen its emergence as a *major* economic support network. We have seen in the previous section how grandparents are nowadays greatly involved in the economic maintenance of
illegitimate grandchildren. We discussed in chapter 3 the great extent to
which "relatives" are involved in visiting back and forth between schemes
in Nzoia and the rural locations of their origins. Ross and Weisner (1977)
found such interaction based on kinship to be significant between Nairobi
and rural areas.

The regulation of marriage is today still a major concern of the clan,
lineage, and extended family. Marriage in East Africa is ideally an "alliance
between families," not usually a decision to be taken only by two individ-

uals who are "in love." Modern people who are "in love" generally continue to believe it is necessary to participate in "negotiations" between their respective families.

The significance of extended family ideology can be observed today in rituals before marriage and in the marriage ceremony itself. We pointed out above that East Africans marry into already existing families. It is for this reason that there is much concern for female fertility as a means of perpetuating a family, and a general interest in the economic standing of a male who will be a prosperous "in-law." The husband is not only a provider of progeny price, but later is a potential benefactor to, for example, his wife's family. A girl's family can expect to receive considerable progeny price if she is educated, possesses a good reputation, and comes from a family with no suspected history of witchcraft or mental illness.

In 1985, Philip Kilbride participated in an "engagement" ceremony of a friend in his thirties who, as a holder of an M.A. degree, had decided to marry a university graduate right after her graduation. This Nairobi friend needed to visit his fiancée's family in the Western province to formally request their approval for engagement, itself a prelude to progeny price negotiation between her family and this friend and his father. One Saturday, the friend (whom we shall call George) came to Eldoret to meet Philip, who was to be the driver for this entourage. Also included were two other men, each boyhood friends, one of whom was the "spokesman," sort of an obligation since George had served as his "best man." We arrived at the fiancée's home dressed in our best clothes, in keeping with our somber and formal mood. Our hosts were about fifty kinsmen, friends, and neighbors of the fiancée. Their mood was one of confidence and slight haughtiness but with polite demeanor. We visitors were directed to a room in one building where we were fed and entertained by two of the fiancée's brothers and her older sister.

The main event occurred when we were led single file into the central house, a multi-room cement structure with a living room furnished with easy chairs and sofas. We four were seated along a wall facing the interior of the room where the fiancée's family was seated. She herself was seated amidst a row of her female relatives of about the same age. The occasion was orchestrated by a spokeswoman representing the fiancée's family interest. She asked us formally to state who we were and why we had come. Our own "spokesman" introduced us one by one, and we each stood in turn. Philip was so nervous that his *KiSwahili completely* failed him when he was asked to "say a few words." When it was announced that we were there to request an engagement for George, the spokeswoman expressed (mock) surprise. George was then asked to "come forward" and identify his fiancée from among the row of young women. When he did so, everyone applauded. After this, the mood seemingly relaxed a bit as we were then taken back to the previous building (or brother's home), where we ate lavishly (meats, chicken, rice, cakes, cookies, etc.). Most of the fiancée's family ate in the main house with the exception of her three siblings, who ate with us. Their mood was relaxed and convivial.

A sum of money was given to the brother to seal the engagement, a sum that had been informally agreed upon beforehand. One brother felt more should be given and, in fact, some subsequent discussion ensued on the subject. Money was given to the fiancée's father and the father's relatives who sponsored the event, some to the fiancée, but more than half was given for her mother, who had "suckled the fiancée while she was a baby." Interestingly, the church received a portion of George's gift in a token payment for their successful role in his fiancée's moral upbringing. In general, this was an East African Christian ceremony, as reflected in the content of the formal speeches and the prominent seats held by church officials during the ceremony. After the meal we left in Philip's car to the loud convivial cheers of our hosts; some of the women were ululating and singing.

The wedding mass took place in Nairobi several months later. This ceremony was held in the Catholic Cathedral, which was filled with about five hundred people. The homily given in English and KiSwahili stressed "equality" in marriage since "the woman came from Adam's rib, not his foot to be tramped on or his head to be superior." After the double ring ceremony, the wedding party exited slowly to regroup in a nearby reception hall. The best man was the groom's friend who had recently served as "spokesman" at the engagement ceremony. Various "grannies" could be seen outside the church dancing and ululating with joy. The reception hall was swelled to capacity, including the balcony seats as well as those on the main floor. The wedding party sat on the stage, where speeches were given by the four parents, previous teachers, and the bride's pastor. Refreshments (cake and soda) were served, after which the guests departed by passing through a reception line where a gift could be given while congratulating the newlyweds. Many guests from both families had traveled to Nairobi from the Western province from where the groom comes. Some members of the groom's family known to us resided with relatives in Nairobi. One of them expressed satisfaction that his rural relatives brought garden produce with them. The monetary expenses for the wedding, reception, and a "party" later that night were borne entirely by the groom and his family. Thus in this wedding, itself typical of others we have attended or read about in East Africa, one sees both persistence of tradition and cultural absorption of the modern. Delocalization can be seen in much of the ceremonial verbal content and events as described above. Moreover, this wedding was interreligious, and the wedding party contained members from several ethnic groups.

Events do not proceed quite so smoothly, however, when interethnic marriage is at issue. This is so since the "extended families" for whom a person's marriage is ideally the basis for group exchange and reciprocity between the families being joined cannot function if one partner does not have an extended family for whom social and economic interaction can, in principle, occur. It is this "group ideal," itself derived from tradition, which runs counter to a more recent ideology of individualism, free marital choice, and true love. Nevertheless, interethnic marriage is not only a modern phenomenon. Mere Kisekka (1976) found that when interethnic marriages occur in Uganda, it is believed they ideally should involve individuals from the same language family (e.g., Nilotic, Bantu, etc.). In some areas, intertribal marriage is long-standing, even across language barriers (e.g., Luo and Abaluyia). Among the Baganda, women are welcome from neighboring Bantu tribes because they will "bear children for the tribe," but women who marry out cannot do this and thus are discouraged from marrying into other tribes. What the delocalized present affords is the opportunity through travel and education for individuals, often with cosmopolitan values, to meet potential spouses from "distant" ethnic groups. One of our informants pointed out that the interethnic marriage question was of concern to his "elders" from his western province home who were concerned that he and others might marry a woman from the "the coast." They were not, however, concerned about his marrying a Luo from the West. On one occasion, a Kenyan friend (Kamba tribe) who works as a secretary said that she had never married. Since this was strange for a woman in her early thirties, we probed further. She said that some years ago she had become pregnant by a Nigerian man whom she loved, and he wanted to marry her. Her parents refused because they felt his relatives would also ask where the couple would go on holidays. What language would they speak? They advised her that it would be even better for her to marry a European since among them it is well-known that family and kinship are not important. It was this conversation that provided Philip

Kilbride a clue about the issue of extended family as a barrier to interethnic marriage. This issue, along with extreme differences in language and culture, are also of importance. Our informant was heartbroken and although she still loves her child's father, decided to follow the instructions of her parents. They have proven to be excellent providers for her child, who has been raised by them. Thus we see that interethnic marriage, a custom derived from tradition, exists nowadays in somewhat delocalized form. Traditional values about the significance of family involvement and cultural similarity are sometimes incompatible with outgroup marriage into now quite distant and culturally different ethnic groups, marriage that results from geographical boundary expansion in nationhood and international travel. In one of the more successful cases of polygyny known to us, there has been cooperation among co-wives from different tribal groups within Kenya as well as among these co-wives and one from Uganda. In chapter 10, we will present this case, but first we will examine the practice of polygyny which can, like interethnic marriage, be problematic in delocalized form when compared to its localized traditional counterpart.

10

POLYGYNY
A Modern Contradiction?

"He who did not see his mother when she was a girl might think that his father wasted cattle."

The institution of polygyny is closely related to delocalized extended family ideology, particularly the practice and belief that a "consanguineal core" is not as economically significant as in the past. Nevertheless, cultural practices concerning its perpetuity and symbolic elaboration persist, more often than not with stressful consequences for women. The levirate, for example, is a form of polygyny in which a dead man's wife is "inherited" by his surviving brother. (Incidently, this marital practice is described in the Old Testament.) In modern Kenya, this practice and polygyny in general have not received symbolic ideological support from many Christian churches or from schools. Such negative sanctions serve to exacerbate further anxieties already in evidence due to the reduced "function" of polygyny in a post-agrarian economy. For this reason, as we shall see below, many women now strongly oppose the levirate and other forms of polygyny.

We consider now the general status of polygyny in modern East African society. In a previous chapter, we introduced the problematic status of polygyny as it is portrayed in the news media. That material and our earlier ethnographic comments highlight the "reasons" why polygyny "made sense" in the agrarian past. Today, as we have seen, the institution is delocalized, although polygyny is not uncommon in the family experiences of numerous East Africans. Many young monogomists, Catholic priests, prominent citizens, and others, for example, have parents or other close relatives who are polygynists. Nevertheless, the society's cultural ambiguity over polygyny can be seen in the marriage laws of Kenya, where separate statutes exist for Christian marriages, Hindu marriages, Moslem marriages, and African customary law marriages. In general, the legal status of polygynous women in "customary" law is ambiguous with no clear law concerning their own and their children's rights of inheritance. In the late 1970s, there was a marriage bill, quite controversial, which attempted to outlaw "adultery," among many other provisions. This bill, which received general support from female politicians and many women, also attempted to improve the legal rights of women in polygynous situations. The bill, however, did not pass. On the cultural level, the ideal of "romantic love" and monogamy is quite strong among younger people, especially school students. We sponsored an essay contest in a local school where we asked seventh and eighth grade students to write an essay on either monogamy or polygyny. The vast majority wrote approvingly of monogamy and disparagingly of polygyny. The latter served as a kind of ideal "scapegoat" responsible for virtually all social evils in Kenya, including poverty, crime, prostitution, sloth, and violence.

Polygyny as a Cultural Value

We will present an example of "inter-cultural" experiential contact to illustrate how difficult it is for the Western mind to grasp polygyny while also showing how modern East Africans sometimes experience conflict in a delocalized behavioral environment. First, however, some more general examples of intercultural interaction might be helpful.

On several occasions Philip Kilbride has taken college students to Uganda and Kenya where they have lived with families in both urban and rural locations. Both students and their hosts had some preconceived expectations. For example, Afro-American students have generally found the experience of living in a country where all the political leaders are black to be a powerful experience at both a symbolic and affective level. Rural East Africans, on the other hand, sometimes expressed surprise that Afro-

Americans did not speak KiSwahili, since it is thought "natural" that all blacks can do so. White students inevitably spend a portion of their time (as we did) visiting "game parks," "Masai Mara" or similar "primitive" locations all assumed to be essential experiences in Africa (particularly by friends and relatives back home). Over the last twenty years, we have learned much from observing the interactive encounters between students and hosts just as our hosts have learned, no doubt, from observations of our encounters with students and Africans. One student, for example, was "surprisingly impressed" when Philip stopped an impending fight between East Africans and some European tourists by employing a strategy of cultural manipulation. This involved jumping up and starting to do *kiganda* dances (with rapid hip movements) with some prostitutes, thus reducing the mob to laughter and in some cases imitative dancing. Philip knew that the traditional dance generally evokes passionate response from Africans while the curiosity of a European doing so, or more precisely attempting to do so, fascinated everyone.

The topic of polygyny is one that has received no favorable comment that we can recall among the dozen or so students (all female) with whom we have intentionally discussed the subject. On occasion the subject has even evoked direct hostile "theoretical" commentary. This is so even though with no exception the students have been outstanding intellectuals with quite keen observational skills, and by training sympathetic to cultural difference. From our experience, there does appear to be a female bias against the institution of polygyny among modern European and, according to Ware (1979) African *educated* women too. Ware, for example, reported in a survey of studies that rarely have women even studied the subject. None of the women who have studied it has commented favorably about it and, to further restrict our information, the male writers on polygyny have themselves not usually considered the female point of view about it. Perhaps for this reason, men who interview men often write approvingly of polygyny (cf. Hillman 1975). Nevertheless there is nowadays considerable variation of opinion in East Africa, particularly between men and women.

The cultural gap between western "educated" female and East African male values was highlighted in a fascinating encounter that took place one evening over drinks in a Nairobi pub. The group included two students and a married man with whose family the students had been living for several weeks in an urban location. During that time the students had become quite close to their married female hostess. This was not surprising to us since she was in fact a charming woman, mother of both boys and girls, employed, and therefore in a position to support relatives back "home" and in town with occasional employment in her house. Her husband drove a car, held a prestigious job, and was perceived by all to be a responsible father. Like most men, he regularly drank at a pub before coming home from work and "missed" many evening meals. In general, he insisted on "respectful" public submission from wife and children. In our opinion, the husband is a person of the highest caliber, one who in our observations over ten years is a fine person, a judgment shared by his colleagues at work and in his home community. In fact, the students liked him very much, if not his "husbandly" role, which did without doubt depart from their Western ideal. Moreover, in the opinion of one student, he seemed to her (perhaps correctly) to "favor" his son over his daughters by giving him more attention.

A value difference on marriage became clearly apparent to us when our friend stated to the group that he was contemplating taking a second wife. In response to our prompting, he gave the following reasons. First, his mother in the village wanted him to do so. She was alone; there was an abundance of unmarried girls, *and* land needed to be farmed. She could not do the work alone, and moreover she also wanted more grandchildren. Why was her son so selfish to live in the city so as to forget about her at home? He further pointed out that his wife was opposed, since he needed to make sure there was enough money for his present children's school fees. Our friend said he told his wife that he would ensure that his second wife "stayed" on the farm. An African man with us voiced his support for monogamy by commenting that this would be unlikely since she too would want to come to the city. Philip jumped in again and, as one not hostile to polygyny (in the right circumstances), pointed out that our friend would actually be conforming to the wishes of a woman, his mother, should he take a second wife. Would not a "feminist" perspective look compassionately on her position too?

Philip then decided to introduce a further cross-cultural dilemma into the discussion, by now heated and animated. He asked what the group thought about the practice of two men being given permission to marry and adopt children. This was then under discussion as a legal option in the United States. The students thought that this was a fine idea, fully consistent with their "liberal" point of view (hopefully enhanced by anthropological training!). The several African men who had been divided on the polygyny question all listened in stunned silence before asking Philip to repeat himself. After he did so, they broke into loud laughter and, after quieting down, said this was impossible; it was "unnatural." "You mean you, Philip, and I would marry?" "Quite impossible." While sitting in the back of a pick-up truck on the way home, the authors could still hear our Kenyan friends laughing loudly over the to them comical ideas discussed earlier.

This cross-cultural encounter was an experiential opportunity made possible in interactive ethnography where encounters are genuine, spontaneous, and unrehearsed. That the conflictive nature of polygyny, so strikingly revealed in this personalized encounter, is quite real in African modernizing society will be seen in other materials to be presented below. According to our materials, its frequency as an experiential problem is not inconsequential.

The practice of polygyny is still, on the whole, an optional cultural ideal for most men and numerous women in East Africa. There is considerable evidence, however, that this ideal is under serious attack, with the status of "co-wife" in particular giving way to a female preference to be involved in a monogamous marriage only. We will in the next chapter provide some data on the "evil eye," itself interpreted as a salient form of indirect aggression among co-wives, emanating from commonly felt "envy." The co-wife relationship is, for example, often nowadays designated by the term "my rival." It is likely that modern-day conflict observed among co-wives has greatly increased from previous generations where social conditions were much more reinforcing of the institution and where women had fewer options than today.

The rate of polygyny varies throughout rural East Africa, although the value is ubiquitous. Monogamy, of course, is the actual dominant form of marriage in all areas, a fact supported by the belief that only wealthy men should have multiple wives. We found *no* examples of polygyny in a rural parish of 109 households in Uganda, although we know of some Baganda polygynists. A low rate of Kiganda polygyny may be due to some vestigial tendency for polygyny to be associated primarily with the kingship, where wives served as important centralizing political-economic links between the Kabaka and clans. In the early nineteenth century, for example, kings had as many as 20,000 wives and armies as large as 50,000 troops. These figures are obviously proof of the economic context of polygyny. In our work in Western Kenya, we found that the Babukusu tended to have polygynous marriages in greater proportion than, for example, the Marogoli, a finding also reported fifty years ago by Wagner (1956). The Samia have many polygynous homes, sometimes with fifteen wives. In the Nzoia area, our census shows only four wives as the highest, with about five to ten percent of the homes having a polygynous union. Our census data revealed, interestingly, an economic factor in the rate of polygyny in Nzoia. In the "richer" large-farm schemes (from ten to hundreds of acres), there was a *higher* proportion of polygynous homes compared to the "poorer" rural area just mentioned above. This is so even though the schemes are, on the whole, more modern than the smaller farms as measured by such things as material goods, education, and occupation.

Delocalized Polygyny: Local Views

We now consider ideals about polygyny by showing what our respondents reported as its advantages and disadvantages in response to our systematic questioning. What our respondents believe are the "ideal" characteristics of a good co-wife will then be discussed. Following this, we will turn from ideals to the actual experience of polygyny as revealed in the lives of several of our best informants. In these lives will be seen the importance of economic factors as shown here from our surveys. It is the breakdown of economic conditions favorable to polygyny that has proven the practice to be less functional in the modern world.

As part of an interview concerning family relationships administered to forty-one married males and females (M = 18, F = 23) from Nzoia and Samia, Janet Kilbride and her Kenyan assistants asked "What are the advantages of polygyny?" Some of the married people were monogamous (N = 11), but we consider here all married people together since all monogamists may in principle become in time involved in polygyny. We received a mean number of responses of 2.84 for each person, with a range between one and four responses. Responses were clustered in eight areas of concern to families with only a few respondents stating that they couldn't answer because they didn't know (N = 2, one male, one female) or that there was no advantage to polygyny (N = 2, one male and one female). The eight areas which were derived from their responses included: (1) economics, (2) protection, (3) reproduction, (4) child care, (5) emotional factors, (6) magico-religious activity, (7) influential power/politics, and (8) sexual domains. Table 14 presents a brief description of the types of responses that

Table 14 Advantages of Polygyny Code

Category	Descriptive Examples
Economic	Quicker, cheaper, easier labor; more wealth, help for extended family
Protection	Defense from attack by outsiders
Reproductive	Better chance of having more children of both sexes; better chance of getting a good child who will help you in old age
Child care	Someone to care for co-wife's children in case she is away visiting, is working, is sick, or dies
Emotional	Less bereavement by husband and less fear of being left alone when one wife dies; co-wife makes up for what is lacking in other wife in terms of love, trust, pride, greed, etc.; stronger family ties if husband is a good leader
Magico-Religious	Less fear of witchcraft, poisoning, evil-eye; one way of serving God who said to go and multiply
Power/Political	Personal fame or influence; nation-building; increased labor, defence, population; better intertribal communication
Sexual	Enjoyment of different types of lovemaking; extramarital affairs of husband are fewer; wife has more of a chance for extramarital affairs; husband remains strong sexually and physically from not having to do a lot of gardening
Don't Know	
No Advantages	

we included in each category. There was strong agreement (31 of 41 respondents = 75.61%) between both married males and married females that economic factors were the most important perceived advantage of being polygynous (males 77.7%, females 73.9%). Because polygynous families are usually large, there are plenty of laborers to farm the land so that one need not pay wage laborers. Labor is also, in general, more readily available when needed. Traditionally polygynous families were ideally wealthy families, and this is still the ideal today. With a larger labor force, more food is available for family consumption and marketing. Thus there is more money for school fees and for helping relatives of extended families.

The second most frequently mentioned advantage of polygyny concerned personal and political power (17 out of 41 = 41.5%; females = 47.8%, males = 33.3%). By having many children one becomes well-known and thus locally politically influential. There is also the increased possibility that one will give birth to a "big man" of the future (e.g., president, ministers). Married males considered emotional factors to be of equal importance with political influence (33.3%). Men considered having several wives as security against being left alone with children to care for if one wife died. A co-wife may also be used as a "rival" by the husband to keep a lazy, proud, or greedy wife in her place. It is thought that a husband who is a good leader and treats his wives "equally" will have a family that gets along well together.

Married women reported the protective area as an advantage the next most frequently after economic concerns (34.8%). A large family was viewed as a means of physical protection against thieves and other enemies. Women also felt that if one had problems, these could be solved within the polygynous family with no need to involve "outsiders." Only 8.7% of married women, however, considered emotional factors related to the advantages of polygyny.

These same Samia and Nzoia respondents also were asked what they considered to be disadvantages of polygyny. The major disadvantage reported was an emotional one for both married males and females (87.8%). The major emotional problems involved jealousy, envy, and hatred among co-wives and their children, usually as a result of the perception that the husband's love and resources were not shared equally among wives and children. Related to this is the second most often reported disadvantage of polygyny: that of magico-religious activity (41.5%). Witchcraft, poisons, charms, herbs, and the evil eye are all means of attempting to rectify "unfair" treatment by the husband or co-wives or a means of obtaining a greater piece of the economic pie for oneself. Among unmarried individuals, the magico-religious and reproductive areas were third in order of disadvantages (23.5%). The third disadvantage of polygyny mentioned by married people (34.1%) and the second disadvantage mentioned by single respondents (52.9%) was the economic factor. In this case, economics referred to inadequate income, food, work, and/or land.

Many of the same factors are seen as possible advantages and disadvantages of polygyny. One can conclude, therefore, that the decision for or against polygyny has little to do with polygyny *per se,* but with the current economic, political, emotional, protective, or magico-religious factors mentioned above that serve to influence the quality of the marital relationship. To be successful, the advantages must obviously outweigh the disadvantages. With delocalization, the advantages of polygyny for many Kenyans are clearly decreasing. This will be illustrated in our case materials to be discussed below. As we shall see, the position of co-wife is particularly problematic nowadays. Present circumstances simply do not permit her to "live up" to her ideal role. The same respondents as above were asked to describe the most important characteristics of a good co-wife. There was overwhelming agreement that a good co-wife is one who is "respectful," "obedient," and "hard-working." Perhaps her profile can best be portrayed by a quote from one respondent who said that a good co-wife was "like a daughter of the husband because she does all jobs that would be done by the firstborn plus she shares a bed with the husband."

The major problem with polygyny in the modern world is that the institution no longer receives careful moral scrutiny through communal sanction of localized clan, community, and family. Contemporary marriage is much more a matter of personal choice than was once the case. Sometimes, therefore, people enter into polygyny in violation of the traditional idea that only wealthy men or men able to be sufficient "providers" should do so. In one instance, for example, public health officials and Philip Kilbride visited a house in Western Kenya where the "man of the house" was impoverished. He could not afford bean seeds and the rains had destroyed his maize. His wife and their four children were hungry and also without school fees. Nevertheless, the husband had just "chased away" a second wife (and their child) because he "could not maintain them," he said laughingly. This man with no animals and one acre of land had "tried" polygyny because he had observed that "big" or "important" men did so. In his failure, he felt he had learned his lesson!

A second major problem with polygyny in the modern world as we have seen is that contemporary moral entrepreneurs of church and state are ambiguous about or usually hostile to the institution. This is so in spite of its widespread current practice. As stated above, our school-student essays overwhelmingly condemned polygyny and blamed it for many categories of social problems. Moreover, press accounts, also reviewed earlier, revealed a negative public image. A third pattern that emerges from our material is a growing gender division (as in family planning and other family issues). Men are seen on the whole to be more favorable to the practice than are women, especially educated women. Whether this was always the case is not known. The Baganda word for co-wife is *kujaa* (similar to the word jealousy), and "jealousy" is certainly structurally understandable given the economic significance of polygyny. Sorting out precisely what conflict is due to polygyny or just plain marriage in any form is impossible. Many East Africans today, however, hold up "monogamy" as the ideal, invariably thought to be free of conflict and jealousy, and a haven for cooperation. How much of this is school and church propaganda or grounded in actual practice is hard to determine. In general, our material shows that East Africans *now* (1) have both positive and negative memories about "growing up in a polygynous home"; (2) report both in the past and the present more favorable impressions about life in a polygynous home as parents or as children if the family is rich compared to poorer homes; (3) report conflict as often acute between or among co-wives, especially over real or imagined economic injustices and (4) state that powerful men still aspire to polygyny. The latter's success at it would seem, in fact, to correlate somewhat with their actual economic power. We turn now to specific case material to illustrate these themes.

Polygynous Lives: Wealth and Polygyny

We first consider the case of a high-school-educated Ugandan woman now about forty years of age. Her father is a wealthy Ugandan agricultural officer who went to school in Kenya. He regularly employs large numbers of porters and farms hundreds of acres for cash and subsistence. He has twenty-five children with four wives, although only three wives are discussed below. The following account illustrates general family relations in a home that was overall viewed as favorable by our informant as reported here in her own words. (Pseudonyms are used throughout this book.)

> *Marjorie*. I remember seeing my father bringing a new wife. When she came my mother was taken by my father to my home district where my father built a shamba, and she stayed there while the new wife was staying with my father in the place where he was working. The place where my mother was now staying was near the school where my sisters were boarding, so they could come home during the weekends. They could come to see my mother.
>
> When I passed to Class 6, I went to study where my father was working. By then he had two more wives. All these women had children. We were all going to school together, staying in the same house. We were doing everything as sisters. I like my stepmothers; they were good. I never know who my father loves best, whether my mother or the others. But I knew he gave "respect" to my mother,

being the first wife. This was according to the traditional way. The wives gave respect according to how one comes, first come, second come, and so on. These women gave so much respect to my mother. Myself and the stepsisters, we don't say, "Who is your mother?" We are all like sisters and brothers.

My father's wives had many gardens. They could plant six acres of cotton for the wives. There was no famine in my family. It was a large family. I used to go to the garden with my stepmother. I could tell them a lot of stories, and they laughed so much. I went back to my mother's house for holidays where I stayed with my two sisters. My mother was so strict with me! It was my future. She had to teach me cooking, responsibilities like doing dishes, all as a woman's duties. My favorite relative was my mother's elder sister. We used to like spending holidays at her house. She gave us a lot to eat so we liked her so much. She had only one son, but mother had ten of us. When my father went to see auntie I cried when he left, I liked him so much.

That was all before I started schooling. Then I went to stay with father as I said before. Actually, I stayed with my stepmother, next to mother. She was a bit bad when she came. She used to give me so much to do. But I didn't mind. I never thought about my mother. My mother never liked us so much, I don't know why. When my father went on safari I used to miss him. One time he brought me a puppy for a pet. Mother came for a visit and I wanted to go back with her but she couldn't take me because father is away. My father could discipline us. He never beat me, but my mother was always beating me. It was my elder brother, however, who was very strict. With him it was all study and no time for playing! My elder sister was responsible for me in school. She made me do all things like eating, studying, and dressing.

The above nicely illustrates the "pragmatic" aspect of polygynous life. Residential decisions, for example, were made in conformity with family educational and farming needs. Child-rearing proceeded according to fixed ideas of kinship and gender hierarchy. Polygyny was thus part of a wider kinship ideology of sibling duty, co-wife cooperation, and male economic "provider" capability. In fact, polygyny delocalized from this wider socio-cultural context would be an institution devoid of meaning.

The following narrative was collected from a boy in his mid-twenties for whom growing up in a home where his father was not wealthy has left a residue of some unfavorable memories about polygyny. We now report his impressions in his own words.

> *Robert: Growing up in a Polygynous Family.* I was born in 1963 in the Ludodo area [and come] from a polygynous family. My father is married to four wives, my mother being the second wife. Actually when seven years old, I started experiencing that it is a home of many. So it forced me to ask some of the relevant questions. How comes that we are so many like this? Who is my really mother? But all the questions were not answered in the way I wanted. Because they forced me to call the first and second wife mother. But eventually I came to realize that I am with one father who is married to four wives of different tribes.
>
> When [I was] eight years old, I was forced to accompany my brothers [of that first wife] to school (Primary School) which was very far (ten kilometres) to join Standard 1. From there I came across many hardships, such as being beaten by children of the first wife, forcing me to carry for them their books to and from the school and also forcing me to borrow for them money from my mother for their lunch. Due to those problems I decided not to continue with the course, but that was not the case [because] I was transferred to another school which was nearby, [the] Primary School where I complete from Standard 1 to Class 4.
>
> From there I was forced to join another school that is Primary, now under the control of the fourth wife. Actually I came to realize that it was a problem to some great extent. Sometimes I was forced to sweep the house, cook, look after the livestock, clean the house, and clean the inner clothes of the children of the fourth wife, and also sometimes I was forced not to get lunch until the suppertime. Therefore, polygyny is a problem insofar as I have expressed concern over it. When doing something, such as welcoming my colleagues (friends), my stepmother would say rough words such as "Do you think that or this is your home?" or "this is not a house of your mother." It made me feel that I was born somewhere else but was now under the control of another person.
>
> The advantages which I have experienced under polygyny are that with work like planting, cooperation works, and when one of the family is sick, contributions occur in great number. Biblically, that is

a time for showing love, peace, and unity as the commandment says to love your neighbor. Another advantage is that barrenness cannot occur. African tribes, particularly the Bunyala, believe that immortality is recaptured in one's issue (offspring). They believe that the more wives one gets, the more children he expects, and the more chances of purportedly capturing immortality. If robbers have appeared at the compound, the polygymous family can react seriously to defend whatever is to happen. Also, no money is wasted employing some people to defend the home. And some believe that polygyny is a sign of wealth.

Some of the disadvantages that I have experienced in a polygynous family are so many. When my mother is given something by father such as money for buying new clothes that is the time when rough words come from the first, third, and fourth wives that their children also need clothes or whatever she has gotten. Who to educate becomes also a problem because of financial difficulties in obtaining school fees. Feeding the family becomes impossible, hence stealing other people's properties results sometimes. Clothing also becomes a hard task for such a family. As most people in Kenya depend basically on farming, a shortage of land to plant some crops which earn cash also brings arguments. Jealousy generates among such a family. For instance, maybe one of the sons of the second or third wife is employed somewhere. The rest of the wives complain that what he gets is only to feed his "really" mother (i.e., biological mother).

Actually the favorite members of my family are mother and my elder sister. What made me to say that mother is a favorite member among our family is that she has struggled a lot for my education and also for my clothes. She always says that what she has she must share with her son. And on the side of elder sister, she stepped down so that my mother would have adequate money for educating me.

Some of the things that I have experienced basically on the side of eating are that when eating we do not assemble at one particular place, each mommy with her children. This results in jealousy because the wives cook different types of food. And also one may be eating only one type of food, such as *Ugali,* without changing. So it results in admiring the food of the other mommies. There is no particular time of eating. Food like loaves of bread, meat, and chapati are eaten when celebrating particular events.

Actually there is no sharing of clothes because of maybe ruining them. Some are so careless while others like different types of clothes. So sharing is limited.

The family always pays visits to friends and relatives. They carry some gifts so that the one being visited would feel consoled.

Each mother works on her gardening without sharing the work, and what she gets she does not share. During the time of holiday, the family assembles together and arranges how they are going to share (in eating). That is the time of unity. Harvesting, each mother works on her own farm, and what she gets she stores for herself.

During the time of famine, actually, that is the time of selfishness; each mother finds a way of feeding her own children without looking sideways (without sharing). It was last year (1984) when the same problem (famine) appeared. Each mother suffered a lot. Then father decided to disappear for a period of two months.

On my side (in my opinion), I find that to be a polygynist is another way of adding problems so that I do not like to be.

Robert's description of his view of his polygynous family illustrates many of the advantages and disadvantages mentioned by our survey sample. Advantages included available labor, protection against enemies, and child care in times of emergency such as ill health. Disadvantages included emotional ones such as jealousy and envy among co-wives and their children as well as economic self-interest, especially in times of famine. Delocalization can be seen in his father's marrying wives from different tribes and in his "disappearing" for several months during a time when there was a shortage of food.

We will now illustrate the importance of economic considerations in polygynous marriage by describing a marriage context characterized by an overextended resource base, if no actual poverty. Later we will contrast this with the case of a wealthier polygynist family.

Our informant, here referred to as John, is currently married to four wives, and has thirty-one children thus far. We presented the view of his son Robert above. Three wives live together in a large compound with their children and the grandchildren of the senior wife. Each wife has her own hut for herself and her children. The youngest wife and her children live some fifteen miles away in their own house. John is a car mechanic who earns a regular, semi-professional salary. He is not "poor" by comparative standards in Kenya, but his resources are not adequate for the large, polygynous family that he seeks to maintain. We present here some of John's own thoughts about his marital history, material obtained by Philip Kilbride in an interview in response to prepared questions.

John: A Polygynist. We married in 1961. No, then I didn't think I would become a polygynist. Millie (pseudonym) had children; everything was fine. I decided to marry after I moved to Nairobi for a period of seven years. I visited the "reserve" every month. In 1969, Millie agreed that I should marry Harriet. She helped me in Nairobi with the housework. Millie gave me four cows which I gave to Harriet's father. Harriet is from my tribe and then lived on the reserve. I knew her brother in Nairobi where we lived in the same house. He said, "You are a good man. Take my sister to marry." I married Mary (third wife) in 1974. I worked with her father in Eldoret. I had helped her father purchase some land, so he said, "You are a good man. Take my child to marry." She was very pretty with very beautiful breasts. In 1979 I married Jane. I worked with her father. One day his wife was sick in hospital so I gave him 800 shillings for her care. When his wife got well, he said, "Take my daughter," so I went to buy some land for her father. She was beautiful like Mary.

Some of the good things about polygyny are as follows. When one wife has her "monthly" I go to another one. When one is angry with me I can go to another and get good food and good treatment. When visitors come they get served faster. There is a good division of labor around the house. On the negative side, I could mention the problem of getting land since each wife needs land for her children. There are multiple demands, one wants food, another clothes. Really difficult is the demand for school fees and uniforms.

Overall, I think the man with several wives is happier than the man with one. He can go to several fathers-in-law for help. I think a woman married to a monogamist is happier than one married to a polygynist. A woman wants *everything* from her husband's pockets. If he does not have money, the wife will run away. I also think monogamy is best for children. This is because of my problems in getting school fees. Nevertheless, most of my friends and relatives are polygynists. My grandfather had two wives, but my father has only one. If a man is a polygynist, two or four is the best number. Three brings trouble. Two will be friends, and the third is left out.

I want no more wives since the burdens are great. There are now a lot of children to support given my income. The obligation of a good father is to educate his children and feed and clothe them. The wife should take care of her children and husband by keeping a good clean house and clothes. She should care for my mother and visitors at large. Co-wives should share cooking and washing clothes and should care for each other's children when necessary. A wife should be consulted before bringing a co-wife; I asked them all for permission.

The only big problem that I have experienced is disagreements over things I give to the children. The stepmothers want the same for her children too. This is true for such items as clothes and a radio. I disagree with them over this issue and also over the amount of work each does in her shamba. Sometimes, I think too little work gets done. Nevertheless, I love all of my wives equally. I sleep with each on a regular schedule. Four days with each one. I prefer that my unmarried sons have only one wife because they have no work. For my daughters, I want them to marry a rich man, preferably a monogamist, but to be rich is the important thing.

We will see below that John's wives do not perceive his marital history in exactly the same way as he does. His narrative does, nevertheless, recognize the crucial role of "riches" in the interpersonal nexus of the multifaceted polygynous home. In general, he is aware of the problematic nature of his low wealth and its effect on his marriages, but these perceptions are more acute among his wives and children. Therefore we will now present the wives' points of view in response to formal and informal interviews with them by Janet Kilbride. We will provide extended comments from his first wife, Millie, with brief comments to follow about the other wives. The latter materials are abstracted from our interviews with these subsequent three wives.

Millie: The First Wife. I was not consulted about my husband's decision to have all his additional wives. The disadvantages of marrying a polygamous man are the shortages of school fees. When I was alone, there was smooth running of our affairs, but now many of my children are running short of school fees, most of them stopping in Standard 7. In polygyny, the husband has a problem dividing things equally—otherwise co-wives will feel jealous. In monogamy, everything runs smoothly. When a child is sick he will always care for it; or if school fees are wanted, he will always provide easily. In our case, polygyny is difficult because we all stay in the same compound and dig in the same fields. Each wife should have her own home and land so each will be able to accumulate wealth in their various places.

In polygyny, the best number of wives is two. This helps cooperation between wives. If one dies, the other can care for all the children and her husband. The evil eye or witchcraft is common in polygynous homes due to jealousy among co-wives. The levirate is fine for young wives, but not for first wives like me. We are older and don't need a husband's brother to protect us; we have grown sons for that. Sisters as co-wives is also the best. Sisters will usually stick together.

We quarrel here mainly over the children. Sometimes when our children fight each other the mothers will take sides and will start quarreling. Another thing is that our husband will be seen with something going into one of the homes. If another wife sees that, she will feel jealousy and say, "Am I not a wife like you? Why is everything being brought into your house alone?" Then fighting starts. Quarrels end when one invites the other to come for breakfast or to share some meat bought from the store.

My husband gets annoyed if his food is not ready or his water for bathing. It is his right to beat his wife for such misbehaviors. My husband has beaten me before because I deserved it. He must also discipline the children, but he does not beat them.

I liked it better when I was the only wife. Now with all these co-wives my husband's money is not enough. My husband took additional wives because his relatives wanted a child yearly, not every two years with me alone. I was happy about Harriet, the first co-wife, but not Mary the third wife. She was brought home without my consent. She was hidden from me. With too many wives there was not enough land and so not enough money for school fees. I did not attend the marriage of Mary, and I would not accept the idea. She was jealous of me. I also didn't like the idea of John's marriage to Jane. One time when I stopped at Jane's compound to rest after going to the dispensary for treatment something terrible happened. I was laying on my co-wife's bed but got up to go to the toilet. While there, my co-wife threw a pan of boiling water on the bed while I watched from the doorway. I grabbed my child and ran home.

I still sleep with my husband. He goes into one of our houses when he comes home and does so in rotation. When I am sick, it is Harriet who helps me. She is my favorite co-wife because we come from the same village. She helped me deliver some of my children. My children and I own land, about one acre for each child. Jane has no land. Mary sometimes practices witchcraft against me, but I pray that the evil goes back to her. All in all I am pleased with my choice of husband, but I prefer monogamy. I am the mother of eight children.

Millie's co-wife, Harriet, with whom she is on very good terms, is the mother of eleven children. Harriet knew her husband was married, so she entered into a polygynous situation knowingly. She was persuaded to do so by her father, but there are problems. There are not enough things to go around. Her views are similar to those of Millie. She reports, additionally, that her husband visits the compound every weekend, remaining during the week at his workplace and living there with Jane. Harriet does not know his salary, and says he favors girl children equally among his wives.

Harriet was much happier when there were only two wives. In fact, she says she could have almost cut Mary with a Panga, so opposed was she to the idea of a third wife. The first time she met Jane, the fourth wife, they had a fight with their fists. She had gone to Jane's house to get some money from John when the quarrel broke out. She says she had a "right" to be there because she needed soap.

Millie helps with Harriet's children; nowadays Mary does, too, but less frequently, and Millie is still her favorite. Harriet prefers monogamy because she has experienced a lot of suffering in her marriage.

Mary, the third wife, is the mother of six children. She knew that her husband was married when she married him, although she now favors monogamy. She says that the primary disadvantage of polygyny is getting enough food for her children.

Mary, like her co-wives, values support for her own natal family from her husband, but he is not able to do so adequately. For this reason, she believes that even a rich man who is polygynous should not have more than two wives; instead he should help his extended family (e.g., in-laws).

Mary's husband doesn't pay school fees, so she pays herself by selling vegetables at the local market. She now regrets having "fallen in love" and subsequently eloping at age fifteen with John, against her parents' wishes. John took a fourth wife against her wishes, but when she asked him about it she was told she had no right to ask.

Mary occasionally visits and is visited by Jane, whom she now likes because she has children, a mutual concern. She doesn't know how Millie and Harriet feel about her "inside," but she has no ill will toward them. She has never practiced witchcraft against her co-wives, but is suspicious that Millie might have used witchcraft against John. Recently he came to her house from Millie's and began to beat her with a lantern. He then apologized, and said that he didn't know why he had hit her. She then realized that he often beats her after coming from Millie's house. She will talk this problem over with her mother.

Jane, the fourth wife, reported that John indicated to her that he suspected that Mary used money he had given her for school fees to practice witchcraft against Millie. Someone had reported to him that Mary had been seen "roaming" far from her home, suggesting a sickness as a symptom of bewitchment.

Jane is the mother of six children; her youngest daughter is under a year old. John had given her father beer when they worked in the same company, and she married after John negotiated with her parents. He promised to pay more, but gave her family only 200 shillings (around $30). He hid the fact that he already had three wives.

Jane ran away to her uncle's house, but after a week her father found her and forced her to marry John. She doesn't like polygyny because there is no money for school fees, and her husband doesn't have enough land. She is beaten by John if she asks him for money; it is his "right" to do so. John, however, never beats the children. Jane's father and brother are disappointed because John has not ever given what he promised for her bride price. Her brother recently came to ask about it, but her husband always "goes away" when he does. She likes all of her co-wives. They all care for each other's children.

The above accounts indicate support at the "experiential" level for data described earlier from our survey. These accounts, in addition, illustrate the ill effects of modernization as argued in this book. We can, for example, observe in the marital life of John and his co-wives the significant cultural themes identified earlier. First, the *economic factor* pervades much of the conscious discourse of these individuals. The idea that the husband should be a "provider" is the most consistent value that John is not able to satisfy in his marital life. There is not sufficient land for each wife to have her own garden, nor does he have nearly enough money to provide for clothing and school fees, a modern necessity. Economic delocalization has therefore brought about circumstances quite unfavorable to polygyny on the scale desired by John. Second, the *reproductive-childcare* concerns of John and his co-wives are clear. The welfare of all their children is valued, even though in practice such cannot be achieved. One can even beat one's wife, but he should not beat the children. Next, the *emotional tone* of this marriage is quite negative, but not hysterically so. Conflict and negative affect are clear; however, when we made numerous spot observations at the main compound, we never observed any overt aggression. Finally, the *magico-religious belief system* seemingly provides a fertile channel for the expression of indirect aggression through suspected witchcraft practices. Nevertheless, violence is not absent, as we have seen, in the relations among co-wives and between John and each wife.

The idea of polygyny is itself an ambivalent one for John and his wives. The wives are opposed to it in practice, although not so much in the abstract as a moral imperative. Both John and the wives do point out, however, that the Catholic church, of which they are members, is opposed to polygyny. John prefers polygyny for men mostly for what we termed emotional reasons.

This family's experience would support the widely held idea that "odd" numbers of co-wives are not desirable. Mary is certainly the odd person out in John's family among the three wives living in the same compound. John also seems to have practiced more deception as his marital career developed. As a person delocalized from the "reserve" through occupation and residence, he more successfully promised things through deception to prospective in-laws and subsequently failed to fulfill his obligations—not a likely occurrence several generations ago. The moral obligations of the polygynist cannot, in his case, be monitored by local people very effectively.

Nevertheless, conflict is to no little extent the result of discrepancies between the narrations of a husband and wife (or wives) about their marriage. These accounts are particularly susceptible to "social construction" and selective memory (cf. Burger 1977). Modern Kenya society frequently holds polygyny to be "wrong," so that as our informants evaluate for us their "polygynous" careers, some negative reconstruction is not surprising. We see in John's marriage the growing rift between men and women over polygyny. His account is *more favorable* than that of each of his wives. Millie, who enjoys some "senior wife" status is also more favorable than are her younger co-wives. Nevertheless, the woman's overall experience is basically more negative than the man's on the polygyny question, as we see in this marriage and the material discussed earlier. Economics, rather than sexual jealousy, a Western idea, is the primary determinant of this gender rift in value and experience. We turn now to consider another case in which the "woman's point of view" on polygyny is provided, including in this case an example of intertribal marriage and widowhood.

A Polygynist Widow

A not-uncommon factor in polygyny is intertribal marriage. This is common for example, in Western Province, where interethnic contact is generally quite high. There is considerable Luo-Abaluyia intermarriage, a sometimes problematic practice given the many "ceremonial" obligations among Luo in comparison to some of the Abaluyia groups, such as the Samia. We will later see that Samia-Luo intermarriage sometimes produces a broken "moralnet" for some abused children, who are caught outside the moralnet of ethnic group, clan, and community when parents prove irresponsible. Traditionally, Luo men were welcome suitors given their large cattle herds, and wealthy Samia men could earn prestige by acquiring a Luo wife known to fetch considerable cattle. Delocalization has made this prestige value difficult to realize.

In one home well known to us in Western Province, a polygynous marriage involving modern contradictions can serve as an illustrative case of delocalization. A Luo widow now lives alone with her children, two girls in secondary school and a son in primary school. She is a devout Roman Catholic who, for this reason, refused to be inherited by her dead husband's brother. She now survives on several acres of land and occasional assistance (e.g., school fees) from the church. She had married her deceased husband, who was a rich Samia man, because cows were needed at home for her three brothers, who obtained wives with her progeny price at marriage. She is not unfavorable to polygyny because co-wives make work easier, and when she is away from home her children would be fed. She favors monogamy, however, because then the husband's role of "provider" is not divided. "Understanding" is higher, she assumes, in monogamous homes. She refers to her husband's third wife (the Samia first wife is dead) as "my rival" and believes that this wife uses witchcraft for her downfall. Although she married a man who was not from her Luo tribe, she wants her daughters to marry Luo boys because of the importance of carrying on "tradition."

The third wife chose to marry into a polygynous home because such homes are comparatively rich. She chose this home because her now-dead husband and his family had herds of cattle. She likes polygyny because the co-wife cares for her children when she goes on extended trips. She believes, nevertheless, that monogamy offers better family planning and thus a better opportunity to prevent children from becoming thieves (due to lack of resources and discipline). As a Samia, she does not like intertribal marriage because of the difficulty of participating in Luo ritual.

We see in the above case some of the "ambivalent" opinions held by many polygynists, particularly women. The church is a key moral force in opposition to polygyny. Sometimes, as in the present case, it even makes it economically possible for some women to avoid levirate remarriage. Interethnic marriage also has the potential for being problematic, but to what extent modernization might make this more common than previously remains unclear. We conclude our discussion of polygynous lives by considering two cases involving "wealthy" men where polygynous marriages are much more favorably perceived than in the cases so far reviewed.

The Big Man as a Polygynist

Both husbands to follow have sufficient capital measured in shillings to sustain polygyny in modern economic terms. Land and cattle unconverted to money are no longer sufficient as a utilitarian means of wealth adequate to sustain polygyny when a modern life-style is also valued. The first case concerns a man who has also successfully married across several tribes. This would suggest that intertribal marriage need not be problematic if the economic basis of the marriage is sound.

Our first "wealthy" man, whom we shall call Joseph, is a rural Kenyan polygynist. Joseph is actually now wealthy because he has judiciously managed his marriages to maximize the monetary wealth potential of what is a "polygynous family business." Joseph is a vibrant, energetic Luyia man in his late fifties. He speaks with enthusiastic optimism about his "plans" to educate his children. He was hopeful that his friendship with us would translate into educational opportunity in America for them. Currently, he lives in the Kitale area of Western Province along with his four wives. His first wife is a Muganda. They met while Joseph worked for the East African Corporation in Uganda. She now lives on a 58-acre farm and is responsible for producing food for herself and subsequent co-wives married by Joseph. He now resides not far from his first wife's farm on a three-acre plot with his other three wives and some of their children. This residence is, in fact, a small trade center in its own right located in a semirural location. His second wife, a Kikuyu, runs a general store (*dukka*) next to her son's tailor shop. A third wife, a Marogoli, operates a nursery school there. The complex also has a dispensary employing a nurse and a mid-wife who are both from the same tribe as the first wife. Behind the public buildings are several residential cement structures. These are prosperous homes with such things as radios, record players, and soft leather chairs.

Joseph has twenty-three children, some of whom work "in the business" (one daughter, for example, acquired skills as a seamstress). The homes usually contain one or another of his school-age children, home for holidays or from nearby schools. His children also number at least one educated at the university level. This daughter and her stepbrother, who runs the tailor shop, are well-mannered, gregarious, and articulate. In our discussions with them, we found them to be quite well adjusted, responsible and eager to achieve success in modern terms (e.g., education). They report some conflict at home but nothing one would not expect in any marriage, be it monogamous or polygamous. They stated that Joseph does have some problems satisfying all of his children's needs but also observed that he "managed" his home well. Each child, for example, was consciously placed with a stepmother to minimize conflict. KiSwahili is used as the common family language, so that individual tribal languages are unknown to the children, thus minimizing speaking "secretly." All the children regularly work on the large farm maintained by the senior wife. Absent in Joseph's family, as far as we could tell, were persistent concerns about witchcraft and wife-beating, commonly observed in polygynous unions with less favorable economic foundations than that of Joseph.

We now turn to another polygynous arrangement, this one being a wealthy man's solution to the modern preference for monogamy. Our informant, "Paul," is the same man described in an earlier chapter as a modern businessman, one who uses traditional conversational means of sociability to achieve success in the modern world. In the course of his marital career, he in time (fifteen years) acquired a large number of girlfriends, one of whom he set up in a home and provided with a business. He has also had a child with her. Paul's marriage to his first wife is a "Christian" marriage, but he considers himself to be a "polygynist" even though he cannot officially marry his second wife. Paul is presently "divorced" from his second wife, who has subsequently remarried in a "ring wedding" another prominent man.

In the fifteen years or so since the "business trip" described in chapter 3, Paul has become quite wealthy. He holds financial interests in a commercial fruit farm and several entertainment clubs as well as having joint business interests with investors from abroad. He remains committed to business success with the same intensity of earlier years when he used to "dream" (literally) about his business activities frequently. He has survived in Uganda in spite of numerous political upheavals primarily because he is essentially "apolitical," although he is nationalistic and proud of his African heritage. In another problematic context, he would be a superb example of a successful businessman, a social role that has received comparatively little theoretical work in the development literature. There are quite enough accounts of African business "failures" (e.g., Marris and Somerset 1971) due to traditional values of family loyalty which clash with modern ideas of impersonal bureaucracy. For our present purposes here, we can consider Paul a "big man," a potentially attractive person for women in the modern world of delocalized marriage and family life.

Paul considers European men strange to comprehend. He notes their "workaholic" characteristics with respect, but laments their seemingly "barren" social lives. He is committed to business as a means to obtain money for his family's personal comfort and success and his own material pleasure. He also sees it as a means of courting and winning as many beautiful women as possible. His interest in women is generally reciprocated by women of all acceptable social categories. He considers girls from sixteen on up to be potential mates but *never* at the expense of his "dignity." He is liberal with his gifts to girlfriends and has gained "considerable good reputation for his generosity." On one occasion, Philip Kilbride asked several women at a party hosted by a good mutual friend of Paul and himself, "Why do women like Paul so much—his good looks or his money?" Paul is, in fact, considered to be handsome, but the unanimous response was "his money." In the same context, European men who "fall in love" with local women are sometimes greatly disappointed to learn that "money" is easily accepted or even requested. This is so even if the woman is rich and the European is poor. Paul is aware of this necessary link between personal attraction and monetary power as evidenced by his almost countless friendships (the number of alleged affairs of former President Kennedy would be quite small in comparison).

Paul's marital history began in the early seventies, when he married a well-educated nurse/midwife from his own ethnic group. At that time, he was locally considered in Kampala to be a "senior bachelor" (in his early thirties and also a "junior tycoon." He had fathered four children, a fact which he concealed from his wife-to-be. Their early years produced a major problem since his wife did not conceive. On several occasions, he said he wanted to marry "someone else," which prompted his wife to "run away." Nevertheless, Paul did not divorce, in part because his wife was "beautiful" and "good." She is, in fact, an intelligent conversationalist who, while quiet, is extremely hardworking and reliable. She eventually had five children with Paul and now operates a successful business in Kampala. (She previously left nursing because Paul was "too jealous.")

In the late 1970s, Paul, by now a father and a successful businessman, decided to take a second wife. A friend of his whom he admired had recently become a polygynist. Paul had fallen in love with another "beautiful" woman, a nurse from his own ethnic group. At that time, she was dating a university student, but Paul courted her with zest. He eventually provided her with a home and set her up in a seamstress business after helping her with school fees for further training. By 1985, their marriage had ended, although his plan to impregnate her resulted in a daughter who at this time was six years old. Mother and child now reside with a professional man who accepted them both when he married Paul's former wife. Paul continues to provide his daughter with money through her mother. His original intention was to bring all his children "under the same roof," but his first wife was not happy about this. Moreover, his first-born son was "disowned" because he refused schooling, failed in several business ventures, and got girls pregnant irresponsibly. Another "outside" child born before his marriage is a prominent athlete. All in all, Paul leads a vigorous life in which he conforms to the cultural standards of a "good provider," one with a reputation for personal conduct that is admired, sometimes with jealous envy, by his male friends. His wife enjoys material comfort, the security of a good provider for her children, and a husband who is respectful and conscientious about his in-law relations (he is well-liked by his brother-in-law, whom Philip Kilbride knows well). This is so in spite of the fact that Paul plays out his "big man" role in a delocalized context where his wife is sometimes angry with him over his women (and he with her over her anger) and where much of his conduct with women must remain secret.

In previous generations, Paul would have had numerous wives, primarily because his motive is to dominate women while at the same time remaining

committed to them. He abhors prostitution or other forms of casual pro-
miscuous sex current in some quarters of East Africa and abroad. His
having an "outside" wife was accepted by his first wife as preferable to
divorce, a practice which is disruptive to the family. Likewise, East African
"outside" women rarely demand that their partners "get divorced" for their
sake. Nevertheless, divorce is a growing practice in East Africa, particularly
in urban Nairobi.

The status of "outside" child is not always as easily resolved as that of
Paul's daughter referred to above. We shall see in the next chapter, and have
briefly alluded to this situation in the last, that such children are often "left
behind" with their grandmothers. This is not infrequently troublesome for
all parties concerned. We have also seen that some men who have children
before marriage and who do not wish to become polygynists may decide
after their marriage to bring all their children "under the same roof." A
variation of this occurs when an already married man has children outside
of wedlock and brings his children home to live permanently with his wife
and present family instead of becoming a polygynist. In another pattern,
children born out of wedlock are formally recognized and not neglected but
are left with their mother for most aspects of economic support. The
following case will illustrate this common pattern, itself almost entirely
culturally modern as a form of delocalized polygyny. We consider this
material from the perspective of a woman born outside of wedlock since her
father was already married in a "ring" marriage (i.e., a legal marriage).

Joanne, a woman in her late thirties, is a university graduate with a
graduate degree. She is a bright, articulate person who has always enjoyed
academic success in the best schools in Uganda and abroad. Her father is a
professional man who is quite cosmopolitan and wealthy. He has numerous
"outside" children besides Joanne in addition to those with his wife. Joanne
used to visit his farm as a child, where she formed close friendships with
some of her half-siblings. Her closest siblings, however, are the three who
have a common mother with her. These three are, like Joanne, all quite
successful, having gone to university or professional school. Joanne's
mother runs a health clinic which has enabled her to support well her
children, who have been fathered by three different men (all white-collar
professionals).

Joanne describes a very happy childhood on her mother's shamba; particularly fond memories include such things as "singing," rides home in the
family car after a long safari, and large feasts on holidays. Indeed, siblings

who have the same mother (often identified by the same nomenclature) are usually the closest throughout East Africa. Joanne's relations with her father's "outside" children are variable. She sometimes (casually) meets them either in Kampala or elsewhere where she has friendly conversations with them. Her sibling ties are, in order of felt closeness: first, children of the same mother, second, children of her father and his wife, and third, children of her father and some other woman.

Joanne's feelings about her mother are warm and affectionate. Her mother is accepted locally as a remarkable woman, one who is very dignified in manner and widely respected in her community. She has achieved what she wanted most in life: a successful business and successful children (and avoided *perhaps* what one of our anthropology colleagues refers to as "the monotony of monogamy!"). Joanne's thoughts about her father are ambivalent. She carries his name and is on friendly terms with him but she has never really fully understood why he had so many "outside children." He once wrote in a letter to Joanne at school that "one day" she would understand when she was older. Joanne feels that her father was quick to rush in and claim full credit whenever she won an award or a degree. Her mother, according to Joanne, provided all her economic support. Nevertheless, she is not hostile to him, probably in part because he is a hardworking respected man in Uganda.

The tale of Joanne is quite common in East Africa. In it, we see cultural flexibility in a situation of economic and ethical delocalization where polygyny is no longer as solvent as previously. It is commonly accepted that "big men," like the three discussed here, can and should have numerous children by more than one woman. There is prestige and power involved in the man's inclination to fulfill these public expectations of him. His options range, as we have seen, from full-scale polygyny (Joseph) to semi-polygyny (Paul) to outside children (Joanne's father). The children of all these forms of "big men's" reproductive achievements, as possessors of multiple women, are themselves at no great disadvantage socially. These children are not unduly stigmatized by society and, depending in part on their own efforts, can achieve public success. The real issue in East African terms is not so much with the structure of the marriage but with the quality of the relationship between parents and between parents and children. The cultural norms are still flexible on structure (in spite of delocalization) but are inflexible on the issue of wealth. Our materials show that East Africans are quite correct to believe that unsuccessful marriages, particularly polygynous ones, are due primarily to lack of money and perceived favoritism in doling out the "limited good." Conflict is the usual result when resources are insufficient.

In the next chapter, we will first consider one of the major forms of conflict in polygynous homes where poverty is a factor. The "evil eye," as we have mentioned previously, is an example of such conflict and a subject that will be made theoretically relevant to our primary consideration of child abuse and neglect.

11

FROM THE EVIL EYE TO THE BATTERED CHILD
Child Vulnerability in Modern Society

"When a woman dislikes you, she accuses you of witchcraft."

One of the objectives of cross-cultural comparisons is to ascertain if cultural practices are entirely "relative" or if such practices, although seemingly different, are better understood as "functional equivalents" or "universals" (cf. Price-Williams 1975, Bourguignon 1979). In comparative research on child abuse, there is a need to recognize, at least in the first instance, that specific cultural values do vary in regard to what extent physical aggression against children is acceptable or not. There is also a need to recognize that such values differ in what constitutes physical aggression against children (cf. Korbin 1981). For this reason, we follow Segal, who defines child abuse as occurring "when the child suffers non-accidental physical injury as a result of acts—or omissions—on the part of his parents or guardians that violate the community standards concerning the treatment of children" (1979:58). We further follow Rohner (1975: 45) who makes a distinction between abuse as "aggression toward the child" and neglect as "indifference toward the child." Thus in our preliminary definition, we hold that child abuse and neglect cross-culturally can be compared according to general criteria (e.g., "aggression," "indifference") but that such criteria need to be grounded in specific cultural practices (e.g., functional equivalents). In this chapter we limit our discussion to Kenya, where our materials on child abuse have been recently and systematically collected with a topical focus.

In the Kenya context, it would be surprising if children, a valued resource, did not provoke envy or jealousy among persons for whom such resources are or were viewed as a competitive advantage. In a "behavioral environment" where supernatural forces such as spirits, ancestors, and the evil gaze are considered phenomenologically "real," it follows that such spiritual forces are considered as a meaningful avenue to bring harm or misfortune to one's antagonists. The "evil eye," in which the aggressor hopes to inflict a child with sickness or death, is now a common form of aggression against children. A common victim today (and probably to some extent in the past) is the child of a co-wife, a not surprising fact given the potential for conflict among co-wives in modern Kenya's delocalized economy.

The evil eye differs from child abuse (and is, therefore, not a strict functional equivalent) in several ways. First, the intended victim is just as much the mother (or other relative) as it is the child. To destroy, for example, a co-wife's children is to render her powerless. Second, the aggression is presumably not performed in the context of obvious "rage" or strong affect, although what a person who "gazes" actually "feels" is not known. Third, the evil eye is not directed at one's "own" children but is done to "related" children and unrelated ones. Nevertheless, when the evil eye is directed against "related children" as an intended form of aggression to cause physical injury, it does constitute a variation that would clearly be considered child abuse by those who actually do believe in supernaturalism (as do many East Africans). We follow here Hallowell (1955), Obeyesekere (1975), and other anthropologists who have theoretically interpreted supernatural means as an indirect channel for the expression of hostile feelings. Obeyesekere, for example, holds that it is not unreasonable to consider cases of "witchcraft" comparable to "homicide" when calculating homicide statistics for Sri Lanka. Accordingly, we begin our consideration of child abuse with the "evil eye." We situate our discussion as a continuation of co-wife conflict raised in a previous chapter and now considered here as "background" to the evil eye. Our discussion will then move from the evil eye to child abuse as experienced in the "modern" form, as in classical "child battering" (Kempe 1969). The latter type of abuse was quite rare in the past (according to numerous ethnographic sources). There is no way, however, to actually determine if the "evil eye" against co-wives is more or less frequent than previously. Our suspicion is that it is more frequent, based on the assumption that the occasion for co-wife conflict is greater today than previously.

The evil eye was and is a common practice among Abaluyia peoples, for example, although it is not found in all East African communities (Wagner 1949). Our own materials would suggest that the primary victims are children and sometimes animals. The aggressors are most frequently women who are neighbors or kin. Jealousy or envy (often over material property) prompts an often intended gaze (unlike Europe or India where the gaze is not so controlled.) The aggressor stares at the intended victim's face or shadow. A commonly seen precaution includes having children wear beads or leather bands on the body. Stomach problems and high fever are symptoms which can be cured by visiting a curer. Among other things, he makes incisions in the stomach and then "sucks out," in the words of one informant, "white things, grass, and frogs."

We will illustrate the commonly held belief that co-wives are "evil eye" protagonists by considering here some material collected from a woman who lives in Western Province. These data are based on what are believed to be evil-eye practices. Unlike some of our other data, we have no direct accounts of co-wives who discussed with us their own evil-eye practices. Philip, however, was able to interview some people who were "born again" Christians, and therefore eager to discuss their previous "sinful" attempts to harm others through evil-eye throwing. One informant's son, who is now a university graduate, carries stomach scars from his visit to a curer at the age of ten. At that time the co-wife of his father's sister became "envious" of the good brother-in-law relation enjoyed by her husband with her "rival's" brother. She therefore, it is thought, threw the evil eye at the brother-in-law's son to bring trouble. In another case, an informant reported that an old woman felt envious of her own daughter's co-wife and therefore over a period of time cast the evil eye on her daughter's rival's children. This would be likely to tie her son-in-law more closely to her daughter, who also had children.

We see in these two instances that the co-wife relationship is itself embedded in a wider context of competing consanguineal and in-law relationships, each a potential source of conflict. The attribution of evil intent to another is, of course, a projection which tells one as much or even more about the accuser's own perceived notions of conflictual interaction.

Nevertheless, what is common is the belief that co-wives are the primary or secondary cause of evil-eye throwing. Monogamy, however, is not without its conflicts. This is so because all marriages are potentially conflictual and because, as transactions which occur in an extended family context, they often involve in-laws in such disputes. Accordingly, my informant reported a "well-known" (as were the others) case of a woman who is the wife of a man who has an older brother whose wife has given him both male and female children. The woman herself has had no male children. She therefore threw the evil eye at the children of the son of the elder brother and his wife. This informant said this occurred due to conflict between the wives of brothers, who, we should note, are having children for the same consanguineal kin group.

We will see that while the family can sometimes be a source of conflict, envy, and jealousy, it is nevertheless still an important support network as in the past. How this support network functions will be examined in instances of child abuse and neglect in the western form, noting here that the above victims were cared for by some relatives who were not "envious" of them. We turn now to examples of child abuse in Kenya.

Child Abuse: A National Problem

One of the suggested antecedents of child abuse is a "cultural" focus on violence. The national Kenyan cultural context is not excessively violent, certainly not when compared to the United States. Kenya achieved independence only recently (1963) and probably for that reason national cultural symbols are just emerging. The national sport is soccer, which is not overly violent nor associated in Kenya with extreme public violence. The military is not usually observed in public or prominent in the media. There are no "national" enemies, and children's toys and common songs on the radio show little evidence of systematic violence. Crime is primarily directed against property, although homicide is sometimes the result. Infrequently there are armed bandits along highways or armed gangs that rob and kill members of affluent homes. It is illegal, in fact, for citizens to own firearms. Moreover, a Kenyan does not experience episodes of random murder or other forms of violent aggression directed at strangers apart from a pragmatic context. Thus the public will generally tolerate "mob justice" in response to thieves who are caught in the act.

It is difficult to ascertain if modern Kenyan society is more or less violent than the smaller more provincial cultures of previous generations. Warfare was present traditionally, but was mostly sporadic. Certainly the militaristic "ethos" of such groups as the Maasai has been greatly exaggerated (Rigby 1985). Domestic life was and is comparatively tolerant of "wife-beating" but not wife battering as such. We have occasionally seen wives with bruised faces or arms, although our male and female informants generally state that husbands only have a right to "beat" their wives for disciplinary reasons and should not be excessive.

Domestic violence was infrequently observed in the course of our field-work, although cases were obtained through informant interviews. Corporal punishment of children is acceptable as long as it is not excessive. In general, community violence does not appear to be pronounced. Of eighty arrests recorded at a local police headquarters in Western Kenya from 1981 through 1984, no homicides and only two rape attempts were included. Commonly, cases involved illegal brewing or theft of items such as cows, food, or household possessions. There were, however, several house burnings, and such have been observed elsewhere by us to result in deaths. Public rowdiness and fighting while drunk occasionally appeared among the cases recorded, as well as episodes of physically threatening to "beat" or "bewitch" someone. There were also several cases of beating and robbing people on the road at night. Stealing from absent victims, however, was the most frequent crime, comprising 35% of the cases.

A perusal of the English-language Kenyan newspapers (*Daily Nation*, *The Standard* and *Kenya Times*) over a nineteen-month period beginning January 23, 1984, and ending August 7, 1985, revealed the following information concerning child abuse and neglect in Kenya. Looking at the age and sex of abusers, we found that adult women are reported to be the primary abusers. Of the 62 cases of abuse/neglect we discovered, abusers were adult females in 39 cases (62.9%), adult males in 16 cases (25.8%), and female children in 3 cases (4.8%). In four cases, the sex of abusers was not reported. Of the 76 children mentioned in these cases of abuse/neglect, 26 of the children were males (34.2%) and 29 of the children were females (38.2%). In 21 cases, the sex of the children was not given. Thus it appears that both boys and girls are victims of abuse in similar proportions. We discovered only one case of incest (father-daughter) in our reading of the Kenyan papers. There were six cases of rape by non-relatives and two cases of physical threats and beatings by male teachers. The only other males involved were the fathers of the abused/neglected children. Two grand-mothers (one paternal, one maternal) and one stepmother were the only female relations other than the children's mothers who were abusers. Twenty of the 39 cases involving mothers were cases of unwed or single parents abandoning their children or attempting infanticide of an illegitimate newborn. The major cases of neglect very much resemble the syndrome of latchkey children in the United States. Very young children, usually under six years of age, are left home alone while their mothers in the rural areas work in the field or their mothers in the city work at various low-salaried jobs that do not provide enough money for child care. Fires are all too frequently the result of leaving such young children unattended by an adult.

Common forms of child abuse in Kenya involve getting rid of an unwanted infant or child by abandonment and attempted or actual infanticide. We can see from table 15 that both boys and girls are at risk and that the pit latrine is a common location to dispose of unwanted children. Press reports of child torture, burning, scalding, battering, prolonged confinement, and the like are not uncommon. Editorials are encountered with such titles as "Our Sad Problem of Battered Children" and "State Urged to

Table 15   Sample Headlines from Kenyan Newspapers Concerning Child Abuse

---

"Boy Found Buried in Mole Hole"
"Two-month-old Girl Abandoned at Bus Stop"
"Five-month-old Boy Rescued from a Church Latrine"
"Baby Wrapped in a Paper Bag Abandoned"
"Two-month-old Girl Abandoned in Hospital"
"Unwed Teenager Mother Abandons Four-month-old Baby"
"Two-year-old Boy Abandoned Is Rescued from Ants"
"Two-day-old Boy Rescued from Ditch"
"Four-month-old Infant Abandoned in the Rain"
"Infant Dumped into Toilet Pit"
"Newborn Boy Abandoned in Primary School"
"Five-day-old Girl Found in Maize Plantation"
"Mother Abandons Two-week-old Girl"
"Eight-month-old Infant Found in Sewage"
"Two-week-old Baby in Plastic Bag Found on Wayside"
"Dog Digs Out Baby's Body"
"Mother Throws Three-year-old Boy into Latrine"
"One-year-old Boy Abandoned by Grandmother"
"Unmarried Mother Throws Two-day-old Baby into Pit Latrine"

Tighten Laws on Child Abuse." Table 16 provides a sense of the type of instances one is likely to encounter in the news media.

In recent years, Kenyan scholars, politicians and other concerned citizens have sponsored or attended seminars or workshops on the subject of child abuse. In December of 1982, for example, such a workshop was sponsored by the World Health Organization in collaboration with the University of Nairobi (Onyango and Kayongo-Mole 1982). The workshop included a Minister of Parliament and specialists from the fields of pediatrics, psychiatry, and sociology. The topics of concern included child labor, battered child syndrome, sexual abuse, institutional child abuse and neglect, government attempts to reduce child abuse, and legal and policy issues. Two papers from the seminar are specifically relevant to our present concerns; therefore we will briefly discuss them.

Bwibo (1982:11), a Kenyan pediatrician, states that "recent figures show that in 1980/1981, 21 children with battered child syndrome were admitted to Kenyatta National Hospital of whom 5 died." Of significance to our present discussion, Bwibo notes that victims of child abuse frequently included (1) "The babies of single mothers thrown along the road, dropped in pit latrines or dust bins," and (2) "the babies whose hands are burnt because they stole a piece of money from the homes" (1982:11). His cases included male and female abusers who, apart from the parents, included stepparents and child caretakers. There is no systematic data available on gender, but our strong impression, reported above, is that women are

Table 16   Example Extracts About Abuse/Neglect Reported in Kenya Newspapers

---

After quarreling with stepson's father, stepmother punished six-year-old stepson by holding his hand over hot charcoal stove.

Sixty-year-old father batters fifteen-year-old daughter to death; she played a small trick on him and he "went beserk."

Barmaid mother leaves two-year-old son and nine-month-old daughter asleep while she goes to work; fire starts by a candle and children burn to death.

Stepmother and father tie 12-year-old son to a tree for 2 months because he wanted to run back to his natural mother.

Father hits 7-year-old son with stick until death because he hadn't done a chore assigned to him; father was drunk at the time.

Mother angry at 10-year-old son who stole 10 shillings (about $1.00) from her; severely beat him on face, neck, and trunk.

---

substantially overrepresented in the pool of abusers. Women are the primary child caretakers, and in their unique status as "co-wife" and "single mother" are frequently reported (e.g., in the press) as abusive.

In another paper, Nyanyintono (1982:25) summarizes the overall institutional Kenyan situation as "particularly urgent when you consider childbearing practices like sibling care, polygamy, and patrilineal family systems, untrained pre-school teachers, poverty and high birth rate. These and related factors expose large proportions of the young to conditions which are harmful to their growth and development."

Child Abuse and Neglect: The Rural Pattern

In our own research in rural Kenya, we found that child abuse is, at present, still a rare (but perhaps increasing) phenomenon. What is more common in rural Kenya these days are cases of child neglect and parental rejection rather than physical abuse. For example, abandonment or failure to provide necessities such as food and clothing (and sometimes school fees) can be observed. We earlier presented examples of parental, and even grandparental, neglect most commonly arising from the high rate of premarital pregnancies in modern East Africa (P. Kilbride 1986). Other causes of neglect include heavy drinking, divorce, and ambiguous ethnic-group or extended-family obligations.

The LeVines (1981) report for the Gusii of Kenya that if only the father drinks the repercussions for the family's welfare are considerable, but that they are more severe if the mother is a serious drinker. Gusii children of drinking mothers are often left alone for many hours and may not be provided with adequate nutrition. The LeVines also found that Gusii children born out of wedlock or from marriages ending in divorce or the death of one parent constituted 25% of malnourished children but only 2% of their study group.

Child malnourishment, is, of course, not always due to parental neglect. Some poor Samia women, for example, cannot afford to adequately feed their children with protein sources. Many others believe that malnourishment is caused by the "evil eye" rather than deficient nutrition (P. Kilbride 1977). Nevertheless, some Samia parents do not feed their children even when able to do so. Such cases are more likely to occur when social supports by the extended family are minimal.

Sometimes interethnic marriage results in ambiguous family responsibility. In the Samia area, as we saw in chapter 10, intertribal marriages frequently occur between Samia and Luo. In one instance which was observed extensively (Fraser and Kilbride 1981), a Luo woman had run away from her Samia husband, leaving behind her two daughters of about five and three years. All four grandparents were dead. The husband had not participated in any clan activities such as house-building or farming. In fact he had not cooperated very much with any of his neighbors, and his wife's uncle complained that he had not completed his bride-price payments to her family. The father drank heavily and did not work very hard on his farm. Both children were suffering from severe malnutrition resulting from frequently being left alone in the home all day without food. The neighbors eventually stopped caring for the children, primarily since it was believed that the mother had a lot of money due to a friendship with a wealthy man. The children, due to the father's lack of participation in clan activities, had little opportunity to be helped by clan members. The state did not interfere because the children were not orphans.

Child abuse in the form of direct physical aggression against children is, at present, seemingly limited in rural areas in comparison to Nairobi. In eight months of field research in Western Province, we were not informed of any current instance of child battering by medical authorities in the area, nor did we find any ourselves. There were a few cases of burns, although it was claimed that these were accidental. Obviously detection is difficult in such matters. Nevertheless, it was possible to locate two past cases of what constitute clear instances of physical child abuse in severe battering. Moreover, one case of attempted homicide did occur during our research. We will now consider social, cultural, and economic factors in the etiology of these cases.

Case 1

A fifty-two-year-old woman (our informant) has been living in Sisal for ten years. She was married in 1950, when her husband brought two cows to her parents. Soon after their marriage, they moved to Taita, where they cut sisal to earn a living. They lived on the Coast for twenty-four years, during which time she gave birth to three sons. Their marriage was fine until around the mid-1960s, when she left work due to deteriorating strength. After this time, for the next several years, her husband became violent— beating the children when they asked for such things as food, clothing, and school fees. She too was beaten whenever she tried to protect the children.

This pattern continued until 1974, when she ran away to Sisal area where she is now maintained on land owned by her brother. She earns money herself by selling pottery. When she came to Sisal, her sons were thirteen, five, and three years old. Her husband came to Sisal for a short time, during which she conceived a daughter. He ran away permanently, however, when he was warned by his brother-in-law that he would be arrested by the police for his violent beatings. His wife reports that he did not have a drinking problem but was not a Christian. He never felt remorseful after his beatings but would leave for several days. He felt he had done a "good job of discipline." Up until now, her legs have bothered her, and her thirteen-year-old son has a permanently swollen hand which was twisted by his father ten years ago.

Two factors should be emphasized in the above case. First, the informant believes that her husband's violence coincided with her own discontinuation of work. The resulting diminution of the family budget could very well have produced stress, then triggered violent reactions in her husband. Second, the informant's brother continues to serve as an important resource person for her and her children. From the standpoint of these children, their mother's brother intervened to disrupt violence which could very well have continued in his absence. We see, therefore, both economic and social support factors (e.g., extended family) implicated in the pattern of child abuse illustrated in this case.

Case 2

A woman in her fifties (our informant) has been living with her two sons and a granddaughter in Sisal since 1982. She is divorced and has another son who lives elsewhere. The latter son is the father of her granddaughter, who is ten years old. This girl is very pretty and a student in Primary 2. She has a scar on her forehead where she was beaten with a cooking stick by her stepmother three years ago. Her father had lived in Mombasa in the 1970s, where he had three children (two are now dead) with a woman labeled as a "prostitute." He subsequently married another woman with whom he has had a son and a daughter. This wife became jealous on those occasions when he would "sleep out" and would aggress against her husband's "outside" child. When interviewed, the child said she was beaten about four times a month but never when her father slept at home. She got along well with her siblings, but she was the only one ever beaten. Her father would beat her stepmother whenever he discovered that she had beaten his daughter. The stepmother was remorseful after beating the child as indicated by her taking the child to a hospital for treatment. The child now lives with her grandmother, who was happy to take her because she has no daughters. Her stepmother sometimes brings her clothes, but neither she nor the father provides any other assistance. Her mother frequently visits but is closely monitored by the grandmother for fear that she will steal the child.

First of all, this example shows, as in the previous case, the positive role of the extended family in alleviating child abuse. Were it not for her grandmother, this young girl would probably still be vulnerable to family violence. Second, the stepmother is mentioned frequently by informants as one who is often aggressive to her stepchildren as a result of conflicts with her husband or co-wives. There do not appear to be any economic problems contributing to child abuse in this case. My informant said that "the only problem was jealousy."

A common form of child abuse reported in the Kenyan press is the throwing of a newborn into a pit latrine by a schoolgirl. During our research, as mentioned earlier, one such instance occurred in which the infant did not die. One day in May 1985, while preparing to "bow out," we observed a large crowd gathering at the local secondary school. Joining the crowd, we arrived just in time to see a newborn infant being lifted out of one of the school's pit latrines. The infant's mother, Sarah (a pseudonym), who had attempted the infanticide, was being hustled into her dormitory for interrogation by local officials and nurses while we observed the proceedings and the crowd continued to gather outside. Through observation and interviews, this incident and its aftermath were followed for several weeks, sometimes with the assistance of a female research assistant. Settings included school, hospital, jail, and home situations. Discussions were conducted with the girl herself, various members of her family, police, school officials, and many other members of the general public.

It became clear through personal involvement with Sarah and her family that our "bridgehead" into their social field (Hollis 1982) was one of mutual self-interest. Financial assistance for the infant's needs was offered in exchange for the chance to acquire "data" by involving ourselves in their present misfortune. (Our genuine concern for the infant's well-being would have motivated our participation even if we had not been "studying" child abuse.) Throughout our encounter with them, we all cooperated as agreed although we resisted continuous attempts, though understandable, to have us take on economic responsibility for the mother. It was apparent that she was suffering from economic deprivation and related inability to control her own fate. She seemed a passive depository for decisions concerning her, but made by others, such as relatives, the police, school officials, and so on. Her male relatives were also feeling monetary obligations, not in terms of their own personal needs, but in relation to stresses associated with extended-family responsibility for helping Sarah and her infant. Their social-power potential and responsibility were greater than Sarah's (and her mother's) and probably for this reason they appeared to be under almost as much personal stress as Sarah herself concerning their "family" tragedy. The most powerless actor in the above episode is, of course, the infant. This is so because he has little apparent value for his mother and his absent father.

That the attempted infanticide described here is tragic can be easily determined by the range of negative affect it elicited during audience appraisal. Anger, rage, fear, and the like clearly qualify the episode as an instance of child abuse, defined as an extreme violation of community standards about proper child care. Such expressions of negative affect were displayed by school officials, nurses, police officials, and others as the "public" responded to Sarah. These observed and reported experiences of negative affect proved to be meaningful phenomenological criteria for establishing the behavioral realism under consideration as constituting child abuse in this non-Western culture.

The mother is now on three years probation and would like to return to school to continue her education, something that can hopefully be arranged. This sixteen-year-old became pregnant by a man she hardly knew, a married man visiting the rural area from the city. Until this incident, she had been an average student in matters of school rank and attendance. She comes from a polygynous family but has been raised by her stepmother (who is barren) and her father. Her mother and father were divorced some time ago. The girl and her maternal family members revealed that she did not get along well with her stepmother and seems to be, in the opinion of her brother, the victim of a broken home. He also believes a factor was lack of money for school fees. In recent years, her mother's brother had provided school fees for her. The schoolgirl did not report her pregnancy to anyone due to "fear." According to her, she did not even realize she was pregnant until she was seven months pregnant! She waited about thirty minutes after giving birth before deciding to kill her baby. During this time, she considered such things as "Where will I take the baby" and "How can I get my school fees back for this term?" In the days and weeks after she attempted infanticide, her mother and her maternal relatives proved to be a key resource group as they visited her in the hospital and in jail. To our knowledge, her father and stepmother did not even write a letter, much less visit their daughter after being informed of the incident and being asked to come see their grandson. In particular, her maternal uncle, at considerable cost and time, looked after his niece and her newborn during this time of duress.

This case shows, as do others, the important function of the extended family in alleviating, if not in this instance preventing, family violence. It is quite possible that were the unfortunate young mother without their financial and emotional support, she would have tried again to mistreat her child. Mother and child were doing well the last time we visited them and since that time, according to the mother's last letter. The problems of school fees, divorce, and stepmother are all in one way or another implicated in this case. It would seem that the young girl's "lover" has an important sociological role in this episode; however, we know nothing about this at present. The girl reported that she had no immediate plans to tell the father of the infant about the birth of their son.

This is, of course, precisely the sort of gender asymmetry in parental responsibility that is at the heart of our argument that there is a significant delocalized ethical morality which serves to reinforce the relatively powerless social position of many contemporary East African women. Our direct encounter with an instance of child abuse in our research area allowed us to enter into the existential reality of our hosts through direct involvement in this mutually shared consciousness. This interactive experience provided the key "economic" insights which proved to be theoretically (comparatively) useful in the interpretation of locally conceived child abuse.

Child Abuse as a Moralnet Problem

Elsewhere we have discussed some theoretical ideas about the etiology of child abuse (P. Kilbride 1986). Among the various causes of child abuse, we noted the significance of isolation from a social network. Such isolation is considered to be a major causative factor, along with both economic and psychological factors (Korbin 1981, Garbarino 1977, Kent 1979). Our Kenyan materials also demonstrate the importance of the "extended family" as a moral community—one whose members act to alleviate child abuse and neglect through intervention and continued child care. We saw too in our previous research the significant role played by grandparents in the case of illegitimate children even though these children are sometimes unwanted. In our concluding chapter, we will discuss the work of R. Naroll on moralnets. Concerning child abuse, our materials are in agreement with his views as expressed in his book *The Moral Order.* He writes:

> For young children the leading social problem is child abuse. And child abuse is largely linked to weakened moralnets. This is to say, it is parents with weakened ties to their extended families who tend to become child abusers. (1983:35)

Our material from rural Kenya would suggest that from the vantage point of the child, abusive behavior stops when an extended family member intervenes to protect him. Thus the child's extended family ties are significant also.

Considerable cross-cultural research exists to support Naroll's moralnet theory. A by-now classic book entitled, *They Love Me, They Love Me Not* (Rohner 1975), provides a comprehensive world societal survey of parental acceptance—rejection beliefs and practices. Rohner found that reasons for parental rejection included such things as no father at home, little help from fathers at home, absent grandparents, children not wanted before birth, and co-wives in the same house. We have seen in Kenya that modern society has witnessed a decline in paternal support, a decline in the positive value of children, overburdened grandparents, and increased co-wife problems. Naroll, using data from Whiting, found global support for the idea that societies with larger households tend to indulge their babies more than societies with smaller households. He concludes, "The world around, parents are warmer to their children when mothers get help in childcare from other adults in the home" (1983:249). It is not simply a matter of demography, however, as research shows that the particular social relationship does influence the quality of adult-child interaction. In the famous "mothers of six cultures" project, Minturn and Lambert (1964) found that parents are warmer when there are also grandparents in the home, but colder when co-wives and sisters-in-law are present.

It should not be concluded, nevertheless, that child abuse is simply a function of the mere presence or absence of moralnets such as extended families. The underlying economic patterns of a society must also be considered. These, in turn, give rise to cultural values about children. Korbin's

(1981) book on child abuse contains chapters on China and India where extended families are strong but where child abuse, particularly for girls, was widespread (cf. 71–96, 166–86). Dowry problems in India, for example, cause considerable tension between mothers- and daughters-in-law, too often resulting in burning the latter. In China, extreme codes of patricentric authority in property ownership and household authority can be contrasted with Africa. In sub-Saharan Africa, including the societies of East Africa, marriage is an exchange between consanguineal kin groups. One family exchanges goods, such as cattle, for the progeny rights to the children of a woman who marries into this family. There has been no strong dowry system as in India, where wealth is needed in order for a female to marry. In East Africa, females are able to bring wealth into the family when they marry out. In other words, sons produce children for the family whereas daughters produce progeny-price wealth. For this reason, it comes as no surprise that in East Africa, for example, both boys and girls are valued. Divorces are sometimes requested if a woman has only sons or only daughters. A more frequent solution to this problem is polygyny. Nowadays, illegitimate girls are preferred over boys because the former will bring progeny wealth whereas the boys will require land, which is becoming scarcer than in the past. The reader is referred to the work of Esther and Jack Goody (1982, 1983) for an analysis of the role of inheritance and other economic factors in a comparative evaluation of marriage and family life in Africa, the Middle East, and Europe.

In our final chapter we will consider the contemporary position of children and family life in East Africa as we view it from the vantage point of our own fieldwork, research findings, and interpretive framework. In so doing, we hope to provide the impetus for others to direct their expertise toward further investigation of the relationship between child abuse/neglect and the value of children within the family, extended kin network, community, and society.

12

WOMEN AND CHILDREN AT RISK

"One who cares too much for oneself causes problems for oneself."

T he traditional strengths and present-day challenges to East African families which have been discussed so far contain a significant message for better understanding the unfortunate plight of abused and neglected children. We have seen how political economy and values interact over time such that "modernization of tradition" means loss of power for women and children in East Africa. Put simply, children are now at risk because political-economic and value-cultural conditions unfavorable to women and extended family life are presently in evidence.

Kenya and Uganda, like many third-world nations, presently occupy a peripheral structural position in a global, capitalist economic order (cf. Wallerstein 1974, Rodney 1974). That is, they do not have a capitalist mode of production with a localized evolutionary history. Capitalism in East Africa contrasts with capitalism in Europe, for example, where family life, religion, and other institutions evolved gradually over several centuries to the current locally derived economic order. The rapid spread of North Atlantic capitalism into East Africa in the latter half of the nineteenth century brought not "localized" capitalism per se but only certain capitalistic "elements." Rodney for example, writes, "so often it is said that colonialism modernized Africa by introducing features of capitalism, such as private property in land, private ownership of the other means of production, and money relations. Here it is essential to distinguish between capitalistic elements and capitalism as a total social system" (1974:215). Such peripheral capitalism, one consisting only of elements but not constituting a local integrated system, results in what Rodney and others refer to as "development by contradiction." In Kenya formerly, for instance, kinship was everywhere the essential idiom of social relations in what was a subsistence mode of production. The traditional African family structure is best understood as resulting from a principle of "consanguinity" or blood descent whereby social groups beyond the nuclear family, as in East Africa, are social units for economic cooperation (see Sudarkasa 1982). Therefore children are links in a generational family ideology, and spouses are linked to each other by their reproduction of children for specific consanguineal groups of relatives. The significant family unit in Africanity is not the two-parent household but the extended family in some form. Moreover, African polygyny results in an emphasis within the household where *wives* and their husband, or wives together, or mother and children, in addition to the husband-and-wife unit, are economically functional family relationships.

Today both kinship and the capitalistic element of monetary relations are salient, but often contradictory, idioms of social interaction. Specifically, modern East Africans still care and provide for children since they are highly valued as formerly, but nowadays they are costly in terms of clothing and schooling while their labor, although important, is less significant than in the past. We argue here that one of the consequences of such a contradiction, itself resulting from delocalization in a peripheral capitalist economy, is child abuse and neglect.

In this book, we have considered how economic and moral delocalization can serve to cause family life (and other) disjunctions in a pre-modern social order undergoing modernization. Our emphasis here has been concerned primarily with moral delocalization, but this is not intended to necessarily support either a materialist or idealist view of historical change in East Africa or elsewhere. Unlike Western modernity in capitalistic Europe, traditional cultural norms of sociability and communalism significantly persist into the delocalized modern social order. The extended family as a significant support group, attendance at family and neighborhood funerals, weddings, and so forth, for example, provide an ongoing context to "enjoy" life and to "anchor" most individuals in an ongoing life of meaningful social experience.

Nevertheless, there have been some devastating effects of modernization. Uganda, in particular, has recently gone through several major national traumas following the dictatorship of Idi Amin and the presence of AIDS. In this context, it is not surprising that a "priestess" has arisen, claiming that she and her followers are immune to bullets, and that they will reassert Lango tribal power through defeat of the national armed forces (hundreds of her followers have been slain in battle as of fall 1987). Similarly, the "prince" of the former kingdom of Buganda is now home and there is a lot of discussion about a restoration of his kingdom. Nativistic or cultural revitalization movements, such as Lango Power or the Baganda Kingship, seek to restore the "good old days." Such movements are very common, particularly as responses to the impact of modern or other foreign "powerful" belief systems (Wallace 1970).

In Kenya, there are frequent "tensions" between the government and the national university over issues of political economy, but on the whole, Kenya as a nation enjoys about as much stability as can be reasonably expected for a nation in the "peripheral" corner of the world economy. There are in East Africa serious government and private programs to combat social problems. In Kenya, compared to Uganda, the political philosophy assumes more self-help commitment at the grass roots level (for instance "*harambee*" or "Let's Pull Together"). What is the case, however, is that the state resources in both countries are not sufficient to cope with the massive social problems posed by modern life. Ugandans are now attempting to care for numerous orphans, *Bayaye* (a new word), resulting from modern political-economic turmoil. Cases of child abandonment and pregnant teenager "pit latrine" homicide are occasionally reported in the Ugandan media.

Policy

We propose here that a solution to East African social problems of the sort discussed in this book resides in a recognition of at least three important principles based on social research. First of all, there are power differentials which structure relations among individuals, among social groups (gender, ethnic group, clan), and among nations. Those nations, social groups, and individuals who are powerful and who are therefore in a position to be moral entrepreneurs are called on to both recognize the consequences of their power *and* then to act upon this awareness. A second principle is that action or awareness is a *cultural* activity involving, therefore, a need to be cross-cultural, interethnic, and self-reflective when acting to modify power structures and their consequences. Policy based on this plan assumes, of course, as does most social policy, that the human condition is modifiable through directed action. Third, we argue strongly that effective social action in the future requires a universal, international policy and cultural understanding, one that recognizes the interconnectedness of the world order as supported by Wallerstein, Wolf, and many others.

Specifically, we propose that the problems of child abuse, feminization of poverty, and distortion of family life in East Africa are, first of all, locally perceived as social problems. Empirical research, including our own, has established this. Second, we recommend that solutions to these problems can be achieved through a *convergence of interpretive frameworks*. We propose here that a Kenyan and Ugandan national policy be supportive of, and based upon, the convergence of the following interpretive frameworks: general humanistic social science (socionomics), feminist theory, and child-centered ideology such as represented in Africanity.

Socionomics

The anthropologist R. Naroll is best known for his theoretical work concerning the perfection of the cross-cultural survey methodology (Naroll 1983). Toward the end of his career, his thoughts turned to the moral and ethical implications of a general social theory of mankind then emerging from cross-cultural comparisons. Naroll writes "I see socionomics as a scientific discipline to be used in and by all the behavioral sciences . . . I see it as a means by which the work of behavioral science can furnish mankind at large with a common ideology to guide its affairs" (1983:28). Behavioral science, he believes, is value-free observation and value-free theory directed at the "overall" condition of mankind. In his book *The Moral Order,* for example, Naroll shows through worldwide empirical correlations that when *moralnets* such as family and neighborhood are weak or weakened around the world, such behavior as alcohol abuse, child abuse, youth stress, and so on, are exacerbated. Naroll proposes that "a universal theory" of human behavior be further refined through research, with subsequent results evaluated and implemented for the eventual creation of a better worldwide moral order. The role of the academic researcher thus assumes social significance as an eventual replacement for supernatural beliefs and structures.

We have been stimulated by Naroll and other cross-culturalists to a great extent. Our study here, for example, assumes functional interpretation theoretically relevant to Naroll's holocultural functionalism. We agree further that a worldwide moral order is desirable and that behavioral science is important to that vision. Our specific finding concerning increased child abuse in Kenya is in direct support of his "moralnet decline" predictions about its concomitant increase. His work on child abuse is an excellent version of the "ecological" theory which we favor as argued in chapter 11. We cannot, however, fully accept his interpretive framework. Science is still largely a property of the industrial world, particularly given its high cost. Third-world social scientists cannot often afford the free time and expense involved in such research. Social science research is long-term, a further luxury difficult to sustain in nations where problems are in need of immediate solutions. The industrialized nations' control of social science usually results in programs of study that are often not relevant to a truly worldwide ideology. This is so because "behavioral science" is never "value free," as Naroll assumes to be the case. Finally, as a practical matter, we do not envision religious beliefs in *Africa* being replaced by socionomics. Religion, we believe, is "there to stay," and the secularist must work to improve its structures and policies to make them more consistent with the findings of "behavioral science" wherever this is necessary.

Feminist Theory

There is by now a widely accepted view in social science that women are "on the march." We enthusiastically support this progressive view, hoping very much that our book will be seen as in step with our sisters. Ruth Sidel, for example, has nicely described a feminization-of-poverty crisis in America for which she has suggested concrete steps to eradicate (Sidel 1986). She writes:

> The agenda I am proposing includes three major areas of reform: the arena of work; universal entitlements specifically connected to the lives of families, particularly those with young children; and the welfare system. This is a broader agenda than is usually considered under the rubric "family policy," but I believe it is extremely impor-

> tant to recognize that employment policy is family policy; welfare
> policy is family policy; and surely the amount of maternity leave,
> prenatal care, and day care a society provides constitutes this policy
> as well. (2)

We commend this agenda. We do not agree with Sidel, however, that
"family policy" must be primarily directed at strengthening "both a two-
parent family and women's place in society." We are cautious about the
place of values in family preference as shown in East Africa. Instead, we
hold that women's place in society must be strengthened in its own right.
Family form is too *relative;* if there is to be a preference in East Africa, we
believe that the *extended family* be so elevated. "Feminist" European researchers in East Africa frequently argue that traditional African society was
"oppressive" to women due to polygyny and restricted public participation
in community life. To be sure this may be partially true; however, we
encourage feminists to work first through *local* women's groups and to take
into consideration their views of proper family form and male/female
relationships. O'Barr, for example, suggests that "development" should not
assume a two-parent model. She further advocates that development for
women in Africa should be channeled through an *international* African association of feminists called DAWN (Development Alternative for Wom-
ens Group).

Child-centered Theory: Africanity

The ideology of Africanity could provide an excellent experiential life-style
rationale in support of maintaining a child-centered public policy. We agree
with President Kaunda of Zambia and others that Africa's gift to humanity
is a "people-oriented" perspective, something he calls "African humanism"
(contrasted with Western technological expertise and Eastern mystical wisdom).

A commitment to Africanity in East Africa would seek to preserve a
child-centered ideology, work to strengthen grandmother networks in
modern society, and also support traditional leaders of wisdom (P. Kilbride
1986). The modern extended family and polygyny would be assessed
through the lens of an African historical heritage, not from the vantage

point of European-derived political or religious ideology. The particular status of women, now delocalized and relatively powerless, must be understood not as a conscious attempt by men to oppress women, but the result of a historical process. Social change and power differential are social problematics, not male oppression existing in some kind of historically decontextualized isolation.

We suggest that increased awareness of Africanity will contribute to regional and ethnic unity in East Africa. A child-centered ethos transcends ethnic group and national boundary. Asian-African and indigenous African, Kenyan, and Ugandan, all have a common experience grounded in family and children. The nation-state is, for example, a modern social invention, a structure quite foreign to African thought (Doob 1970). Sapir, writing years ago, argued that cultural units below the state level were in need of ultimate integration with a world order sufficient for maintaining a "genuine" cultural experience. In East Africa a multi-state, region, or district within the state would appear to be a cultural unity, not the "tribe" or even the nation-state as now constituted (Nkruma's Pan Africanism expresses the same sentiment).

Conclusion

We recommend that our East African brothers and sisters continue to work out meaningful national and regional social policies designed to improve the lives of all citizens. Three principles applicable to East African policy were set out earlier in this chapter: namely, power differentials, intra- and cross-cultural action, and a universal perspective. Moreover, it is to be hoped that all international "development" organizations, secular and religious, be understood as coming from a specific interpretive frame. (We have suggested three useful ones above.) Thus, for example, if one is to incorporate family values based on Euro-Christianity into an African context, then decisions must be made as to what, if any, "theological" revisions are necessary. As Rigby (1985) has observed, all too often Christianity has served as an excuse to steal land in exchange for the Bible. It cannot be denied, however, that East Africans are culturally religious and that certainly, as Rigby has also pointed out, apostolic Christianity of the first century is not incompatible with brotherhood along traditional African lines. Similarly, in response to "feminists" who singularly and often selectively decry, for example, female circumcision as symbolic of "male oppression," we suggest to Africans that these feminists also be made aware of Baganda female genital elongation practices designed to *enhance* sexual pleasure for both men and women. In any case, *all* foreign and domestic ideology has a cultural agenda, and it is for this reason that we argue for an "interactive ethnography" for those who set out to do research on social problems of their own or some other ethnic group. As a general rule, we agree with the following Kenyan editorial:

> The lesson that many developing countries have to learn from the Chinese experience is that it does not pay in the long run to blindly copy foreign systems of thought and then, without digesting them, seek to apply them. *Sunday Nation* (December 9, 1984)

While "foreign" ideologies are not the exclusive, wholesale answer to East African problems, we suggest that the experience of locally derived child-centered Africanity is a useful starting point for public policy. The above editorial continues:

> African countries, in particular, should be very careful in choosing their development strategies. More care and thought should be given to selection and formulation of national ideologies. Selfserving ones that cannot spur development activity should give way to more meaningful ideologies that have strong roots in the respective local settings . . . that is the Chinese lesson. *Sunday Nation* (December 9, 1984)

Policy should, according to the logic of this editorial opinion, always question how much modernity is a good thing. Nevertheless, whatever the answer to this question is, there is one fact that must be realized: There is no turning back. As the Baganda say, "He who has not traveled likes his mother's cooking." Rather than turning back, we advocate going forward, but with one eye on East Africa's past while the other is on the future.

Thus we were pleased to find that one of the guidelines for preschool education in Kenya (see Olouch) concerns a respect for and development of cultural heritage. It states:

> Education shall respect, foster and develop Kenya's rich and varied cultures. It should instill in the youth of Kenya an understanding of

past and present culture, and its valid place in contemporary society. It should also instill in them a sense of respect for unfamiliar cultures. (1984:3)

The previous chapters have set out the interpretative framework within which we have chronicled our own encounter with the modernization of tradition in East Africa. Over the years, we have learned much both personally and professionally. We shall always cherish the importance of social involvement so thickly cultivated in East African tradition. We feel that this rich social context, now under threat, is favorable to children. Professionally, this inclines us to favor strongly those theorists who emphasize a social-ecological understanding of the etiology of child abuse and neglect. Methodologically, we believe that there must be a consistent recognition of a value dimension in child development research. Our term "interactive ethnography" is intended to capture the flavor of this argument not only for child study but for all cross-cultural ethnographic research as well.

Finally, we believe our work has important implications for social policy both in East Africa and in the United States. There is renewed interest in America, for example, in attempting to improve the quantity and quality of a potential child abuser's social network. Studies show that when such networks are enriched through intervention that child abuse can be minimalized. Our material on the significance of the extended family in East Africa is one other example of an enriched social support network, one that both in the past and at present contributes to a much lower incidence of child abuse in East Africa as compared to the West. Rugged individualism, now so common in American life and advancing in East Africa, does not in our judgment compare very favorably with social interactionism, particularly insofar as children are concerned. Let us keep in mind the challenge made by the noted psychologist, educator, and child advocate, David Elkind: "The child is a gift of nature, the image of the child is man's creation" (1987:6).

REFERENCES

Ainsworth, M. D. 1967. *Infancy in Uganda: Infant Care and the Growth of Love.* Baltimore: Johns Hopkins University Press.
———1977. "Infant Development and Mother-Infant Interaction Among Uganda and American Families." P. H. Leiderman, S. Tulkin, and A. Rosen, eds. *Culture and Infancy: Variations in the Human Experience.* New York: Academic Press.

Ambler, C. 1988. *Kenyan Communities in the Age of Imperialism.* New Haven: Yale University Press.

Arens, W. 1976. *A Century of Change in Eastern Africa.* Paris: Mouton.

Aswani, H. 1972. "Luhya (Bunyore) Oral Literature." Taban lo Liyong, ed. *Popular Culture of East Africa.* Nairobi, Kenya: Longman.

Bahemuka, J. M. 1983. *Our Religious Heritage.* Nairobi: Thomas Nelson and Sons.

Bateson, G. 1979. *Mind and Nature: A Necessary Unity.* New York: E. P. Dutton.

Bayley, N. 1969. *Manual for the Bayley Scales of Infant Development.* New York: The Psychological Corporation.

Benedict, R. 1959. *Patterns of Culture.* Boston: Houghton Mifflin.

Berger, P. 1977. *Facing Up to Modernity.* New York: Basic Books.

Bernard, H. R. 1987. "Sponge Fishing and Technological Change in Greece." H. R. Bernard and P. J. Pelto, eds. *Technology and Social Change* (2d ed.). Prospect Heights, IL: Waveland Press. 167–207.

Bernard, H. R., and P. J. Pelto. 1987. *Technology and Social Change.* Prospect Heights, IL: Waveland Press.

Billington, W. R., H. F. Welbourn, K. C. Wandera, and A. W. Sengendo. 1963. "Custom and Child Health in Buganda: Pregnancy and Childbirth." *Tropical and Geographical Medicine* 15:121–23.

Booth, N. S. 1977. *African Religions.* New York: Nok Publishers International.

Bourguignon, E. 1979. *Psychological Anthropology.* New York: Holt, Rinehart and Winston.

Bronfenbrenner, U. 1974. "Developmental Research, Public Policy, and the Ecology of Childhood." *Child Development* 45:1–5.

Bruning, J. L., and B. L. Kintz. 1977. *Computational Handbook of Statistics.* Glenview IL: Scott, Foresman.

Bwibo, M. 1982. "Battered Child Syndrome." P. Onyango and D. Kayongo-Male, eds. *Child Labour and Health.* Nairobi: Acme Press.

Carew, J. V. 1980. "Effective Care-giving: The Child from Birth to Three." M. Fantini and R. Cordenas, eds. *Parenting in a Multi-cultural Society.* New York: Longman.

Cohen, A. 1969. *Customs and Politics in Urban Africa.* Berkeley: University of California Press.

Cryns, A. G. J. 1962. "African Intelligence: A Critical Survey of Cross-Cultural Intelligence Research in Africa South of the Sahara." *The Journal of Social Psychology* 57:283–302.

Davis, K. 1971. "Sexual Behavior." R. Merton and R. Nisbet, eds. *Contemporary Social Problems.* San Diego: Harcourt Brace Jovanovich.

Dean, R. F. A. 1961. "Health Education and Protein Calorie Malnutrition." "Health Education and the Mother and Child in East Africa." Seminar at Makerere Medical School, Kampala, Uganda, November 1961. Reprinted from *Journal of Tropical Medicine and Hygiene,* November 1962–January 1963.

Demos, J. 1982. "The Changing Faces of Fatherhood: A New Exploration in American Family History." S. H. Cath, A. R. Surwitt, and J. M. Ross, eds. *Father and Child.* Boston: Little, Brown.

———1987. *Past, Present, and Personal; The Family and the Life Course in American History.* New York: Oxford University Press.

Devereux, George. 1967. *From Anxiety to Method in the Behavioral Sciences.* Paris and The Hague: Mouton.

———1978. "The Works of George Devereux." G. D. Spindler. ed. *The Making of Psychological Anthropology.* Berkeley: University of California Press.

Doob, L. W. 1964. "Leaders, Followers, and Attitudes Toward Authority." L. A. Fallers, ed. *The King's Men.* London: Oxford University Press.

Doob, L. W., and collaborators. 1970. *Resolving Conflict in Africa: The Fermeda Workshop.* New Haven: Yale University Press.

Egan, Sean, ed. 1987. *S. M. Otieno: Kenya's Unique Burial Saga.* Nairobi: A Nation Newspapers Publication.

Elkind, D. 1987. "The Child Yesterday, Today, and Tomorrow." *Young Children* 42(4):611.

Etienne, M., and E. Leacock. 1980. *Women and Colonization: Anthropological Perspectives.* New York: Praeger Publishers.

Fallers, L. A., ed. 1964. *The King's Men: Leadership and Status in Buganda on the Eve of Independence.* London: Oxford University Press.

Fallers, M. C. 1960. *The Eastern Lacustrine Bantu: Ganda and Soga.* London: International African Institute.

Feldman, H., and M. Feldman, eds. 1985. *Current Controversies in Marriage and Family.* Beverly Hills: Sage Publications.

Foster, G. 1969. *Applied Anthropology.* Boston: Little, Brown.

Foster, G., T. Scudder, E. Colson, and R. V. Kempe, eds. 1979. *Long-Term Field Research in Social Anthropology.* New York: Academic Press.

Fraser, G., and P. Kilbride. 1981. "Child Abuse and Neglect—Rare but Perhaps Increasing Phenomena Among the Samia of Kenya." *Child Abuse and Neglect: The International Journal* 4(4): 227–32.

Freedman, D. G. 1974. *Human Infancy: An Evolutionary Perspective.* New York: Wiley.

Friedl, E. 1975. *Women and Men: An Anthropologist's View.* New York: Holt, Rinehart and Winston.

Freilich, M., ed. 1970. *Marginal Natives: Anthropologists at Work.* New York: Harper and Row.

Garbarino, J. 1976. "A Preliminary Study of Some Ecological Correlates of Child Abuse." *Child Development* 47:178–85.

———1977. "The Human Ecology of Child Maltreatment." *Journal of Marriage and the Family* 39(4): 721–35.

Geber, M. 1956. "Développment Psycho-moteur de l'enfant Africain." *Courrier* VI:17–29.

———1958. "The Psycho-motor Development of African Children in the First Year and the Influence of Maternal Behavior." *The Journal of Social Psychology* 47:185–95.

Geber, M., and R. F. A. Dean. 1957. "The State of Development of Newborn African Children." *The Lancet* 1:1216–19.

Geertz, C. 1964; 1973. *The Interpretation of Cultures.* New York: Basic Books.

———1984. "Anti-Anti Relativism." *American Anthropologist* 86(2): 263–78.

Gelles, R., and J. Lancaster. 1987. *Child Abuse and Neglect: Biosocial Dimensions.* New York: Aldine, Walter de Gruyter.

Gerschenfeld, M. K. 1985. "Couples Have a Right to Divorce even if They Have Children." H. Feldman and M. Feldman, eds. *Current Controversies in Marriage and Family.* Beverly Hills: Sage Publications. 167–179.

Goffman, I. 1963. *Stigma.* Englewood Cliffs, NJ: Prentice-Hall.

Goldschmidt, W. 1965. "Review of L. A. Faller's, *The King's Men: Leadership and Status in Buganda on the Eve of Independence.*" *American Anthropologist* 67:785–88.

Goodale, J. C. 1971. *Tiwi Wives: A Study of the Women of Melville Island, North Australia.* Seattle: University of Washington Press.

Goodenough, W. 1966. *Cooperation and Change.* New York: Wiley.

———1970. *Description and Comparison in Cultural Anthropology.* Chicago: Aldine, Walter de Gruyter.

Goodman, N. 1978. *Ways of Worldmaking.* Indianapolis: Hackett Publishing.

Goody, E. 1982. *Parenthood and Social Reproduction.* Cambridge: Cambridge University Press.

Goody, J. 1983. *The Development of the Family and Marriage in Europe.* Cambridge: Cambridge University Press.

Gordon, I. 1980. "Significant Sociocultural Factors in Effective Parenting." M. D. Fantini and R. Cardenas, eds. *Parenting in a Multi-Cultural Society.* New York: Longman.

Hallowell, A. I. 1955. *Culture and Experience.* New York: Schocken Books.

Harms, I. E. 1962. "Average Age in Months of Attainment of Certain Motor Skills as Reported by Different Investigators. Unpublished report, The Pennsylvania State University.

Harris, M. 1964. *The Nature of Cultural Things.* New York: Random House.

————1968. *Rise of Anthropological Theory*. New York: T. Y. Crowell.

Hayley, T. T. S. 1940. "Changes in Lango Marriage Customs." *Uganda Journal* 7(4): 145–63.

Henry, J. 1963. *Culture Against Man*. New York: Random House.

Herdt, G. H., ed. 1982. "Fetish and Fantasy in Sambia Initiation." In L. Herot, ed. *Rituals of Manhood: Male Initiation in Papua New Guinea*. Berkeley: University of California Press. 44–99.

Hillman, R. 1975. *Polygamy Reconsidered*. Maryknoll, New York: Orbis Books.

Hollis, M. 1982. "The Social Destruction of Reality." M. Hollis and S. Lukes, eds. *Rationality and Relativism*. Cambridge, MA: MIT Press. 67–87.

Hollis, M., and S. Lukes. 1982. *Rationality and Relativism*. Cambridge, MA: MIT Press.

Hopkins, B. 1976. "Culturally Determined Patterns of Handling the Human Infant." *Journal of Human Movement Studies* 2:1–27.

Horton, R. 1982. "Tradition and Modernity Revisited." M. Hollis and S. Lukes, eds. *Rationality and Relativism*. Cambridge, MA: MIT Press. 201–261.

Hsu, F. 1983. *Rugged Individualism Reconsidered*. Knoxville: University of Tennessee Press.

Hymes, D. 1974. *Reinventing Anthropology*. New York: Vintage Books.

Izard, C. E. 1978. "On the Ontogenesis of Emotions and Emotion-Cognition Relationships in Infancy." M. Lewis and L. A. Rosenblum, eds. *The Development of Affect*. New York: Plenum Press.

————1983. "Emotions in Personality and Culture." *Ethos* 11(4): 305–12.

Jelliffe, P. B. 1963. "Custom and Child Health in Buganda." *Tropical and Geographical Medicine* 15:121–23.

Jensen, A. 1969. "How Much Can We Boost I. Q. and Scholastic Achievement." *Harvard Educational Review* 39(1): 1–123.

Johnson, O. 1981. "The Socioeconomic Context of Child Abuse and Neglect in Native South America." J. Korbin, ed. *Child Abuse and Neglect: Cross-Cultural Perspectives*. Berkeley: University of California Press. 56–71.

Jones, D. 1970. "Toward a Native Anthropology." *Human Organization* 29:251–259.

Kagwa, Sir A. 1952. *Ekitabo Kye Mpisa za Baganda*. London: Macmillan (Book of the Customs of the Baganda).

Kaunda, K. 1966. *A Humanist in Africa: Letters to Colin M. Morris from Kenneth D. Kaunda*. Nashville: Abingdon Press.

Kayere, J. 1980. "Rural Female Roles: Some Reflections." July, 1980. Seminar paper number 142, Institute of African Studies, University of Nairobi, Kenya.

Kempe, C. H. 1969. "The Battered Child and the Hospital." *Hospital Practice*, October, 44–57.

Kent, J. 1979. "Helping Abused Children and Their Parents." *Families Today*. Drew Publication, No. (Adm): 79–85.

Kenyatta, J. 1984. *Facing Mount Kenya*. Nairobi: Heinemann Educational Books.

Kilbride, J. E. 1969. "The Development of Rural Baganda Infants." Master's thesis, The Pennsylvania State University.

————1973. *The Motor Development of Rural Baganda Infants.* Kampala, Uganda: Makerere Institute of Social Research.

Kilbride, J. E. and P. L. Kilbride. 1975. "Sitting and Smiling Behavior of Baganda Infants: The Influence of Culturally Constituted Experience." *Journal of Cross-Cultural Psychology* 6(1): 88–107.

Kilbride, J. E., M. C. Robbins, and P. L. Kilbride. 1970. "The Comparative Motor Development of Baganda, American White and American Black Infants." *The American Anthropologist* 72:1422–29.

Kilbride, J. E., and M. Yarczower. 1976. "Recognition of Happy and Sad Facial Expressions among the Baganda and U. S. Children." *Journal of Cross-Cultural Psychology* 7:181–94.

————1980. "Recognition and Imitation of Facial Expressions: A Cross Cultural Comparison between Zambia and the United States." *Journal of Cross-Cultural Psychology* 11(3): 281–96.

Kilbride, P. L. 1970. "Individual Modernization and Pictorial Depth Perception among the Baganda of Uganda." Ph.D. diss., University of Missouri.

————1974. "Modernization and the Structure of Dream Narratives among the Baganda." M. Robbins and P. Kilbride, eds. *PsychoCultural Change in Modern Buganda, Kampala, Uganda.* Nkanga Editions: Makerere Institute of Social Research.

————1977. "Early Psychomotor Development and Cultural Practices among the Samia of Kenya." Seminar Paper No. 82, Institute of African Studies, University of Nairobi, Kenya.

————1979. "Barmaiding as a Deviant Occupation among the Baganda of Uganda." *Ethos* 7(3): 232–55.

————1980. "Sensorimotor Behavior of Baganda and Samia Infants: A Controlled Comparison." *Journal of Cross-Cultural Psychology* 11(2): 131–52.

————1986. "Cultural Persistence and Socio-Economic Change Among the Abaluyia: Some Modern Problems in Patterns of Child Care." *Journal of Eastern African Research & Development* 16. Nairobi: Gideon S. Were Press. 35–52.

Kilbride, P. L., and J. E. Kilbride. 1974. "Socio-Cultural Factors and the Early Manifestation of Sociability Behavior Among Baganda Infants." *Ethos* 2(3): 296–314.

————1983. "Socialization for High Positive Affect Between Mother and Infant Among the Baganda of Uganda." *Ethos,* Special Edition. 232–46.

Kilbride, P. L., and H. W. Leibowitz. 1977. "The Ponzo Illusion Among the Baganda of Uganda." L. L. Adler, ed. *Issues in Cross-Cultural Research.* Annals of the New York Academy of Science, vol. 285:408–18.

————1982. "The Ponzo Illusion Among the Baganda: Implications for Ecological and Perceptive Theory." L. L. Adler, ed. *Issues in Cross-Cultural Research.* New York: Academic Press.

Kilbride, P., and M. C. Robbins 1969 "Pictorial Depth Perception and Acculturation among the Baganda." *American Anthropologist* 71(4): 634–47.

Kingsley, P. 1976. *Research into Conceptions of Intelligence in Africa.* Lusaka: University of Zambia Press.

Kisekka, M. 1973. "Heterosexual Relations in Uganda." Ph.D. diss., University of Missouri.

———1976. "Sexual Attitudes and Behavior Among Students in Uganda." *The Journal of Sex Research* 12(2): 104–16.

Kiste, R. 1987. "Relocation and Technological Change in Micronesia." H. Bernard and P. Pelto, eds. *Technology and Social Change.* Prospect Heights, IL: Waveland Press. 73–111.

Kitching, G. 1980. *Class and Economic Change in Kenya: The Making of an African Petite Bourgeoisie, 1905–1970.* New Haven: Yale University Press.

Kluckhohn, C. 1949. *Mirror for Man.* New York: Whittlesey House.

Konner, M. 1977. "Infancy among the Kalahari Desert San." P. H. Leiderman, S. R. Tulkin, and A. Rosenfeld, eds. *Culture and Infancy: Variations in the Human Experience.* New York: Academic Press.

Korbin, J. E. 1981. *Child Abuse and Neglect: Cross Cultural Perspectives* Berkeley: University of California Press.

Kroeber, A. L., and C. Kluckhohn. 1952. *Culture: A Critical Review of Concepts and Definitions.* New York: Vintage Books.

Kuhn, T. S. 1962. *The Structure of Scientific Revolutions.* Chicago: University of Chicago Press.

Landis, J. T. 1977. "The Trauma of Children when Parents Divorce." J. DeBurger, ed. *Marriage Today.* New York: Wiley.

Langness, L. L. 1975. "Margaret Mead and the Study of Socialization." *Ethos* 3(2): 97–112.

———1981. "Child Abuse and Cultural Values: The Case of New Guinea." J. Korbin, ed. *Child Abuse and Neglect: Cross-Cultural Perspectives.* Berkeley: University of California Press. 13–35.

Langness, L. L., and G. Frank. 1981. *Lives: An Anthropological Approach to Biography.* Novato, CA: Chandler and Sharp Publishers.

Laye, C. 1954. *The Dark Child.* New York: Farrar, Straus and Giroux.

Leakey, R. E. 1981. *The Making of Mankind.* London: Michael Joseph.

LeVine, R. 1970. "Personality and Change." J. N. Paden and E. W. Soja, eds. *The African Experience,* vol I. Evanston: Northwestern University Press.

———1977. "Child Rearing as Cultural Adaptation." P. H. Leiderman, S. R. Tulkin, and A. Rosenfeld, eds. *Culture and Infancy: Variations in the Human Experience.* New York: Academic Press.

LeVine, R., and S. LeVine. 1981. "Child Abuse and Neglect in Sub-Saharan Africa." J. E. Korbin, ed. *Child Abuse and Neglect: Cross-Cultural Perspectives.* Berkeley: University of California Press. 35–56.

Levi-Strauss, C. 1962. *Totemism.* Boston: Beacon Press.

Little, K. 1973. *African Women in Towns.* Cambridge: Cambridge University Press.

Liyong, T., ed. 1972. *Popular Culture of East Africa.* Nairobi: Longman.

Lwanga, G. n.d. "Health Worker Report." Nangina Hospital, Kenya.

Mackay, A. 1892. *Mackay of Uganda by his Sister.* London: Hodder and Stoughton.

Mair, L. B. 1934. *An African People in the Twentieth Century.* London: Routledge and Kegan Paul.

Malinowski, B. 1953. *Argonauts of the Western Pacific*. New York: E. P. Dutton.

Maquet, J. 1972. *Africanity: The Cultural Unity of Black Africa*. London: Oxford University Press.

Marcus, G. E., and M. J. Fischer. 1986. *Anthropology as Cultural Critique: an Experimental Moment in the Human Sciences*. Chicago: University of Chicago Press.

Marris, P., and A. Somerset. 1971. *African Businessmen*. London: Routledge and Kegan Paul.

Mazrui, A. 1975. *The Political Sociology of the English Language: An African Perspective*. Paris: Mouton.

Mbiti, J. 1986. "The Encounter of Christian Faith and African Religion." D. Ferm, ed. *Third World Liberation Theologies*. Maryknoll, New York: Orbis Books.

Mead, M. 1963. "Socialization and Enculturation." *Anthropology*, 4:184–88.

Messenger, J. 1969. *Inis Beag: Isle of Ireland*. New York: Holt, Rinehart and Winston.

Messerschmidt, D., ed. 1981. *Anthropologists at Home in North America: Methods and Issues in the Study of One's Own Society*. Cambridge: Cambridge University Press.

Minturn, L., and W. Lambert. 1964. *Mothers of Six Cultures*. New York: Wiley.

Moody, R. W. 1961. "Preliminary Notes on the Clan Structure of Samia." Paper presented at a conference held at the East African Institute of Social Research, Makerere College, Kampala.

Moss, H. A. 1967. "Sex, Age and State as Determinants of Mother-Infant Interaction." *Merrill-Palmer Quarterly* 13:19–36.

Moynihan, D. P. 1987. *Family and Nation*. San Diego: Harcourt Brace Jovanovich.

Munroe, R., and R. Munroe. 1980. "Infant Experience and Childhood Affect Among the Logoli: A Longitudinal Study." *Ethos* 8(4): 295–316.

Mutesa, F. 1969. *The Desecration of My Kingdom*. London: East African Publishing House.

Naroll, R. 1983. *The Moral Order*. Beverly Hills: Sage Publications.

Nasimiyu, R. 1985. "The Participation of Women in Bukusu Economy: the Situation as at the End of the Nineteenth Century." S. Wandibba, ed. *History and Culture in Western Africa: The People of Bungoma District Through Time*. Nairobi: G. S. Were Press.

Nyanyintono, R. M. 1982. "Institutional Child Abuse and Neglect." P. Onyango and D. Kayongo-Male, eds. *Child Labour and Health*. Kenya: Acme Press.

O'Barr, J. December 2, 1987. "Women and the Politics of Development in the Third World." Presentation at Haverford College.

Obeyesekere, G. 1975. "Sorcery, Premeditated Murder, and the Canalization of Aggression in Sri Lanka." *Ethnology* 14(1): 1–23.

Oboler, R. S. 1985. *Women, Power, and Economic Change: the Nandi of Kenya*. Stanford: Stanford University Press.

Ojiambo, J. A. 1967. "Maternal and Infant Dietary Practices of the Abasamia of Busia District, Western Province, Kenya." *East African Medical Journal*, 44(12): 518–23.

Olouch, C. P. (and Staff of Pre-School Education Section of the Kenya Institute of Education). 1984. *Guidelines for Pre-School Education in Kenya.* Nairobi: Jomo Kenyatta Foundation.

Ong, W. 1969. "World as View and World as Event." *American Anthropologist* 71(4): 634–49.

Onyango, P., and D. Kayongo-Male. 1983. "Child Labour and Health: Proceedings of the First National Workshop on Child Labour and Health, Nairobi, Kenya." December 2–3, 1982. Nairobi: Acme Press.

Orley, J. H. 1970. *Culture and Mental Illness.* Nairobi: East African Publishing House.

Osogo, J. 1966. *A History of the Baluyia.* London: Oxford University Press.

Otaala, B. 1973. *The Development of Operational Thinking in Primary School Children: an Examination of Some Aspects of Piaget's Theory Among the Iteso Children of Uganda.* New York: Teacher's College Press.

Owusu, M. 1976. "Colonial and Postcolonial Anthropology of Africa: Scholarship or Sentiment?" W. Arens, ed. *A Century of Change in Eastern Africa.* Paris: Mouton Publishers.

———1978. "Ethnography of Africa: the Usefulness of the Useless." *American Anthropologist* 80(2): 310–34.

Pandey, T. 1975. "India Man among American Indians." A. Beteille and T. N. Madan, eds. *Encounters and Experience: Personal Accounts of Fieldwork.* Honolulu: University Press of Hawaii.

Parkin, D. 1969. *Neighbors and Nationals in an African City Ward.* Berkeley: University of California Press.

Parkin, J. M. 1971. "The Assessment of Gestational Age in Ugandan and British Newborn Babies." *Developmental Medicine and Child Neurology* 13:784–88.

p'Bitek, O. 1966. *Song of Lawino.* Nairobi: East African Publishing House.

———1972. *African Religions in Western Scholarship.* Nairobi: East African Publishing House.

———1986. *Artist the Ruler: Essays on Art, Culture, and Values.* Nairobi: Heinemann Kenya.

Pelto, P. 1973. *Technology and Social Change in the Arctic.* CA: Cummings Publishing.

Pelto, J. P. and G. H. Pelto. 1978. *Anthropological Research: the Structure of Inquiry.* Cambridge: Cambridge University Press.

Poggie, J. J. and R. N. Lynch, eds. 1974. *Rethinking Modernization: An Anthropological Perspective.* Westport, CN: Greenwood Press.

Powdermaker, H. 1966. *Stranger and Friend.* New York: W. W. Norton.

Price-Williams, D. R. 1975. *Explorations in Cross-Cultural Psychology.* San Francisco: Chandler and Sharp Publishers.

Pritchard, J. M. 1977. *A Geography of East Africa.* London: Evans Brothers.

Putman, D. and P. Kilbride. "A Relativistic Understanding of Intelligence: Social Intelligence Among the Songhay of Mali and the Samia of Kenya." Paper presented at the *Society for Cross-Cultural Research.* February, 1980, Philadelphia, PA.

Riesman, P. 1977. *Freedom in Fulani Social Life: an Introspective Ethnography.* Chicago: University of Chicago Press.

Richards, A. I. 1964. "Authority Patterns in Traditional Buganda." L. A. Fallers, ed. *The King's Men: Leadership and Status in Buganda on the Eve of Independence.* London: Oxford University Press.

Rigby, P. 1985. *Persistent Pastoralists; Nomadic Societies in Transition.* London: Zed Books.

Robbins, M., and P. Kilbride, eds. 1974. *Psychocultural Change in Modern Buganda.* Kampala: Nkanga Publications, Makerere Institute of Social Research.

Robbins, M., and P. Kilbride. 1972; 1987. "Microtechnology in Rural Buganda." H. R. Bernard and P. Pelto, eds. *Technology and Social Change.* Prospect Heights, IL: Waveland Press.

Robbins, M., and R. B. Pollnac. 1969. "Drinking Patterns and Acculturation in Rural Buganda." *American Anthropologist* 71:276–85.

Robbins, M., R. Thompson, and J. Bukenya. 1974. "Gratification Orientations and Individual Modernization in Buganda." M. Robbins and P. Kilbride, eds. *Psychocultural Change in Modern Buganda.* Kampala: Nkanga Editions: Makerere Institute of Social Research.

Rodney, W. 1974. *How Europe Underdeveloped Africa.* Washington D.C.: Howard University Press.

Rogers, E. 1969. *Modernization Among Peasants: The Impact of Communication.* New York: Holt, Rinehart and Winston.

Rohner, R. 1975. *They Love Me, They Love Me Not: A Worldwide Study of the Effects of Parental Acceptance and Rejection.* New Haven: HRAF Press.

Rosaldo, M. Z., and L. Lamphere, eds. 1974. *Women, Culture, and Society.* Stanford: Stanford University Press.

Roscoe, J. 1911. *The Baganda.* London: Macmillan and Co.

Ross, M. H., and T. S. Weisner. 1977. "The Rural Urban Migrant Network in Kenya: Some General Implications." *American Ethnologist* 4(2): 359–75.

Sahlins, M. 1976. *The Use and Abuse of Biology.* Ann Arbor: The University of Michigan Press.

Sangree, W. 1966. *Age, Prayer, and Politics in Tiriki, Kenya.* London: Oxford University Press.

Sapir, E. 1962. *Culture, Language and Personality.* Berkeley: University of California Press.

Sayegh, Y., and W. Dennis. 1965. "The Effect of Supplementary Experiences upon the Behavioral Development of Infants in Institutions." *Child Development* 36:81–90.

Scarr-Salapatek, S. 1976. "An Evolutionary Perspective on Infant Intelligence: Species Patterns and Individual Variations." M. Lewis, ed. *Origins of Intelligence: Infancy and Early Childhood,* New York: Plenum Press.

Scudder, J. and E. F. Colson. 1987. "The Kariba Dam Project: Resettlement and Local Initiative." H. R. Bernard and P. J. Pelto, eds. *Technology and Social Change.* Prospect Heights, IL: Waveland Press.

Segal, J. 1979. "Child Abuse: A Review of Research." *Families Today,* no. adm. 79–815:577–607.

Selby, H. 1974. *Zapotec Deviance: The Convergence of Folk and Modern Sociology.* Austin: University of Texas Press.

Short, C. R. 1962. "Health Education for the Expectant Mother." "Health Education and the Mother and Child in East Africa," seminar at Makerere Medical School, Kampala, Uganda, November 1961. Reprinted from *Journal of Tropical Medicine and Hygiene.* November 1962–January 1963.

Shuster, I. 1979. *New Women of Lusaka.* Palo Alto: Mayfield Publishing.

Sidel, R. 1986. *Women and Children Last: The Plight of Poor Women in Affluent America.* New York: Viking Press.

Southall, A. W., and P. C. W. Gutkind. 1957. *Townsmen in the Making.* Kampala, Uganda: East African Institute of Social Research.

Southwold, M. 1965. "The Ganda of Uganda." J. Gibbs, ed. *Peoples of Africa.* New York: Holt, Rinehart and Winston.

Spiro, M. E. 1978. "Culture and Human Nature." G. A. Spindler, ed. *The Making of Psychological Anthropology.* Berkeley: University of California Press.

Spradley, J. P. 1979. *The Ethnographic Interview.* New York: Holt, Rinehart and Winston.

———1980. *Participant Observation.* New York: Holt, Rinehart and Winston.

Stoller, P. 1982. "Relativity and the Anthropologist's Gaze." *Anthropology and Humanism Quarterly* 7(4): 2–10.

Stone, L. 1979. *The Family, Sex and Marriage: in England 1500–1800.* New York: Harper and Row.

Strauss, M., and R. Gelles. 1970. "Physical Violence in Families" *Families Today,* no. adm 79–815:553–77.

Sudarkasa, N. 1982. "African and Afro-American Family Structure." J. Cole, ed. *Anthropology for the Eighties.* New York: The Free Press. 132–61.

Super, C. M. 1973(b). "Patterns of Infant Care and Development in Kenya." *Kenya Education Review.* 64–69.

———1974. "The Development of Affect in Infancy and Early Childhood." H. Stevenson and D. Wagner, eds. *Cultural Perspectives on Children.* San Francisco: Freeman Press.

———1975. "Environmental Effects on Motor Development: The Case of African Infant Precocity." Paper presented as part of a symposium on cross-cultural studies at the meeting of the American Academy for Cerebral Palsy, New York.

———1980. "Behavioral Development in Infancy." R. L. Munroe and B. B. Whiting, eds. *Handbook for Cross-Cultural Human Development.* New York: Garland Press.

———1981. "Cross-Cultural Research on Infancy." H. C. Triandis and H. Heron, eds. *Handbook of Cross-Cultural Psychology: Developmental Psychology,* vol 4. Boston: Allyn and Bacon.

Super, C. M., and S. Harkness. 1974. "Patterns of Personality in Africa: a Note from the Field." *Ethos* 2:377–81.

Wagatsuma, H. 1981. "Child Abandonment and Infanticide: A Japanese Case." J. Korbin, ed. *Child Abuse and Neglect: Cross-Cultural Perspectives.* Berkeley: University of California Press. 120–39.

Wagner, G. 1949. *The Bantu of North Kavirondo.* London: Oxford University Press for International African Institute, vol I.

———1956. *The Bantu of North Kavirondo.* London: Oxford University Press for International African Institute, vol. II.

Wallace, A. 1970. *Culture and Personality.* New York: Random House.

Wallerstein, I. M. 1974. *The Modern World System: Capitalist Agriculture and the Origin of the European World Economy in the Sixteenth Century.* New York: Academic Press.

Wanjala, C. 1985. "Twilight Years Are the Years of Council and Wisdom." S. Wandibba, ed. *History and Culture in Western Kenya: People of Bungoma District Through Time.* Nairobi: G. S. Were Press.

Ware, H. 1979. "Polygyny: Women's Views in a Transitional Society, Nigeria, 1975." *Journal of Marriage and the Family* 41(1): 185–95.

Warren, N. 1973. "African Infant Precocity." *Psychological Bulletin* 78:353–67.

Warren, N. and J. Parkin. 1974. "A Neurological and Behavioral Comparison of African and European Newborns in Uganda." *Child Development,* vol 45, 966–71.

Weisner, T. 1983. "Putting Family Ideals into Practice: Pronaturalism in Conventional and Nonconventional California Families." *Ethos* 47:278–305.

Were, G. 1967. *A History of the Abaluyia of Western Kenya c. 1520–1930.* Nairobi: East African Publishing House.

———1982. "Cultural Renaissance and National Development: Some Reflections on the Kenyan Cultural Problem." *Journal of Eastern African Research and Development* 12:1–11.

———1985. "Ethnic and Cultural Identity in African History: A Myth or Reality?" S. Wandibba, ed. *History and Culture in Western Kenya: The People of Bungoma District Through Time.* Nairobi: G. S. Were Press.

Werner, E. E. 1979. *Cross-Cultural Child Development: A View from the Planet Earth.* Monterey, CA: Brooks/Cole Publishing.

Whiting, B. B. and J. Whiting. 1975. *Children of Six Cultures: A Psycho-Cultural Analysis.* Cambridge, MA: Harvard University Press.

Whitten, N. E. 1966. "Reply: To the Role of the Fieldworker in an Explosive Political Situation." *Current Anthropology* 7.

Wilson, B. 1985. *Rationality.* Oxford: Basil Blackwell.

Wober, M. 1975. *Psychology in Africa.* London: International African Institute.

Wolf, E. 1982. *Europe and the People without History.* Berkeley: University of California Press.

Worthman, C. M. and J. Whiting. 1987. "Social Change in Adolescent Sexual Behavior, Mate Selection and Premarital Pregnancy Rates in a Kikuyu Community." *Ethos* 15(2): 145–65.

Yarrow, L. J. 1963. "Research in Dimensions of Early Maternal Care." *Merrill-Palmer Quarterly* 9:101–14.

Yarrow, L. J., F. Pederson, and J. Rubenstein. 1977. "Mother-infant Interaction and Development in Infancy." P. H. Leiderman, S. R. Tulkin, and A. Rosenfeld, eds. *Culture and Infancy: Variations in the Human Experience*. New York: Academic Press.

Author Index

Subject Index